Shannon Molloy is an award-winning journalist and author with more than fifteen years of experience working for major media outlets spanning print, digital and publishing. He began his career at Fairfax in Brisbane as an award-winning news reporter and has since covered property, business, entertainment and human interest. He spent seven years working for News Corp as an entertainment reporter and feature writer, and then as News Editor of news.com.au. He is currently the News Editor at realestate.com.au. Shannon was the 2020 recipient of Journalist of the Year at the Mumbrella Publish Awards.

His debut book, *Fourteen,* a memoir about growing up gay in regional Queensland, is a critically acclaimed bestseller that was turned into a sell-out hit stage production and is now being adapted for the screen.

Shannon also contributes to various charity organisations, and founded the annual Clare Atkinson Memorial Scholarship for journalism at The University of Queensland.

SHANNON MOLLOY

YOU MADE ME THIS WAY

FOURTH ESTATE

Except for Craig Hughes-Cashmore, names and identifying details of survivors and perpetrators of childhood sexual assault interviewed for this book have been changed.

Fourth Estate
An imprint of HarperCollins*Publishers*

HarperCollins*Publishers*
Australia • Brazil • Canada • France • Germany • Holland • India
Italy • Japan • Mexico • New Zealand • Poland • Spain • Sweden
Switzerland • United Kingdom • United States of America

HarperCollins acknowledges the Traditional Custodians of the lands upon which we live and work, and pays respect to Elders past and present.

First published on Gadigal Country in Australia in 2023
by HarperCollins*Publishers* Australia Pty Limited
ABN 36 009 913 517
harpercollins.com.au

HarperCollins*Publishers*
Macken House, 39/40 Mayor Street Upper
Dublin 1, D01 C9W8, Ireland

A catalogue record for this book is available from the National Library of Australia

ISBN 978 1 4607 6186 1 (paperback)
ISBN 978 1 4607 1477 5 (ebook)
ISBN 978 1 4607 4667 7 (audiobook)

Cover design by George Saad
Cover image by Wizemark/stocksy.com/2641206
Typeset in Baskerville BE by Kirby Jones

Printed and bound in the United States

This book deals with child sexual assault.

If you, or a person you know, is in need of support,

call Lifeline on 13 11 14, or visit lifeline.org.au/gethelp

For Jarad, whose courage and candour inspired me to confront my past and stop running from it

Prologue

Why am I like this?

It's something I've found myself wondering each time my painful and uncomfortable personality flaws disrupt my happiness, my sense of security, my wellbeing … and most parts of my life.

More often than not, I feel broken. There are days those fractures in my psyche feel beyond repair. And a chance conversation a few years back gave me the realisation that much of those chips and cracks are the result of something that began when I was five.

This is a book that delves into those experiences, but also relies on the shared experiences of many other men who are just like me. It hasn't been easy to write, but it has been necessary.

In seeking to understand more about why I am the way I am, I confronted my dark past head-on. I spoke about it for the very first time ever. I sought guidance from mental health professionals. I opened up to my husband. I told my mother. I let friends in.

I went looking for the insights of men who have come from a similarly difficult place and walked a near-identical path. I went to a support group, and I spoke to experts in the fields of treatment, research and survivor advocacy. I heard from the loved one of a man who didn't survive. I spoke to men who had never told a soul about what happened to them as boys until they said it out loud to me for the very first time.

After all of that, two things became clear to me.

The first is that it doesn't matter whether you are rich or poor, privileged or struggling, set up for success or fighting much harder for a place in the world, child sexual abuse has an unimaginably destructive and destabilising impact on a young life.

It's something that society struggles to comprehend and therefore chooses not to talk about. And that's understandable. When something is too awful to think about, why would you willingly start a meaningful conversation about it? It's simply too hard. It's too sad.

That feeds into the second realisation that writing this book has given me, which is that only a little bit above bugger-all is done to help men who were sexually abused as children. Only some non-government organisations exist, and those are largely run by volunteers.

Those groups each have a waitlist of hundreds of survivors, desperate for a hand, just yearning to be heard, to be understood, and to be believed.

The conversation about child sexual abuse, when it's had, tends to focus predominantly on girls and female survivors rather than boys and male survivors. Perhaps it's the perception that girls are more likely to be the victims of this crime. But experts tell me the gender balance between victims is almost equal. There are a few in the field who suspect instances of child sexual abuse could even be higher in boys, but that it's not going to be represented in the data because many men don't disclose.

The abuse perpetrated against boys isn't more worthy of our attention and sympathy and rage than that endured by girls. One isn't less wrong than the other.

But the fact remains that boys are likely to cope with it – or not cope, as it happens – in a unique way. We're likely to face different outcomes. We're less likely to ask for help, and when we do, we're very likely to find that there is none.

As with everybody affected by diminished mental health, we're more likely to die by suicide. And tragically, when men do suicide, their loved ones – the people who thought they knew them better than anyone else in the world – might be left with no idea why. Some men will take their secrets, their shame, to the grave.

Child sexual abuse is a total destabiliser, one that plucks its victims from whatever road they're walking down in life and drops them in the midst of a living hell. The terrors they endure are similar, and that trauma at such an early age robs them of their innocence. The consequences can be dire and last a lifetime.

Their stories might be different. Their backgrounds could be totally at odds with each other. But they are likely to find stark similarities in the emotional damage done, and the battles they must wage for decades of their lives.

That's the evil of child sexual abuse.

It steals from kids their untarnished potential in life, whatever they might've been. What it leaves behind is hurt, confusion, guilt, a distorted view of the world, distrust, pain, and deep scars that never really fade.

And, especially for boys, it infects them with a crippling sense of shame that is tragically debilitating in countless ways.

Some young men are able to cope and push through life relatively unscathed. Some benefit from early intervention and psychological treatment that helps to ease their suffering and put them somewhat back on track.

For many, though, they're not so lucky.

Young men living in the shadow of child sexual abuse will probably battle depression, anxiety and post-traumatic stress disorder to varying extents. They're likely to struggle to contain their anger.

They are more likely to abuse drugs and alcohol. They might be violent to loved ones. They'll probably struggle to find and maintain healthy intimate relationships.

They might make terrible life choices, knowingly or not, and be prone to self-destructing. They could wind up in trouble with the law or in gaol.

Some might flunk out of school or be unable to hold down a job. Some will gamble away whatever money they manage to make.

A number will find themselves fighting off suicidal thoughts that creep in when the familiar darkness descends. Some will take their own lives, often by violent means.

Almost all will come to know a relentless demon that burrows itself within the deepest recesses of their psyche and can never really be exorcised. Not entirely.

Shame.

For men who survive child sexual abuse, speaking about it to someone – to anyone – is difficult. While female survivors have thankfully been the beneficiaries of a cultural shift towards reducing stigma, boosting support services and creating awareness of the danger signs and red flags, society has not extended the same help to men.

For whatever reason, boys and men don't feel the same level of safety to disclose what's happened to them. The average time of disclosure – that is, how often it takes a man to tell someone what happened to them when they were a boy – is almost thirty years. Thirty years. Up to a decade longer than is the case for female survivors. Just picture the kind of despair those men have carried in secret for all that time. Imagine what they've endured, what they've done to survive, rightly or wrongly.

Across the board, when it comes to mental health, men are significantly less likely to seek help than women. That's the consequence of a range of factors, from the ingrained social view of masculinity and what it means to be a man, to the lack of specialised support services, through to the sheer potency of shame.

So much of the horror that men face after abuse and throughout their lives is borne from shame.

That's why I wanted to write this book. For me and my experience, to understand why I am the way I am, but mostly for other men who've been to hell and dragged themselves back. And I've met so many.

The men I've encountered are incredibly inspirational. They're survivors in every sense of the word. They've endured the absolute worst thing that can happen to a child, and they've pushed their way through. It hasn't been pretty. It hasn't been perfect. There's been unspeakable pain and insurmountable challenges.

But there's also been a lot of healing. There's been a determination to continue surviving and to make something out of these broken lives we find ourselves living.

It would be naive to think that any of us are going to one day wake up 'fixed'. I don't think there's a permanent cure for this kind of trauma. There are treatments to ease the pain and coping mechanisms to deal with persisting symptoms and new challenges.

But these men carry with them their deep scars for life. I do too.

What happened to us all is different. In fact, I think I'm still undecided whether or not what happened to me *is* child abuse. That's part of what I want to work through in this book.

Our backgrounds are different. The struggles we've faced are different. The points we've reached in life are different. The level of healing we've managed is different.

But all of us have been shaped in some way, big and small, by what happened when we were boys. And this book explores how.

Writing about child sexual abuse is difficult, and not just because the content is heavy. The hours and hours of interviews I conducted with survivors, the reams of research I pored over, the conversations with experts and lawyers, and the self-reflection in quiet and unpleasant moments have been overwhelming at times.

I've juggled a combination of choking emotions simultaneously on many of the days I've sat down to fall into this book. Anger, sadness, dismay, hopelessness, fear.

But the hardest part is what I'm not allowed to say. There is much that I can't tell you, or at least that I'm unable to tell you in its truest, rawest form.

That's just how defamation law works in this country, for better or worse. Mostly for worse, in my view, but any journalist who's had a good story torn to shreds by a sympathetic but ruthless media lawyer prior to publication will tell you that.

There are people and stories in the pages that follow that I've had to portray differently in various ways. Names have been altered, locations changed. Details about the perpetrators will, in most cases, not even remotely resemble reported facts.

Unless a perpetrator has been successfully prosecuted, I can't name them, nor can I even come close to identifying them.

If I were to tell you that John Smith was abused by his science teacher at St Something-Or-Other College in the 1990s, there's a chance someone could put two and two together and find out who that man was. And unless he was found guilty of his crimes, he could rightfully sue my publisher and me.

And I'll be damned if I'm going to reward a monster with a pile of cash.

So, where I've had to, to stay within the narrow boundaries of the law, I've made some tweaks to retain the rich complexity of these stories but strip them of any potential identifying factors.

Will's uncle Paul was not a television producer who once danced on *Bandstand.* His partner Franco was not an Italian photographer. Those aren't their real names. Jason didn't grow up in Coffs Harbour. Joey lived in a very different part of Queensland. I've not said specifically where Chris or Luke grew up.

For me, Joshua's name isn't Joshua. He didn't live where I said he did. His parents had different occupations. His physical appearance is vastly different. My reasons for that are a little more complicated to explain. You'll understand why a bit later.

And in a few instances, these changes are at the request of the men themselves. Some have never spoken about what happened to them and therefore don't want to be identified by those in their lives. These men had their agency snatched away from them, and they deserve to reclaim it and protect it however they like.

These stories are not pleasant to write, and I know they are not easy to read. They will likely be especially confronting for anyone with a lived experience, as well as for anyone with a loved one who has been abused.

To anyone reading this who's struggling, I say: A new dawn always follows even the darkest night. There is always, always hope, even when things feel utterly hopeless.

You are *never* alone, even if there's not a soul in the world you feel you can talk to, and even if you believe in the moment that there's no one who loves you, who believes you, or who cares. There is. And they will.

Shame is its most potent when it lives unchallenged within us. Secrecy kills. Going it alone is unnecessarily burdensome and painful.

Speak up when you're ready. Always seek help when the going gets too tough. And don't believe the things your demons tell you.

You can do this. You can survive. I believe in you.

Chapter One

Joshua yanks on the cord of the aluminium venetian blinds, and they collapse on the windowsill in a clang. His bedroom is plunged into almost total darkness, except for the soft glow of a small lamp on his dresser.

'Come here,' he says, quietly but gruffly.

He's standing in the corner of the room. I can faintly make out his face in the darkness, and I'm struck by the harshness of it now.

'Come here,' he says again, this time more sternly. It's a tone I haven't heard before. Demanding. Commanding. It's jarring and makes me jump.

I don't know much about anything at this stage of life. I'm just a little kid. But I know enough that something about this whole scenario feels off. My adrenaline starts pumping and there's a small but not insignificant part of me that wants to run.

But I stay.

It all looks so different in a low light, this space where I've spent almost every single afternoon since meeting him by chance three months ago.

*

I'm just about to turn six years old. Joshua is two and a half years older than me. We live a few blocks from each other in a small seaside Queensland town of about nine thousand people, but our paths don't cross until a fairly typical Saturday spent at the basketball court next to my house.

That day, I'm playing with my brother, Brett. He's eight, and while we're close enough in age that he can tolerate my incessant desire to be best buddies, we're often just a little too far apart in maturity to be on the same page.

He's always looking for someone to palm me off on. I'm annoying, truth be told. A little too eager. Far too chatty. Not good at basketball – not even a little bit.

A boy with perfectly straight jet-black hair in a bowl cut shows up with his mum. She's off to run some kind of errand that would be made cumbersome by him tagging along, so she leaves him here with a bunch of strangers. It's the start of the 1990s and things are fairly nonchalant – that's just what people do. 'Hey, here are some random kids – play with them and I'll be back later!'

He seems awkward. He doesn't know any of the other children hanging around.

I'm a precocious extrovert, and so I skip over to greet him. The big, wide smile on my face is contagious and spreads to him. He's glad to meet me and, together with one of my toy

Tonka trucks, off we run to explore the tall weeds that border the bitumen rectangle court.

Joshua might be a couple of years older than me, but he's consumed by a childish energy, with a vivid imagination and hyperactive tendencies. Life is an adventure to be enjoyed, if he's just given the chance. There is no limit to the trouble that can be gotten into.

I'm enamoured. We bond immediately.

Our parents very loosely know each other. Or rather, know of each other. Yeppoon, a sleepy village on the central Queensland coast, is the kind of place where everyone is familiar with everyone else in some form. That was especially the case for my family, with my mother Donna being the local hairdresser.

We're in the second half of 1991 and I'm meant to be enjoying kindergarten ahead of starting school. I was born in December, and so when I turn five, I'm technically old enough to head off into the world for the first time the following January, learning shapes and using safety scissors and digging in sandpits. The teachers do not agree that I am ready.

'Bring him back next year,' they politely suggest after a month.

Instead of playing and exploring with other kids, I spend long days at the home of a babysitter – one of mum's clients, a woman in her sixties who has retired as a bookkeeper and suddenly has lots of free time. She's lovely and warm. We watch *Play School* together and play games, and she prepares bananas just the way I like them – thickly sliced with a little sprinkle of white sugar on top.

But it's lonely. I wish I could have friends. There aren't too many in my neighbourhood.

Joshua instantly fills that void.

The first time I go over to his house to play, our mums chat excitedly like cockatoos in a gum tree, each clutching cups of tea in one hand and lit cigarettes in the other. Joshua drags me by the wrist to his bedroom.

It's small. Much cosier than the enormous space I share with Brett at our house. But unlike mine, it's packed from floor to ceiling with toys. Every kind of toy imaginable. Giant stuffed teddy bears. All of the action figures currently on the market. A train set. Boxes and boxes full of Lego pieces of every shape, size and colour.

My mouth falls open in surprised delight as I turn slowly to take it all in. And then my heart skips a beat when, in the corner next to the dresser, I spot it. A small colour television. And, nestled on top, a Sega Mega Drive video game console.

I am surely dead and this must be heaven.

Within those four walls, for hours at a time, until the sun has completely disappeared behind the horizon to signal that it's time for me to go home, we play. We dream up all kinds of dramatic scenarios for our figurines to get themselves into. We watch cartoons or, better still, play *Alex Kidd in Miracle World* on the Sega. We construct tall towers from bricks and then cackle as we smash them into a million pieces again.

When we grow restless cooped up inside, we run like wild animals possessed down the tiled hallway and out into the backyard. We chase each other with sticks, dig in the garden, and turn the hose on each other, laughing maniacally.

Most days, all day, our excited and high-pitched laughter fills the air and punctures the quiet of Joshua's street.

Each weekday afternoon when I know he's home from school, and every single weekend from dawn until dusk, I'm there. I run outside the rusting front gate of my house, across the basketball court, through the long grass, up one block, around the corner and then four houses up. I'm breathless by the time I reach Joshua's front door and bash excitedly on it with a closed fist.

Finally, I have a best friend. I have an outlet for my endless enthusiasm for the world. We're each other's partner in crime. For us, there is no such thing as a bad day together.

Until this one arrives.

There's a frustrated forcefulness to Joshua this afternoon. I can feel a tension hanging in the air as he lets me inside his house and ushers me down the hall to his room. He barely says a word to me.

Joshua shoves me to the side and closes the door behind him. He looks around for something to slide up against it.

He spots a heavy wooden toy chest and drags it over. I feel trapped. This all feels wrong, but I don't know why. I look at him, puzzled, and open my mouth to speak.

'Shhh!' he hisses at me in annoyance, his eyes wide.

I do as I'm told and stay quiet. With the blinds closed and his room dark, I hear him clumsily make his way towards me and can just make out the outline of him coming closer and closer. He stumbles over the toys strewn on the floor.

'Come here,' he commands.

I feel his hand clasp my shoulder tightly, yanking me towards him and veering me into the narrow space between the end of his bunk bed and the wall. Even though we're ordinarily not that dissimilar in height, it suddenly feels like he's towering over me.

An unpleasant mix of fear, anticipation and discomfort swirls in the pit of my stomach.

I open my mouth again to speak.

'Be quiet,' he whispers. He's a little gentler than he was a moment ago.

Joshua lowers his head and I feel his hot breath melting the skin on my neck. He's nervous and excited. I can hear my heart beating fast, a thud-thud, thud-thud vibrating in my eardrums.

His hand falls to my stomach and slowly slides down. Lower and lower. I freeze. I feel the fingers of his other hand pull on the drawstring of my shorts.

'You can't tell anyone,' he says, half-pleading and half-threatening. 'You can't ever tell anyone.'

The first time Joshua molests me, it's all over almost as quickly as it begins. He touches me, touches himself, instructs me to touch him, and then he's finished.

He leans down and pulls his shorts up from the ground, pushing himself off me. I'm flung back against the wall in the process, hitting my left shoulder. A shooting pain radiates through my body. My legs are like jelly, so I'm unsteady on my feet.

Joshua turns on his heel and stumbles in the dark towards his dresser. He stands there awkwardly, unsure of what to do next.

'What was that?' I whimper.

Joshua grunts. He pretends to busy himself, shuffling around toys and ornaments, determined not to make eye contact with me.

I stay huddled in the corner, frozen in this shameful place where he dragged me only a few moments earlier. *What do I do? Do I run?* My head is spinning and I feel faint.

What the hell just happened?

'Go home,' he barks at me, interrupting the awkward silence hanging in the air.

I don't move. I'm not even sure I can. There's a hollowness in his voice that I don't recognise, and I almost find it terrifying in this moment. I can't see him, but the way his eyes looked today when I arrived – dark and mean – keeps flashing into my mind.

I take a few steps forward. My legs are shaking, like they do after a really fierce game of basketball. I take a few more steps forward, tiptoeing around the debris of toys and books and stuffed animals littering Joshua's bedroom floor.

I reach the door, pausing briefly to turn back and glance at him. I can feel the sting of tears in the corners of my eyes, tickling the bridge of my nose. I mustn't let him see me cry.

He's standing up perfectly straight. Rigid like a plank of wood. He's staring into space.

I heave the toy chest out of the way, open his bedroom door and lunge through, practically sprinting down the hallway of his house and out the front door. I keep running until I'm home, where I throw myself beneath the covers of my bed.

I stay there until it's dark outside. I quietly cry for what feels like hours. Silent little sobs. I don't want my brothers and sister to hear me. I don't want anyone to get an inkling of what happened.

No one must ever know. What we've just done is very, very wrong – I know that much. I'll be in trouble if anyone ever finds out. My family will be so ashamed. They'll be so disgusted.

Before this afternoon, I have no idea what any of that kind of sexual stuff is. I'm still under the impression that seeing adults kiss is rude; an intimate act I should avert my gaze from. Touching private parts? The notion wouldn't have even crossed my mind.

The instant that Joshua slid his hand inside my underwear, the blood drained from my body. It's as though instinctively, my body's hardwiring – the factory default settings of my brain – recognised some command prompts. It knew what this was. The physiological reactions indicated as much.

How is it possible to be terrified of something without even really knowing what it is? How do we have enough in-built knowledge to recognise something is wrong, but not enough to contextualise it?

The act itself was horrible. It felt intrusive and uncomfortable. It made me feel awkward. A sickness started to brew in the pit of my stomach and its almost acidic toxicity intensified as each second ticked by.

But by far the worst part of it all was how Joshua had transformed. That lingers with me for days afterwards.

This boy I'm almost completely obsessed with, whose every word I hang on, who I wanted to spend every waking minute with, had just turned on me with an icy indifference.

He was calculating. Ruthlessly so. He was imposing and manipulative. And then, when he was done with me, he was brutal in his dismissal of me. I suddenly didn't matter at all.

It's a side of Joshua I'd never seen. It's scary to see a deep darkness seep out of someone, especially as a child, when there isn't yet an understanding that sometimes people do bad things. But mostly, it breaks my little heart. It feels as though our friendship is over.

I don't see him for the better part of a week. I play in the backyard instead of going out onto the basketball court, not wanting to run into him. Or I spend free days inside my room, drawing or napping.

I plonk myself on the couch in front of the television and stay there until someone tells me to get up and go to bed. Or until Mum comes home from a long day at work.

'Help me get tea ready, love,' she will usually say, fatigue oozing out of every pore.

I'm the youngest of four children. In later years, it'll become abundantly clear to me I wasn't part of my parents' grand plan. Mum insists otherwise, that she and Dad had always intended on me joining my other siblings to make four. But even the raw mathematics doesn't add up. My three older siblings – my eldest brother Damien, my sister Trinity, and my other brother Brett – are almost equally spaced apart. Six years each.

Then, abruptly, there's me. Number four. A little over two years after Brett. Surprise!

Mum had only recently gone back to work when she fell pregnant. After I burst onto the scene, she quit hairdressing salon work to take a job at the TAFE college in Rockhampton, forty minutes up the road, as a teacher of new apprentices.

The pay is better, the work is more secure, the hours are much less relentless and don't involve weekends, and she absolutely loves it.

Hairdressing itself is her life's calling. She's been doing it since she was fourteen. There was never any suggestion of some other way of life for her. But to be in a classroom with twenty apprentices hanging on your every word, ready to absorb a lifetime of knowledge? There's something so intoxicating about that.

Mum would've happily taught for the rest of her working life. Fate had other plans.

When I'm two years old or so, I suddenly become ill with a bizarre condition that doctors can never really diagnose, and therefore struggle to treat. In a nutshell, my body suddenly cannot process solid food. It's like the mechanics of my digestive system cease to work. Whatever goes in quickly comes straight out the other end.

It's unpleasant for all involved, but also pretty unhealthy, and my body suffers from being continually deprived of nutrition.

For a year, Mum and I go back and forth to the doctor, to the hospital, to specialists down in Brisbane, to anyone who would see me to try to figure this thing out. Everyone is stumped. Various treatments are tried and fail. Sometimes I'll get a little better, then much worse.

It's stressful. And it's very time-consuming. Mum has to miss so much work that eventually her bosses at the TAFE college suggest she stop coming entirely and focus on her family. Of course, they won't be paying her when she doesn't come, but they wish her all the best.

One day, after a year, just as abruptly as this bizarre sickness arrived, it's gone. I get better and I stay that way. It's a mystery, but given it's all's well that ends well, we move on with our lives.

Mum goes back to hairdressing and opens a salon called Beachcombers in downtown Yeppoon. It's *the* place to get your hair done.

Mum is young and trendy. Her staff are women in their twenties and thirties who are vibrant and vivacious. The shop fit-out is innovative – bright and bold in its design. Clients fill every single chair, cackling, sipping on piping hot cups of coffee, and sucking back cigarettes.

The success of the business means Mum works six days a week, leaving home at around seven o'clock in the morning and not returning until seven at night. Sometimes later. She rushes in the door, puts together dinner for the four of us, and hustles us through our evening routines and into bed. Only then can she tend to her own needs, if her exhaustion allows it.

Success demands a great deal of Mum. So too do the regular and unpredictable absences of my father. Although they hide the worst of it from us kids, their marriage is such that blow-ups often lead to Dad storming out in the middle of the night and not coming back for days, sometimes weeks, and once or twice, months.

Half of the household's income disappears with him. He doesn't send money from his semi-regular jaunts.

Even when things are good with Mum and Dad, his job in a coal mine four hours west means he's away for long stretches of time. It's usually an entire week at work, with a half day of travel on either side, then back for a few days of rest before he's gone again.

Occasionally, one of Mum's friends comes over to help get dinner ready if she's stuck late at the salon. There are always women floating in and out of the house to help with laundry, cleaning or babysitting. We're truly raised by a village.

Life is busy. Our home is loud and frantic, like a colourful and chaotic circus. But things are pretty good, as far as I can tell.

Damien is almost finished with high school and will soon be out of the house permanently. He's getting ready to move down to Brisbane to go to the police academy. Even while he's still here, he's not really around much. He plays football, he does competitive kickboxing, he loves to surf, he has a girlfriend, and he's a drummer in a band.

So, really, it's the remaining three of us at home most of the time. Trinity is in her mid-teens and takes care of Brett and me. We're pretty close, when we're not fighting like cats and dogs. Trinity is especially protective of me, even if I *am* annoying, and have no concept of privacy, personal space or boundaries – things important to a young woman.

I go through her things, borrowing cassette tapes without asking and listening to them on the little portable player in my bedroom. I thumb through her fashion magazines. I spray her various perfumes into the air and dance beneath the gently lingering scent.

Trinity gets frustrated with me. Especially when I'm in her room. But her soft spot for me is clear, and I love it.

I'm a precocious and confident kid. Loud and outgoing. An old soul trapped in a child's body, Mum's friends tell me constantly. I love hanging out with and talking to adults, as though we are equal peers. I like to sing and dance, gravitating towards theatrics from the moment I can walk and talk.

I have a sharp mind and a deeply entrenched ambition. Each day during summer, at the height of noon when the temperature is highest, I set up a rickety old vinyl-covered card table in front of our house and sell icy cold cups of cordial for twenty cents each to passers-by.

I learn quickly that the novelty of this, and my certain level of cuteness, means people will often pay much more than twenty cents. It doesn't take long for me to find this hobby fairly lucrative.

I make friends with Carmel, who owns the ceramics store down the road, and begin funnelling my profits into her business. When I have a decent stash of cash, I go in and select one of the undecorated figurines that line her shelves, discuss a colour scheme with her, then leave her to her devices. I check in each day to see how things are progressing. Then, when it's ready, I proudly carry the creation home and gift it to someone in my family.

Mum gets a pink pig with little bits of silver glitter covering its body. My grandmother gets a rose – it's fitting because her name is Rose. Dad gets an enormous wizard holding a trident in one hand and clutching a crystal ball – an actual bit of crystal – in the other.

I'm enthusiastic and easily motivated. I leap from bed each day, excited about what the world has in store for me. I'm a pretty good and easy kid.

The sudden absence of Joshua, my best friend, knocks me off my even kilter. I'm lost. Not running off to Joshua's house whenever I can leaves me with plenty of time alone to think. And flashes of the memories of what happened constantly take over my mind.

His mean tone. The dim light in that bedroom. His fingers fumbling where they shouldn't be.

I'm depressed and hopelessly lonely. But I can't see him. There's no way. The thought of looking at him, at merely meeting his gaze, is enough to make me want to be sick. It's too awkward and too unpleasant.

And so I resign myself to the fact that we aren't friends anymore. It was good while it lasted, but it's back now to me being on my own.

And then, one morning, he shows up at my door.

Trinity yells down the hallway that he's here and ushers him inside. Suddenly, he's in my room.

His skin looks ashen, as though he too has been cooped up inside for several days. His eyes are glassy. He looks sad.

Neither of us acknowledges what happened. We're kids. It's not like we're going to sit down and thrash things out, talking frankly and candidly about how we each feel. That's not how things go. Instead, we're quiet, occasionally looking at each other sheepishly.

'Do you want to be friends again?' he asks me.

I shrug. I do – of course I do. But can I?

I'm so confused and so rattled by what happened. At the same time, I miss being one half of something. Seeing Joshua again has given my heart a little happy jolt, in spite of everything that happened.

He slips his backpack off his shoulder and plonks it heavily on the floor. He leans down to unzip it and lifts out his Sega. He peers up at me and smiles.

'Do you want this?'

My jaw drops in shock. Joshua loves his video game console. He only plays the in-built game, *Alex Kidd in Miracle World*, but he's basically glued to it. The controller is practically an extension of his arm. We both love that game.

And what's not to love? A little jumping dude punching his way through rocks, taking on evil henchmen, traversing all kinds of dangerous and deadly environments until he meets the big monster – the biggest of them all. Alex does all this while taking time out every now and then to treat himself to a burger.

To want to give his Sega to me, with Alex included, is a massive deal. I'm touched – truly chuffed in a way I probably haven't been before. I beam at him and he smiles back at me.

Joshua helps me set up the game console on the second television in the back part of my house, in an unused space that would have once been the outside steps before one of several extensions were tacked on. It's a bit of a sleep-out with a desk, a futon couch and an old television that used to be in the lounge room until recently, when my parents upgraded it for something bigger.

We play for hours that day, him watching over my shoulder and offering words of encouragement and tidbits of advice.

When my eyes are tired and almost square, we take a break and run outside. We watch older kids playing basketball and skateboarding. We wander through the tall, unmowed grass on the vacant block of land next to the court. We chatter happily and, without really deciding to or even thinking about it, we walk towards his house.

Joshua tells me about this cool new toy his mum just bought him. It's a big tyrannosaurus rex that moves its head and roars. That's pretty much the height of cutting-edge technology in the early 1990s, so I can barely believe my ears.

'Can I have a go? Where is it?'

He smiles and nods, dragging me down the hallway to his bedroom. I look around for this toy, which is almost impossible for me to even picture.

'Here it is! Shut the door!' he says, beaming.

As I turn to close it, I hear the blinds clanging shut. That sound. It sends shivers down the back of my neck. The room goes dark and I freeze. I hear his voice, low and quiet, beckoning me over to him.

Chapter Two

Dr Arlo Rolenstein raises his eyebrows and takes a slow and deep breath. It feels as though he is sucking the air out of the room.

'Well,' he sighs, exhaling heavily, removing his delicate round eyeglasses and rubbing the bridge of his nose with his thumb and forefinger. 'This explains a lot.'

It's 2017. For the first time in my life, I've just said out loud the words that have been rolling around in my head for the better part of thirty years. My dirty little secret. A secret I never imagined I'd tell anyone.

They're words that I've said to myself silently countless times. Probably ten thousand times or more, reliving my childhood over and over again as a kind of penance for my sins. But while I might've thought about it endlessly, I'd never verbalised those things that took place.

'He would touch me ...'

The words felt like acid reflux gurgling up the back of my throat from the pit of my stomach.

'Then he'd touch himself and rub until he reached climax.'

To say all of this now – to give voice to these things for the very first time in my life – stings.

These are secrets I've carried with me since I was five. Things I thought I'd never dare to tell anyone for fear they wouldn't understand. Secrets both big and small – countless untold and deeply unpleasant truths. A heavy burden that never became any lighter no matter how much time passed.

Right now, in this moment, perched on the very edge of the ageing leather couch in Dr Rolenstein's office, I feel about as uncomfortable as I ever have. I'm sweltering, and not only from the sharp heat of a Sydney summer, pulsating through the window of his office.

He sits silently for a moment, looking me in the eyes, and then staring off at a point just above my head and to the left. He's done this before, and each time I have to fight the urge to turn around and see exactly what he's looking at.

I think it's the top corner of the enormous abstract artwork that hangs above me. It's a mad swirl of reds, oranges and yellows, like a sunset that has had one too many champagnes at the end of a long day and become a bit fuzzy around the edges.

He looks there occasionally after I've dropped some heavy nugget of new information. It's how he processes things and considers his response. I sit and wait, still and quiet, for him to speak, and for some big insight to be bestowed upon me.

I listen to the world outside. The city is alive and breathing. Cars whizz by. People chat and laugh at the cafe five storeys below. There's the odd sound of a car horn – a disgruntled taxi driver in a rush, probably. Maybe a delivery van trying to access an illegally occupied loading zone. It's the perfect soundtrack for this part of town, right on the fringe of Circular Quay and the historic Rocks district.

Dr Rolenstein has a small office in an old sandstone building. It's beautiful, but horribly inefficient for a modern workplace, with no elevator and zero air-conditioning. Sometimes the heat is so stifling that it's hard for me to dig deep into the recesses of my soul to find little bits of trauma meaningful enough to justify the $380 these fifty-minute sessions cost.

Dr Rolenstein is still pondering. This one is a doozy, it seems. I've been here before, occupying myself with the sounds of the city while he descends into a quiet meditation. In the two years he has been my psychiatrist, I've led him into quite a number of these reflective moments.

His face never gives anything away. He's a consummate professional. I wouldn't know if he's shocked or enthralled. I fear, in this reflective moment, he might feel a sensation of disgust.

Eventually, after a minute or two, sometimes several, his gaze lowers and settles back on me. He blinks sharply, as if returning himself to the present moment, and nods at me gently.

'Right,' he often begins. 'Let's unpack that.'

And so we do, wading together through whatever torrent of terror or deep sadness I've just revisited, not really appreciating its significance until hearing it out loud for the first time.

At almost every session, there's some new self-discovery. Some are grand, some are small, but all of them together paint an increasingly compelling picture of just how truly fucked I am.

I came to Dr Rolenstein at the insistence of my partner, Robert. A psychologist himself, he sees my tendency for self-destruction and my horribly immature and unsustainable way of dealing with my emotions. Anger. Isolation. Alcohol. It's not the best combination.

We've gotten really serious and, if I care about him, I'll make an investment in myself, he suggests.

The thought of opening up the tightly shut lid on the box of my life's worst moments doesn't really appeal to me at all. Why would anyone want to look back? Why would you deliberately disturb calm waters?

Besides, I feel relatively well-adjusted, all things considered. At this stage of my life, I think I'm pretty happy – successful, settled and content, with healthy habits and sound coping mechanisms.

Good Lord, was I deluded.

For the entirety of my adult life, it turns out, I've been barely keeping it together. The facade of effortless living and carefree happiness is complete and utter bullshit. I've been carefully maintaining it for so long, though, that I actually believe I'm fine. I've convinced myself of this grand illusion.

When I arrive for my first appointment, I'm convinced I'm doing well. I'm sure that this shrink will see it too, and send me back to Robert with a clean bill of health. One or two sessions and I'll be done, never having to return to this little hotbox of an office.

Nothing could be further from the truth. Dr Rolenstein doesn't have to scratch very deep below my faintly cracking surface to expose the extent of my lie.

I cry hysterically in our first session while talking about how much I loathe myself. I tell him about the things that go through my head when I look in the mirror, or see my reflection elsewhere – the inner monologue that plays when I catch a glimpse of myself in a shop window as I walk by, shuddering in disgust.

'But everyone kind of hates themselves a bit, right?' I sniff, looking at him for reassurance.

Dr Rolenstein narrows his eyes ever so slightly, but enough for me – an eagle-eyed observer of body language – to notice.

'Do they? I don't know …' he says, his voice trailing off. He continues, more definitively: 'No, I don't think they do.'

I nod, but I don't think I believe him. Surely inside all of us is a little hardened critic who sees everything we do and has some candid and usually cruel notes to share? It's that familiar insider who has analysed the plot of our story, tearing through the holes in the arcs, judging the merits of the cast, and who has given the whole production an overall star rating.

And it's not a great review.

After a few months of seeing Dr Rolenstein weekly, I wonder out loud one afternoon if I'm irreparably broken. We've uncovered so much that has been long hidden, and a lot of it is really troubling. Depression and severe anxiety. A dangerous self-loathing. An unhealthy way of dealing with what's going on inside, as well as the things that occur in the real world. I'm not even sure anymore if I'm a particularly good person.

Dr Rolenstein sighs and tells me how the old cliché of a person being like an onion with many layers is dumb, but actually quite apt.

'It does take time to peel away the layers of time and trauma and repression and shame,' he says. 'But really, Shannon. I've never seen an onion quite like yours. It's not a bad thing. It just means you're complex.'

We work through a lot of the problems that, not long ago, I could barely see. Now they're as plain as day – shockingly so.

Drinking too much – far too much. Needing a few drinks to feel secure in a social setting. Using it as a crutch when I'm unsettled or sad. Not being able to stop after just one or two, and instead needing to finish the bottle. And, if I crack open a second, probably polishing that one off too.

Knowing that a relationship, friendship or otherwise,

is deeply unhealthy, but persisting with it anyway due to boredom, ease, not wanting to rock the boat, or because I think this is probably as good as it gets.

Disliking myself in a way that seems to be deepening more and more by the day. The kind of dislike that, if I think about it for too long, how much I loathe this person I am, makes me tremble with anger.

Sabotaging the good things in my personal and professional lives, as though contentedness is a poison that I need to rid myself of immediately.

Burning the candle at both ends in a bid to distract myself from the creeping darkness that is getting harder to keep at bay. I believe that if you're as busy as humanly possible, there's no time to think about being depressed or anxious or collapsing into a heap. It's true, but only for a while, and it turns out that you eventually run out of candle.

In my early twenties, this kind of internal turmoil is relatively manageable. I'm just so busy squeezing everything I can out of life that there's not much left in the day to devote to my demons. And drinking and partying all the time makes serious self-reflection pretty impossible.

But as time goes on and age wears away at my thresholds for disruption, pain and unease, it's draining. And I've felt very drained of late.

*

It's as though good parts of myself are slowly slipping away and in their place is left a husk of a man who barely wants to exist. Dr Rolenstein helps me to see the kind of dangerous path I'm on and shines a light on the experiences in my past that help explain a little of why I am the way I am.

We have covered a lot of ground.

My parents' disastrous marriage and the unsettling impact that their on-again, off-again union had on me when I was a kid. The precarious nature of the meaning of 'home' it instilled, for example. The financial ramifications of Mum finally leaving Dad for good. The hurt of an absent and uncaring father who had almost no interest in me.

My sexuality, and the long struggle to come to terms with being gay. The severe bullying, both mental and physical, that I endured through most of my adolescence.

The heady mix of fear, shame and uncertainty that I became familiar with at a young age and carried with me through to early adulthood.

It all combined to create self-loathing of a severity Dr Rolenstein says he hasn't come across too often. His brow furrows sometimes when I speak about myself – about how I see myself. The words I use are laced with venom.

'Hey now, just stop for a second,' he'll tell me, shaking his head. 'Think about what you've just said. Does that seem reasonable? Is that a fair way to think about yourself?'

Those words belong to my horrid inner voice, he tells me, and aren't rational. Thoughts aren't real when they come from a place of such hurt; I can't merely accept them as gospel. I need to push back and challenge them before they consume me whole.

I nod emphatically, but I'm not sure I ever really believe him or listen to him fully. I know that voice better than any other. We go way back. And as nasty and toxic as it can be, I'm not about to discard my old mate now, even if he is a total asshole a lot of the time.

But for all of the revelations I've made in this office, for the hours and hours of unpacking and processing, I've never mentioned Joshua's name once. Until today.

I didn't even intend to when I walked in this afternoon. In fact, I firmly expected to take that particular compartment in my trauma box to the grave, never letting anyone take a peek at its gory contents.

'There was this kid growing up ...' I begin.

Once I start speaking about it, I can't stop. The dam is broken. Even though it feels like I'm regurgitating a razor blade, something inside of my soul knows this is long overdue. It's time. It's worth getting all of this out, finally, and worth persisting through the awkwardness and discomfort I feel right now.

I tell Dr Rolenstein about how it started. I relive that day in Joshua's bedroom. I tell him about the second time it happened, after he gave me the Sega Mega Drive and took me to his house to show me the T-rex toy.

I tell him how it happened a third time, and a fourth, and about how I eventually lost count. It probably happened every other day. I think there was an instance like that whenever we were alone.

My memory doesn't hold really specific accounts of the times beyond the third or fourth encounter. Just little snippets. Being in the back row of Yeppoon's sole movie theatre watching the film *Hook*. Hiding in his mum's humid greenhouse in his backyard. Crawling into the back of his dad's ute. Hiding in the bushes near the basketball court next to my house.

I told him how it went on for almost two years, until my family moved away from Yeppoon to live in Mackay, a town five hours north, when I was seven years old.

I told him how it resumed, picking right up where we left off as though nothing had changed at all, when I was ten and we moved back to Yeppoon.

Joshua and his mum had left by then, moving down to Brisbane after his parents got a divorce. But he comes back to town each school holidays to visit his dad, who still lives in the same fibro cottage a few blocks away from my childhood home. And so, each day of his stay in Yeppoon, we resume our long friendship, and for the most part it's pretty great.

The dirty things we do continue. It remains shameful. It feels wrong. But at the same time, it's been happening for so long now that it feels almost normal. Or *typical*, in any case – to me, anyway.

I tell Dr Rolenstein about when it stops. I'm twelve and I go down to Brisbane to stay with Joshua for a few days. We spend the time playing on his computer and watching *South Park*, but each night in the darkness of his bedroom, it happens again.

I'm beginning to suspect that I'm gay and I hate it. I desperately don't want to be gay, but I feel it's going to be unavoidable. There's a sensation in the pit of my stomach that tells me as much when I look at girls and feel nothing, then look at boys and feel a spark. But in the late 1990s, being gay can be a death sentence, and that terrifies me.

The escalating shame is too much. It's a cancer spreading throughout my body, eating away at tissues or organs. Soon there'll be nothing left. This has to end for my sake, before I go completely mad, I think. And so, after that trip, I never see Joshua again.

I pause and look up at Dr Rolenstein, who's sitting quietly and staring at me. There's the slightest hint of a mix of pity and intrigue painted across his face.

'Another layer of the onion peeled back.' Dr Rolenstein nods. 'A lot to dive into next week.'

And so we do, tearing back layer after layer, getting our hands dirty amid the scorched depths of my soul. Each session brings some new self-discoveries that make such perfect sense once a light is thrust on them. It's the kind of time to reflect and take stock that I've never given myself. I haven't been brave enough until this point.

'These kinds of feelings, these kinds of challenges, they're not uncommon with people who've been sexually abused,' he tells me one day.

I jolt upright. The sudden movement startles him, and he shuffles back in his seat. He can see that I'm instantly uncomfortable.

'It's not abuse, though?' I blurt out in a way that's partly a defiant statement but also an urgent question. 'That's not sexual abuse. That's just fucked-up kids doing fucked-up stuff. Right?'

He purses his lips. His eyes begin to drift to that familiar space above my head.

'No!' I interject, heading off his brief mental departure. 'No, no. You just said that I was sexually abused. Is that what this is?'

The silence that hangs above us is crushing in its weight. It feels like we sit there staring at each other across the room for hours. In reality, it's probably a couple of minutes. He's doing the other thing he does – remaining silent so that I fill the void with more words, which often will contain the answer to my question. I'm a journalist in my day job. This is a technique I know well and have mastered over the years.

I'm rattled. I've spent so many years replaying those moments with Joshua and agonising over what he did to me –

what we did together. Not once did it strike me as a kind of sexual abuse. He was a kid too. Kids can't abuse other kids, can they?

But suddenly, in the same way that all of my other flaws and insecurities and challenges have become unexpectedly visible, there's a sense of blinding clarity.

The age difference. The power imbalance. Him knowing which of my buttons to push to get what he wanted, with a kind of sophisticated manipulation that I couldn't withstand. The coercion and threats to stay quiet – to keep our dirty, shameful secret.

As Oprah Winfrey might put it, it's an 'a-ha' moment.

It's not like the 'a-ha' moments I've had before. Figuring out how to assemble the BILLY bookcase from IKEA on my own, when even my own internalised homophobia doubted I was man enough to. Finally realising the 'straight' cowboy I had a brief fling with in my late twenties was never going to love me. Accepting in my mid-teens that I was not in fact bisexual, despite my desperation to identify this way because it was so much more palatable than being a 'faggot'.

This is a whole different ball game. This stark realisation helps put so many of those other puzzle pieces together. So much of why I am the way I am makes sense.

It helps to explain the toxic relationships I leap into and endure, one after the other, even when I know they're shitty.

It helps explain my suffocating fear of being abandoned, my willingness to accept the absolute shittest of situations to avoid seeming impolite or difficult.

It explains the constant uneasy hum of awkwardness drowning out most of my thoughts – especially the positive ones. The ever-present sensation of guilt which is my second shadow. Guilt about feeling too joyful, too burdensome, too insecure, not insecure enough … and, of course, guilt for no reason at all. Sometimes even guilt about feeling guilty.

It explains why I don't value myself or my body, not even one little bit, considering myself utterly worthless to anyone. It explains my deeply held belief that I have nothing much of anything to offer the world. That constant negativity I feel towards myself; the nasty, scathing words, from me to me, inside my head, running on a loop, like a soundtrack to every element of my life. *Ugly. Fat. Stupid. Unworthy. Overrated. Unlovable. Broken. Fucked.*

So much of it makes sense now. I see myself in a new, albeit unsettling light. I understand a lot about why I am the way I am, and the origin of much of my story.

It's him. Joshua. He made me this way.

I see Dr Rolenstein every single week without fail. Sometimes it's twice a week if needed. And for the most part, I'm really enjoying our time together, even if it is heavy.

Looking back, I just can't believe how little of this I understood before now. I really had no idea how troubled I was inside. Now, having discovered so much about myself, I feel like a different person.

Sometimes the revelations I experience are small but fascinating. Take me not liking the sound of especially hotted-up cars with roaring engines – it's probably because one of the bullies who beat me at school tore around town in a noisy Ford Falcon. It's very likely the roaring sound reminds me of him.

Some discoveries are big and core-shaking, like when I am forced to examine the instances throughout my adolescence and early adulthood when I let men use and abuse me. On reflection, they all make sense. The driver of that kind of unhealthy risk-taking behaviour suddenly seems so obvious.

Maybe I could have come to some of these conclusions on my own, without the help of a very expensive professional who mostly lets me do all of the talking, but without him the pieces have never quite fallen into place.

Like, I'm a shocking sleeper and, until now, I've never really understood why. Whether I can't doze off easily and only get two or three hours of slumber, or whether I lose consciousness the moment my head hits the pillow and stay comatose for eight solid hours, I feel the same. Exhausted. Shattered. Like a zombie.

Well, that's probably because my sleep is so often corrupted by vivid and terrifying nightmares. I'll often be jolted wide awake by my own scream. I thrash out, kicking and punching at invisible enemies only I can see. I yell furiously, viciously, hurling all kinds of insults into the night.

My long-suffering husband – we married in 2018 after four years of dating – is used to it and will give me a rundown in the morning of the horrid things I've said in my sleep.

I'm fearful of so many things – some rational, many very much not. Heights. Confined spaces. Being underwater. Being in the open water. Being at a certain height and looking at a completely cloudless sky. Vegetables. Spiders. Spiderwebs. Overly drunk men. Particularly strong wind. Walking barefoot outside. That almost deafening *whoop-whoop-whoop* noise that happens when you're in a car and travelling at speed with only one window down.

I'm prone to sudden, unprompted and inexplicable mood shifts. I can be completely content, even happy – deliriously so – and then, in an instant, totally distraught. Inconsolable at times. Or, more often than not, I go into a blinding rage that can't be eased or contained.

I can swing wildly from a withdrawn state to one that's overwhelmingly clingy.

After I tell Dr Rolenstein about Joshua, he wants to understand more about what I was like as a child before those things happened to me for the first time. He asks when things began to change.

We figure out that my mood swings probably developed around that time. I reckon I was probably prone to being a little emotional and dramatic. It's kind of in my DNA. But around the age Joshua first touched me, I begin to become more emotional, sometimes overly so, and leaning towards the hysterical.

Little things, mostly inconsequential things, set me off into tantrums, uncontrollable crying, and violent outbursts. Over nothing, sometimes – feeling overlooked or disregarded. Looking forward to something and then it not happening. Being second-guessed or underestimated.

Even now, I'm volatile. It's as though my impulse control and coping mechanisms ceased to develop beyond the age of five or six. Honestly, I lose my cool and erupt at the drop of a hat. Even the vaguest perceived slight is enough to set me off.

It was like that when I was a kid. Brett not sharing his toys. Trinity smirking at me in a mocking manner. The pair of them ganging up and excluding me from things. It cuts deep and I'm distraught if I get the impression that I'm being made fun of.

Tiny little things blow up into major catastrophes when I'm involved, as though I only have two speeds – zero and one hundred miles per hour. Some of my most vivid memories are of having an enormous explosion of some kind and uncontrollably crying until I vomit.

Honestly. Much of my recollection of early childhood is stained with tears and spew. That can't be normal.

I remember being eight years old. I'm walking through the showgrounds the day before the annual show weekend, and see the stalls being set up. One of the show-bag stands has a 'help wanted' sign out the front of it and I am instantly consumed by excitement. I can just picture it now. I can work all weekend at the show, make a heap of money, and maybe get a discount on some cool show bags. I run home as fast as I can and tell Mum my plan, expecting her blessing.

'Absolutely not,' she laughs. 'Show people are weird and you're too young to be working there. You're eight, for Christ's sake! No.'

I'm devastated. I mean, completely crushed. I scream and throw myself on the floor, dragging random shit off the kitchen table as I go down. 'You're dead to me', I declare, as I crawl along the floor to my bedroom, suddenly unable to use my legs.

I'm howling like a dying animal. I'm so utterly distraught that I make myself sick. Literally – I vomit all over my bed and almost choke on bits of bile. I never do manage to work at the show.

Dr Rolenstein and I often laugh together while I recount these stories. I was quite a little shit and it's pretty funny. But there's also a shared understanding of what these kinds of insights reveal.

I remember more and more about younger me as time goes on and we focus most of our sessions on this period of my life.

I suddenly remember that I wet the bed. For a long time. It goes on until I'm about eleven years old. Every single night, without fail, unless I set the alarm next to my bed for one o'clock in the morning and force myself to get up to go to the toilet. Even then, I sometimes slip up.

But the bed-wetting – a classic sign of acute anxiety in a child, research tells me – is something I have forced myself to forget until a session with Dr Rolenstein.

'Wow!' he says, betraying a little bit of surprise for once. 'You honestly forgot about wetting the bed until you were almost a teenager?'

'Eleven, thank you – not *almost a teenager*,' I scoff.

I really had, though. It was like it had been completely wiped from my surface memory and pushed way, way down.

I'd forgotten about how sleepovers at friends' houses were all but impossible, and school camps a nightmare to navigate. In Year Five, my class went to Stony Creek and a trusted teacher, told about my problem by Mum, came in every morning to help me drag out my sleeping bag while the other kids were distracted with breakfast, so that we could wash it and hang it out to dry.

For the years this carries on, Mum turns to multiple sources for potential remedies. My childhood doctor is sure I'll eventually grow out of it. A magazine article she comes across about this very topic suggests putting a stick of lavender inside my pillow case. It's got something to do with its calming properties, I guess. The alarm clock idea was hers and is a good stopgap measure.

Apart from that, it's all plastic mattress protectors and a shitload of money spent on laundry liquid.

But when I'm approaching adolescence and this nonsense is still a concern, she pushes the doctor to do more. He agrees that I should've stopped by now. He prescribes me a fairly low-dose antidepressant and it works almost instantly. Within a week, I stop wetting the bed and, aside from one extremely drunken night in my mid-twenties, I never do it again.

For all of my childhood and adolescence, I am pathologically afraid of having my shirt off in public. I'm talking totally crippled with fear.

Wearing a swim shirt at the pool or at the beach, or even just not taking my T-shirt off, isn't super unusual, it seems. It doesn't create much of a stir. I'm just a few shades darker than translucent, so it's probably seen as me being sun smart rather than rocked by a difficult-to-comprehend insecurity.

But the practice of getting changed in the toilet at the local swimming pool, particularly during school lessons, will almost send me into a meltdown every single time. I have my very first panic attack in Year Five when one of the cubicles in the toilet block at the local pool is taped off for maintenance, and the other is occupied by a boy changing out of his uniform and into his board shorts.

'Hurry up and get changed!' one of the male teachers screams at me when I am one of a few still in their uniform.

Dawdling, he probably thinks. He might ask himself why I am standing in the corner of the room, facing the wall, shaking like a leaf, if he cares. He doesn't, though.

I begin to quietly cry as I gingerly slip my grey dress shorts off and pull my parachute-material swim ones on. I clench my eyes closed and tear my school polo shirt off and slide on my rashie as quickly as I can. It's horrible. I feel sick in the stomach just recalling now how it made me feel then.

Apparently, a resistance to fairly routine things, like removing clothing in an appropriate setting, is one of the red flags that abuse counsellors say adults should look out for. The teachers don't notice, and of course I never say anything to anyone about how I am feeling.

A significant change in body weight or eating habits is another warning sign, I've read. When I'm in my early adolescence, around the age of thirteen, I begin to rapidly lose weight. I look gaunt and sickly. The doctor – a different one to my childhood GP – is for some reason convinced that I am bulimic. The diagnosis made as little sense then as it does now. There is no reason for him to jump to such an extreme conclusion, and it just makes things really terrible in my already overwhelming life.

I have to go to see him every single week to be weighed. Mum overhauls my diet and introduces a lot of carbohydrate-heavy foods, as well as fattening stuff, supplement shakes that they give to anorexic kids in hospital, and a heap of sugary desserts and treats. I eat it all dutifully. But I only put on little bits and pieces of weight – a couple of hundred grams here and there.

I'm definitely not deliberately skinny. It's not like I am making myself sick or foregoing meals due to some desire to be thin. If anything, I hate the way I look. It's not attractive to be so bony. I look even weaker to the bullies at school who make my life a living hell.

Of course I am thin. If my body was a car engine, it was one that was never switched off. It ran at full capacity, thousands of revs per minute, all day, every day, thanks to the relentless anxiety that tormented me. When an engine runs full bore without pause, it's going to chew through a shitload of petrol.

Much of it makes sense when Dr Rolenstein and I begin to explore what trauma looks like, especially over a long period of time. How it begins, how it transforms, how it sets in.

'And abuse is one of the biggest triggers of trauma,' he says.

There's that word again. I'm not sure he means to use it in this instance, given my prior reaction. Since then, when I've brought it up again, he's been totally unwilling to tell me if he really sees what Joshua did to me – what we did – as sexual abuse.

'Do you really think it's abuse, what happened to me?' I ask again.

He raises his eyebrows and opens his mouth to speak, but

quickly closes it again. He gives me a look that I can read instantly – one telling me that there might not be a simple answer to that question.

If there is an answer at all, it's probably one I need to discover on my own. And then, entirely by accident, that's exactly what I begin to do.

Chapter Three

It's meant to be a twenty-minute interview for a news story about a relatively new fundraiser. That's all. I've done a million of them in my time – the jobs some other journalists tend to overlook because they're small fry. They don't get a huge amount of clicks. Why bother?

I like this stuff though. It's real. It's human. Some kid somewhere, doing something for charity. A heartfelt but fairly skippable tale of adversity that inspired something good.

It sounds cynical, and it probably is, but most editors don't particularly care about those stories. Simply put, readers don't tend to care either. They click on, read, or watch the salacious, sexy, scandalous and shocking stuff – not the nice stories.

My boss is different. She holds the view that journalism in this modern, audience-devoted era should still be about doing stories that matter – to people and to communities. I've also worked on the other side of the fence in media relations for a not-for-profit, once upon a time, and remember how difficult it can be to get a reporter to pick up a pitch for something very worthy but not at all ground-breaking. And so, as a news reporter, I try to do these little stories whenever I can, and with my editor's blessing.

So when this interview opportunity comes up, I say yes. It's a story about Polished Man, a relatively new part-awareness campaign, part-fundraiser benefitting child sexual abuse victims. The concept is that blokes – both prominent people and everyday participants – sign up to paint one fingernail for a month, to spark a conversation and generate donations from their friends and family.

The publicist who pitches the story to me is lovely. The timing coincides with an annual mental health awareness campaign that I coordinate, so I figure I can slot this in. I agree to do a story if she can find me a compelling case study that I can anchor it to.

Enter Luke.

We meet one evening in late winter in 2018 in the foyer of the News Corp Australia headquarters in Surry Hills in Sydney's inner-east. He's just knocked off work and comes to meet me for a brief interview.

I just need some colour, I think. A little bit about why he's taking part, how much he hopes to raise, a little bit about his own experiences, if he's willing to share – that sort of thing.

It's already dark and the air has turned crisp when we shake hands in the lobby. I usher him past the security gates and deep into the bowels of the building. We set ourselves up at a table in the far corner of the empty staff cafeteria.

I sit my voice recorder in front of him and hit the start button, then turn to a blank page in my notebook, pen poised.

'So, tell me about yourself,' I begin.

Luke is an architect in his late thirties. He has shoulder-length hair that's haphazardly tucked behind his ears, without much further thought or care. His skin shows mild evidence of a life spent almost entirely outdoors, and a happy one at that, with faint little smile lines around his eyes.

He radiates gentleness. His is the kind of personality that could instantly put at ease even the most anxious of people. That old saying 'doesn't have a nasty bone in his body' might've been coined in honour of him, I think.

But his light brown eyes are just a little bit sad. It's probably not noticeable to most people, but I've seen those kinds of eyes before. They betray an otherwise well-hidden internal turmoil.

When he does cry a little towards the end of our interview, when giving me a glimpse of the horrors that were inflicted upon him as a boy, those eyes almost seem relieved for a moment.

They've witnessed much. They've kept many secrets.

This interview, which was meant to be brief, goes for almost two hours. We are both totally engrossed, to the point that we barely notice the office cleaner noisily vacuuming around our feet, knocking the legs of our chairs as she goes.

'I had never said out loud, in public, to anyone except my family and my psychologist, the words "I was sexually abused" before the opening night of Polished Man last year,' he tells me.

'It's kind of hard to explain, but this thing you think about every single day of your life, it's really hard to say it ... as though you might give it life if you do.'

It's uncanny how much he's verbalising things that have been on my mind for several months now. I nod along intently. I feel this immediate connection to Luke. I want to grab him and shake him, to tell him that I know exactly what he's talking about when it comes to a secret coming to life.

I think he feels what I want to say, somehow. My face probably tells him that there's a shared experience here. He pauses and looks at me. I nod again. *There's a meeting of our two life paths*, I silently say.

Then aloud: 'Something happened to me when I was a kid, so I think I kind of get it.'

This is the second time I've verbalised my own shameful, secretive past. First with Dr Rolenstein, for reasons I still don't understand, and now, with this person I don't even know, at my actual workplace.

Luke's face softens. He leans in, nodding gently, all of a sudden lighter and less awkward about sharing his own difficult story.

To unveil a part of myself in a professional setting is unusual. I like to be personable and engaged in an interview, and while

I might sometimes share the odd anecdote, I've always been reluctant to be too candid. It's like I'm playing a fictional role, and straying off-script would break the fourth wall.

There's also a fine line between being relatable and making something all about you rather than the person you've come to speak to. The last thing you want to do in an interview is break the momentum of the conversation you've come to get for your story. Jumping in with your own two cents can often throw your subject off track.

And so this is out of character for me. But it feels almost freeing. To open up and connect with someone like this, a stranger no less, leaves me a little light-headed. Almost giddy.

'I mean, that's a story for another day,' I quickly say with a smile, moving the conversation on. 'This chat is about you.'

We continue and I listen intently as he tells me about his life. He had a fairly pleasant childhood in Sydney's outer suburbs with his siblings, a younger brother and sister, and loving parents, a pastor and his wife.

For the first several years of Luke's childhood, the family lives on a street like most others in middle Australia in the late 1980s – young couples in modest homes, their kids running around squealing, jumping fences and chasing each other, or speeding down the street on BMX bikes.

'We were total latchkey kids,' Luke explains. 'We roamed and did our own thing and we thought we were pretty free.

But there were points we knew we weren't allowed to venture beyond.'

Things are pretty loose and cruisy, as they were in those days, but still, there's a kind of Neighbourhood Watch of parents who keep an eye on all of the kids, who span all ages, as they happily play, he explains. The mums and dads look out for each other. They ensure everyone's littlies are protected from harm.

It's the era of stranger danger and the Safety House community policing program. Kids are told terrifying tales of shadowy figures in strange cars trying to lure them inside, snatching them away from the safety and comfort they know, taking them God knows where to do God knows what.

Unknown monsters that can be hard to spot can be lurking anywhere, ready to strike at any time, it seems. But for eight-year-old Luke, the real danger lurks just over the back fence in the form of an older boy who is seventeen years old.

'He didn't have younger siblings, but friends of mine had older brothers who were his age, so that's how I came to interact with him. It wasn't really unusual for older kids to be around us younger ones. That's just the way things were. There was no reason to think me spending time with this guy was odd or something to think twice about.'

As a young boy, the attention of a cool teenager is exciting. It makes you feel cool too, and maybe a little more grown-up than your peers. And this particular teenager has the things that Luke likes – a computer with heaps of games, and a shiny hotted-up Cortina with its bonnet permanently popped up, just begging you to peer inside with wonder.

'I loved cars. My first great love was a Volkswagen Beetle. My friend's dad drove one – two-tone blue with black panels in the doors. It was beautiful.

'Knowing as an eight-year-old that the Porsche company developed out of Volkswagen felt like this secret, special insight that no other kid had.'

Luke's eyes light up now as he explains that a Porsche 911 sports car is basically a squashed Volkswagen Beetle. That's just one of the countless car facts he unearthed and meticulously stored in his mind when he was a kid.

'I don't remember the first time he abused me,' Luke tells me. 'I have this very vivid memory of being afraid to play in the backyard afterwards, though. I suddenly didn't want to be out there because I knew he would hear me, come outside and pester me to jump the fence.

'I kind of learnt to be where he couldn't get to me. So I don't remember how it started or any of the details of that first time, but I definitely remember how terrified it made me.'

Luke's childhood bedroom is at the back of the family house. From his window, through the gaps in the fence palings, he can see glimpses of that boy's house. From time to time, he can hear his gruff voice floating through the air, reaching him in the safety of his room.

He begins having … not nightmares in the traditional sense. But he wakes suddenly in the middle of the night and is struck by an intense fear that someone is going to climb through the window and snatch him away.

'I had a real fear of him. I didn't like what he was doing and I didn't understand it, and I knew it was wrong. But I was afraid I would be the one who got in trouble for it. I was filled with this constant anxiety about it all. It was horrible.'

While Luke can't remember the first time, he remembers the very last time the older boy tried to abuse him.

It's a fairly typical weekday afternoon and he's out on the street playing handball with his friends. The sun beats down on some kid's concrete driveway that's been turned into a makeshift court, with bright pink chalk marking the boundaries of each boy's square.

That day is the first one in a long time when Luke feels free. The burden of the enormous and shameful secret he's been carrying for almost a year has temporarily lifted. It's a beautiful day. He has successfully dodged the older guy for a week or so and relishes the sense of safety. His mates are here.

The older boy must be able to hear him. He's been waiting to see Luke, it seems. Knowing he's outside, he makes a beeline for him.

'He came out into the street looking for me. He saw me and called me over. I didn't want to go but everyone looked at me and if I didn't go, I feared they'd wonder why. So I went.'

He lures Luke up the street a little and into some bushes on a strip of unoccupied council land. He grabs his wrist and yanks him forward, out of view of the other kids.

'He tried it on in the open. It felt so predatory and premeditated. It was chilling really, thinking about it now. I was like, *no, no way*, and I ran off.'

Mercifully, fate plays a part in ending the abuse once and for all when Luke's dad gets transferred to a new church, on the very opposite end of Sydney, just about as far away as you can get from that street.

'I was very fortunate. It gave me a huge amount of space. Unfortunately, a lot of people are trapped in proximity to the person abusing them. The stories I've heard from survivors are horrendous.

'But for me, I was finally free. It was done. They weren't family friends, so it's not like I had to see them or anything. I thought that would be it and I'd never have to think about it again.

'I couldn't have been more wrong.'

Eventually, realising the time, Luke and I wrap up our conversation, walk to the entrance of the building, and say our goodbyes. I feel changed in some way. I feel a renewed determination to tackle this huge burden I've been dragging around with me.

'If you ever need to talk, man …' Luke begins. I nod and smile. We shake hands and he wanders off into the night.

The story comes out a short time later. I've poured my heart and soul into it, spending much more time piecing it together than I expected to for something like this. I read and reread the draft. On the final run-through, just before I file to my editor, I realise that it's probably one of the best stories I've ever done.

Filing the story is typically the point where the interviewer and subject part ways, but I can't stop thinking about him. I send Luke a link to the story and we email back and forth a couple of times. His story has forced its way into my heart and made a home there. The similarities between us – the things we feel so deeply and the flaws he battles to live with – are strong.

His words echo in my head every couple of days. *If you ever need to talk, man …*

The thought of picking up the phone and asking him to grab a beer crosses my mind. There are so many things I want to ask him. But I reread my notes and listen to the audio of our interview and realise that our experiences aren't that similar at all. Not the things that happened to us, I mean.

I was touched up by a kid a couple of years older than me and it made me feel ashamed and dirty. He was sexually abused by someone who was virtually an adult – a premeditating monster who knew what he was doing. I couldn't really sit down face to face with Luke and share my story, thinking that we're in any way on a similar level, could I?

Meeting him was an extraordinary experience and ignited within me a yearning to understand more about myself and what happened to me. I'm filled with a determination to figure out why I am the way I am, and how much of that is because of Joshua.

And I really want to figure out if what happened was child sexual abuse, or something entirely different. Or maybe it's not that black and white.

'One in five children will be affected by sexual abuse in some form.'

Those are the very first words that Carol Ronken says to me. She's the director of research at Bravehearts, Australia's leading child protection organisation.

I reach out to her by email to see if she might be willing to talk to me, to share her insights. I'm keen to understand how pervasive child sexual abuse is, whether there are different categories of abuse, and whether what I experienced might fall into one of them.

She phones me a few days later. I'm holed up in bed battling a nasty flu, the cat curled up in my lap and a pillow over my throbbing head. But I've read a lot about Carol and her background. She's a big deal. For an expert of this calibre, who is so universally respected by her peers and regarded as one of the leading voices in this field, you don't let the call go to voicemail.

Twenty-odd years ago, Carol was an associate professor at Griffith University in Queensland. She's a criminologist who also did her undergraduate degree in psychology and a graduate degree in applied sociology. She was in the midst of a PhD, focusing on sex offenders, when she switched on the evening news and saw a stern but passionate woman declaring war on one of the most powerful men in Australia.

Hetty Johnstone became a prominent voice for survivors in the 1990s after discovering her daughter, then seven, had been sexually abused by her paternal grandfather. She thrust herself into the spotlight, determined to drag this ugly and often ignored issue into the mainstream.

When Carol saw her on television, Hetty was calling for the resignation of Peter Hollingworth – the former Anglican Archbishop who was at the time the Governor-General of Australia. Hollingworth had been accused of failing to appropriately deal with allegations of sexual abuse within the church, and of brushing off an accusation from a student levelled against a teacher. In trying to defend himself, Hollingworth said he was new to the position of Archbishop when the complaint reached him, and so he didn't have the experience to adequately deal with it. He also claimed to be unaware that the case involved alleged sexual abuse. But in the end, he conceded that he hadn't done enough to support the complainant and stamp out instances of abuse.

After prolonged pressure from Hetty's campaign, Hollingworth eventually stood down. He continued to deny any deliberate wrongdoing.

'She was amazing,' Carol recalls. 'I thought it was important to sort of help support Hetty and her lobbying around legislative reform, and trying to ensure that legislation and policies and programs were always in the best interest of children, and served to protect children from sexual predators.'

What began as a volunteering commitment turned into a full-time job and a lifelong passion, leading research and working with partners to increase knowledge and awareness around the issue.

That work all helps to devise and guide prevention and support programs at Bravehearts.

'That's crucial if we want to bring down that one-in-five figure,' she says.

One in five. Jesus. I start to silently count all of the children I know. My nieces and nephews. My husband's nieces and nephews. My friends' kids. Dozens and dozens of little people in my life. I have to drag my thoughts back from the reality that there statistically could be a one-in-five among them.

Those numbers take into account a number of things, right from the lower end of the spectrum through to the most severe kinds of abuse imaginable. The spectrum is vast and unpleasant, Carol explains. It could be a man flashing a child in a park or an abuser grooming a victim, right up to penetrative rape and physical violence or torture.

'The average age of the onset of sexual abuse is around six or seven,' Carol continues. 'Obviously there's a lot of younger children who are sexually abused, as well as older children, but that's the average age.'

Most adults who have some rare reason to cast their minds to the issue of child sexual abuse, maybe after hearing about a case on the news, tend to have an idea in their head of the likely perpetrator.

Some horrible creature lurking in the shadows, evil and unknown. That's what generations of Australian schoolchildren were taught during the stranger-danger era. I remember it vividly from my own schooling. We had actual workshops from outside facilitators on what to do if an adult you didn't know approached you.

'Yell out "fire!" because no one takes much notice if a little kid is screaming for help, because it's usually nothing,' I remember one instructing us. We were in Year Five.

Faceless monsters. The truth couldn't be further from that.

'The vast majority [of abusers] are someone known to the child and often loved and trusted by the child,' Carol tells me. 'It's not necessarily a parent, but very often it's a family member, a close family friend ... So that vulnerability that most people think about – the stranger-danger concept – is flawed.'

About 90 per cent of the time, the offender isn't faceless at all. It's someone the child knows well. And in three-quarters of cases, the perpetrator doesn't live in the family home. It's an uncle. A neighbour. The local priest. The child's friend's older brother. A teacher. A sports coach.

It's someone Mum and Dad also know and probably trust. It's often the last person they'd expect, which is terrifying for any adult with a young person they love in their lives.

'I think people really struggle with that because it's easy to think of that monster being a stranger on the street who's terrifying but a kind of evil you're not very likely to encounter,' Carol says. 'But if it's someone your child knows, someone in their life and in yours ... that's scary. And the reality is that a perpetrator like that is grooming the parents as well.'

What's worse, though, is the burden that profile puts on a victim.

Put yourself in the mind of a little boy or girl for a moment. If an uncle or a family friend is abusing you, someone that your parents adore, who you love, and who's at your house all the time ... would you speak up? Could you speak up?

'That person being someone the child loves and cares about makes it so much more difficult for them to speak out and disclose what's happening to them. They don't want to get that person in trouble,' says Carol.

So often, the victim will stay quiet. Not because what's happening to them isn't awful. They know it's not right. Not because they don't want it to stop. They do. In many cases, they stay quiet to *protect* the person abusing them. For the victim to reconcile that in their mind later must be horrendously difficult.

Much of the issue of child sexual abuse is still taboo. For all of the awareness, for all the very public cases over recent years, it's just not the kind of thing that people want to confront.

It's certainly not something you bring up when in polite company. That level of suffering inflicted on the most vulnerable in society – children – is just too much to bear. And so, we look away.

Carol Ronkin tells me about some of the worst cases she's come across. Little boys and girls whose innocence has been shattered and whose carefree childhoods have been robbed from them. It's stuff that even she finds difficult to comprehend, even after decades of doing the work she does.

I ask her about a scenario like mine.

'Let's say there's a child and they're molested by another child. What is that? Does that fall somewhere into the broad definition of child abuse?' I ask.

It's one of the most difficult areas to tackle, she tells me. When the perpetrator is also a child, it's almost like no one really knows what to do. How do you even start to address that? It's so confronting that even those at the frontline, who devote their careers and their emotional bandwidth to the issue of child sexual abuse, have trouble coming to terms with it.

'It's definitely an area we don't talk about as much,' Carol said.

Yet, the research indicates that one in three cases of child sexual abuse are instigated by another young person. Hearing this, I gasp.

'Yeah, it's a huge number. I think we do really struggle with understanding that element of the problem and knowing how to respond to it. It's complicated and messy.

'Particularly, we hate thinking of children as being perpetrators. You recoil from using that term in some ways because really, often these young people are victims themselves. It's not an excuse. But the reason is, often they've gone through some kind of trauma and they're looking for control, or they're acting out.'

I tell Carol that I assume most victims are girls, given how much of the focus of the public narrative, in the media and in pop culture, is centred around them.

'Well, that's a tricky question also, and it's one without a simple answer, I'm afraid,' she says. 'Data tells us that girls are more likely to be sexually abused than boys, but the difference depends on the study you're looking at.'

An Australian Bureau of Statistics analysis conducted in 2017 found 11 per cent of women and 5 per cent of men reported having been sexually abused before they were fifteen. That would equate to an estimated 1,410,100 people living in Australia now who were sexually abused as children. More than half of those were sexually abused for the first time before they were ten years old.

A birth cohort study published in the *Journal of Psychiatric Research* in 2016 found that of 3739 participants, 19 per cent of males in the group self-reported that they had been sexually abused as children by the age of twenty-one, compared to 30 per cent of females.

And a policy paper released in 2013 by the Australian Institute of Family Studies concluded that a growing body of research had 'reported that severely intrusive forms of abuse, including attempted or completed vaginal, oral, or anal penetration, did not greatly differ between boys and girls, with the majority of studies reporting prevalence figures in the range of five to 10 per cent for both males and females'.

'So, in some studies, it's twice as likely for girls than boys, in others it's a smaller gap, but I think everyone in the sector agrees that the numbers we have on boys just simply aren't true,' Carol tells me. 'We know it's probably a lot closer to the figure for girls, so pretty equal. It's just that for boys, there are added complexities around disclosure and speaking out. For a number of reasons, some boys will never tell anyone what's happened to them.'

*

There's a lot tied up in it. The Australian concept of masculinity and what it means to be a young man, for one, which is something boys begin absorbing while they're still playing with Tonka trucks in the dirt.

It's the idea that normal boys are tough and don't cry. They are stoic and resilient and push on towards battle – or everyday life – with a steely resolve. Punch on, never look back. That's just how it's meant to be.

You can see it in playgrounds. Very little boys who fall over and cut open their knees on the gravel have no problem crying and expressing their hurt, fear and regret. There's little judgement of boys who are emotional from their peers. It's a typical and very human response, right? But then something happens as they grow up, and somewhere along the way there's a point at which that kind of reaction isn't allowed anymore.

Suddenly, it's not OK for a boy to show his hurt and his pain and his frustration. He can't cry. He should toughen up. It'll be all right, he's told. You're a man now so you've got to act like one.

Instead of being allowed to feel things, the boy, who's on the border of childhood and adolescence, will hold his breath, force back his tears, stiffen his lip, and grunt through the hurt.

Another problematic element with males reporting their sexual abuse is the involvement of a male perpetrator. As open and accepting as parts of society have become, there's still multiple layers of shame that begin to form when a boy is abused by a man because … well, that's just a bit gay, isn't it?

'It's such a shame that we still have some of those images of masculinity because they can stop young boys from speaking out.' Carol sighs. 'Somehow, because it's happened to them, their masculinity is in question. That's a very threatening feeling for a young boy.

'It's just crazy. It's so insane. But unfortunately, these are the things we're still trying to battle.'

And so, many little boys who are sexually abused stay quiet. For a long time. Just like me. Instead of screaming out for help, I retreated within myself and hastily built up a wall to keep out prying eyes. Over the coming months and years, I added reinforcements to that wall, strengthening it, making it almost impenetrable.

As a child, my shame lay just behind the perimeter, out of sight from the outside world, but by no means benign. It sat there, slowly growing bigger and meaner, like a cancerous tumour. Whenever it had the chance, it would rapidly spread through my little body, stretching to all corners.

That shame ravaged my mind, soul and psyche. It strangled the geese that give those goosebumps of surprise, squished the butterflies that deliver flutters of excitement, and stomped on frogs that fill the back of throats with emotion.

Eventually, all that was left was numbness. A heavy, silent void where a beating heart should be.

Carol's words sit with me for a long time. The way she speaks about masculinity in the context of child sexual abuse almost makes it sound like a prison. It's a construct that traps young men in their pivotal years and subscribes them to an archaic list of rules about what's right and what's wrong.

In the dying days of childhood, these boys are sentenced to a lifetime of unhealthy expectation that constricts so many of their natural tendencies. The need to be vulnerable. The desire to live freely and fully. The yearning to ask for help when it's needed.

Michael Salter is an associate professor of criminology in the School of Social Sciences at the University of New South Wales. He's an expert in child sexual exploitation and has studied extensively the issue of complex trauma. He is on the board of directors of the International Society for the Study of Trauma and Dissociation, and he is an advisor to the Australian Office of the eSafety Commissioner and the Canadian Centre for Child Protection.

He wrote an article in 2015 following the conviction of Maggie Kirkpatrick, the acclaimed Australian television actress best known for her role in the hit series *Prisoner*, for abusing a fourteen-year-old girl in 1984. The conviction was later overturned on appeal.

Kirkpatrick's trial came around the same time that fellow small-screen legend Robert Hughes, who starred in the '90s hit *Hey Dad!*, was gaoled for ten years for child sexual abuse offences, also of an historic nature.

Those cases, as well as the trial of entertainer Rolf Harris in the United Kingdom, saw some rumblings about why many victims of child sexual abuse take so long to come forward. As Salter noted, it was a question of a legal nature, but also laced with societal scepticism.

'They recall entrenched myths that a rape victim who doesn't raise "hue and cry" immediately after the event is untrustworthy,' he writes for *The Conversation.*

In his article, he cites a retrospective survey of Canadian adults abused as children, which found that around 20 per cent reported the abuse within a month, but 58 per cent delayed disclosure for five years or longer, and 20 per cent never disclosed the abuse to anyone.

He writes that studies of adult survivors consistently find that most don't tell anyone about the abuse when they're children. As such, a very small proportion of incidents are ever reported to the police.

There are many and varied reasons that a child might not disclose what happened to them when it occurs, or for a long time – or ever.

The victim's age and their level of development plays a role, as does their relationship with the perpetrator and the severity of the abuse they've endured, Salter writes. There are social and cultural challenges that enhance the level of shame a child might feel, as well as the level of blame they apportion on themselves – or worse, the blame some in their family or community might put on them.

In many instances, a victim might not have the knowledge or the language to communicate what's happening to them. And as Carol also noted, they might not want to get anyone in trouble – especially if the perpetrator is someone within their immediate family or an important part of the home's broader social circle.

When a victim speaks up but is ignored or not believed, or not heard, or they sense that they can't disclose what's happening to them out of fear or shame, they're likely to feel betrayed. 'Negative and shaming reactions to sexual abuse disclosures have been shown to significantly increase the risk of mental illness and distress in the victim,' Salter writes.

Children who are sexually abused are often in living conditions where they can't rely on support or understanding should they speak up and ask for help. But at the same time, society relies on these disclosures in order to detect perpetrators and remove them from society.

'In this impossible situation, non-disclosure is a way that victims of abuse protect themselves from further betrayal and harm. Extricating themselves from unsupportive environments and finding opportunities to speak about their abuse is a complex and fragile process that can take many years.

'It seems that the pertinent question in "historical" abuse allegations is not: "Why didn't victims say something at the time?" Rather, it should be: "Why do abuse victims have to wait so long to speak and be heard?"'

As Luke explained to me during our interview, before you speak up for the first time, the notion of ever telling anyone feels just as terrifying as the memory of the abuse. Survivors remember imagining how people would think differently of them, unable to see them in the same light ever again. Survivors vividly recall lying awake at night playing scenarios over and over in their heads, trying to predict how certain people will react – family, friends, co-workers.

And most of all, they shudder at the thought of what might come next. Once they've unleashed that shame beast, where does it go? How on earth do they keep a handle on it?

Chapter Four

I search for Luke's profile on Instagram and start following him. He follows back. We chat a bit and exchange memes about politics, religion and architecture, as well as the occasional cute cat or silly dog video. It's all quite light and airy.

But I decide I want to talk to him again. I want to hear more about his story. I need to know more about what's happened to him in the years since those horrific childhood experiences. How has he fared? What else do we have in common when it comes to our struggles?

Does he think what happened with Joshua is in the realm of abuse, or am I just the grown-up version of a disturbed, deviant child?

We catch up and start talking about shame and how we hide ourselves away from it. He tells me about the first time his deeply held and rapidly growing shame broke through his defensive wall and began to seep out.

He's sixteen and out with one of his best mates, his mate's older brother and one of the older brother's friends. It's a Friday night and the air is warm. Everyone's keen to have a bit of a night. They'll find a house party to hit up, they figure.

Someone buys booze and it's being shared around. Luke hasn't been drunk before. He's not sure if he's even seen someone especially drunk before. His mum and dad drink, and they're not prudes about it – they drink in front of him and his siblings. But they don't get wasted. They drink to enjoy it.

'I'm not even sure if I'd seen them tipsy, really. They enjoy a couple of glasses of wine. That's them. They're happy. They enjoy it that way.'

But on this night, the boys pool their money and buy up big. Luke can't remember what their choice of poison is that occasion. It's probably something cheap and nasty, as teenagers are prone to favour. Maybe wine in a box that somehow tastes both bitter and sweet. That, or a bourbon with an obscure brand name and the consistency of molasses.

'I got rip-roaring drunk,' Luke recalls. 'And something in me changes, and everything I've been holding in comes out.'

He doesn't remember much of the later part of that night. It's just little flashes of unpleasant memories now, but his mate is there to witness the absolute carnage that follows.

The house party they're at is on a road with cars whizzing by in both directions. His chest tight and his eyes welling with tears, Luke steps out onto the bitumen and begins to run.

'I'm jumping in front of cars, apparently. I don't recall making the decision, but I have this sense that it seemed deliberate.

Like, when I think about that night, I suspect that I probably wanted to hurt myself. I'm drunk and my guard is down.

'I'm blind drunk, and as alcohol does, all of this stuff that's just below the surface is brought up and out. I'm pretty hysterical, crying and trying to jump in front of cars. My mate tackles me and drags me back to the gutter.'

Luke sits by the side of the road slumped over, crying so hard that he's choking, his face drenched in tears. His mate envelopes him in a bear hug from behind. He squeezes tight, keeping him still. It's more of a case of him being pinned down rather than being comforted. His friend is absolutely terrified.

'He didn't know what was going on. He'd never seen this side of me. As far as he was concerned, as far as everyone was concerned, I was happy. I'm the good boy, I'm from the good family. I'm responsible, I get good marks at school, I'm the eldest so I take care of everyone around me, you know? Then all of a sudden something has changed and I'm a wreck.

'The way I describe it is that a wall went up between me and everyone else after I was abused, and I was living life inside of it. There was a projection on the outside of who I was supposed to be, while on the inside, nothing made any sense to me.'

Luke starts talking for the very first time about what happened to him when he was a boy. He can't stop. Once the slurred words begin pouring from his mouth, they flow freely. There's a kind of relief in some way. This is his best mate. He's holding him – yes, to stop him running into traffic, but also because he cares.

It's a watershed moment. With his friend's encouragement and support, he tells the youth minister at his church, who encourages him to confide in his parents.

He does, and while the revelation absolutely devastates them, they swing into action to get Luke the support he needs. He starts seeing a counsellor, he begins university, and he moves out of home at twenty-three.

He is supported. He pushes on with his life. But the road to healing is a bumpy one.

'When I was nineteen, there was a pretty serious suicide attempt. It was close. It was a pretty scary realisation afterwards [how close I'd come].'

He lurches from one type of self-destructive behaviour to another.

'My twenties were a disaster. I would cycle through these deep feelings of shame and guilt. The level of distress I would feel was extreme and hard to comprehend. I struggled with super self-destructive behaviour.

'I was smart enough never to get into drugs. I think I was educated and scared enough. But I drank a lot. I have self-destructive tendencies but thankfully I never struggled with day to day alcoholism. Just a lot of binge-drinking.

'I have been compulsive with other things over the years, though. I got really into long-distance running in my thirties, but then I did my knee and got depressed that I couldn't run anymore. It was a healthy habit that became almost unhealthy because I relied on it so much and needed the adrenalin.

'And money. I spent money like there was no tomorrow, to make myself feel better. I got lost in that.

'The shame and the guilt … it impacts all aspects of your life. There were a bunch of people watching me anxiously for a number of years. I think my therapist is a big part of the reason I'm still alive. It was a tough period.'

Shame is potent and destructive. It's something that isn't often acknowledged or confronted, but rather ignored and squashed deep down, again and again, until it compacts and eventually combusts.

With Luke's story ringing in my ears, I start to search for others. I know they're out there, walking a similar path to us, enduring the same sorts of stumbles and falls. Maybe if I find them, their experiences will help me understand more about my own. Perhaps I can finally come to terms with this turmoil and put it behind me.

On one forum, there's a section devoted to the loved ones of adult male survivors. I notice the words of a woman named Kristy, who speaks about the terrifying and ugly reality of shame in a way that echoes Luke and myself. We begin talking about her partner, Joey.

Joey hates the taste and smell of mango. And it's quite a pungent smell, especially in north Queensland where he's spent the entirety of his life, where mangoes are about as famous as sugar cane and the NRL State of Origin.

In his late teens, while nursing a nasty hangover at his girlfriend Kristy's house, he's reminded of just how violently he loathes mango. Kristy's mum plonks a big plate of bacon down in front of him, along with a glass of juice, and playfully pats him on the head.

'That'll fix you up,' she declares.

Joey groans. His mouth tastes like a rum-soaked ashtray. He must've smoked at least two packets of cigarettes last night.

That wasn't unusual. While just seventeen years old, Joey's been drinking like a hardened farmer in his forties since he was in his early teens. Smash them back with no regard for the consequences, that was his style. Worry about that later – that's a tomorrow problem.

And here he was, enduring yesterday's tomorrow. Head thumping and stomach churning. And he is absolutely parched, so he takes a big swig of the orange juice.

Except it's not orange. It's mango.

The moment it hits the right spot on his taste buds and that sickly familiar taste and scent fills his palate, Joey's brain begins to scream. He slides the chair back and throws himself from it, running at full speed through the kitchen, down the hallway and out onto the front veranda, where he vomits for a good ten minutes.

Kristy and her mum laugh and shake their heads. What a horrible hangover, they must think. So much worse than usual. Joey has never been quite that sick the next morning.

This has nothing to do with booze, though, and everything to do with mangoes.

When he's younger, Joey lives in a small fibro shack on the outskirts of Townsville. His mum works at a supermarket in town managing the deli section. His dad is a labourer with no specific skill set or interest, but more of a general 'shit-kicker', as he puts it.

It's just the three of them. His parents are pretty good – they're busy, so not always around, but they're loving and kind.

When Joey is about nine, his dad's brother comes to stay with them for a few weeks. He lives in Innisfail, three hours north, and has had a pretty normal, pleasant life. That is until recently, when his wife abruptly died in her thirties. They were hoping to start a family at the time. His uncle has a total breakdown.

Joey's dad takes him in to keep an eye on him, fearful of what he might do if the grief becomes too heavy.

It's meant to be a brief visit. Just until his uncle gets back on his feet. But months later, he's still there, camped on the couch and living out of a duffel bag. No one seems to mind, though. He cleans up after himself, and he does bits and pieces around the house, like finally fixing the broken bathroom door and sanding back the peeling paint on the windowsill in the kitchen.

And he looks after Joey when his mum and dad are working late or have gone out with their friends.

A few weeks before Joey's tenth birthday, Joey's dad surprises his mum with a weekend away to Magnetic Island for their wedding anniversary. They take off on Friday afternoon and are gone until early Monday morning. Joey's uncle minds him while they're away.

That weekend is the first time his uncle abuses him.

Late on the Friday night, but probably more like early Saturday morning, his uncle stumbles into his darkened room. Joey has been asleep for hours, but the sound of the thumping footsteps down the hall wakes him.

His uncle plonks himself down on the edge of the bed. Joey lifts his head, but his uncle holds his finger to his lips.

'Go back to sleep, mate,' he slurs. He's drunk. Joey can smell the rum on his breath and he sways from side to side even though he's sitting.

Joey doesn't go back to sleep. How can he? Instead, his body is frozen and he clenches his eyes shut as his uncle slides down his Mickey Mouse pyjama shorts. He tries to focus on something else. The sounds of crickets chirping outside. The *tick-tick-tick* of the rickety old ceiling fan overhead. The smell of fermenting mangoes that have fallen from the branches of the giant tree outside his bedroom window, becoming food for the bats.

In the north Queensland heat of high summer, which keeps the mercury at about thirty degrees Celsius all day and into night, the scent of slowly rotting mangoes fills the back of Joey's house most of the season. It's sweet but tart. It's always been there. He's never really noticed it quite like this, though.

But now, to make the time pass a little quicker and distract him from what his uncle is doing to him under the sheets, he thinks of nothing else but the smell of that stone fruit.

He does this the four or five other times his uncle abuses him that weekend, pushing things a little further and further each time. It starts as touching and rubbing, then more. Then more. As the terror inside Joey grows, he focuses more of his energy on thinking about those mangoes outside.

He pictures the thick trunk of the tree soaring into the sky. He can see the leaves sprouting off branches and the big, golden ovals of fruit clinging to them. He imagines the fallen mangoes nestled in the thick grass below. He thinks of the half-chewed fruit, the soft, smooth skin pierced by the tiny teeth of bats in the dead of night.

He visualises the odour wafting up from the ground like steam and dancing through the air gently, making its way into his bedroom through the louvre windows.

If he focuses enough, he can almost see it swirl around above his bed, like the southern lights, only bright orange and pale yellow intertwined.

Joey is eighteen when he kills himself.

*

A motorist heading off to work at dawn one morning sees something strange out of the corner of his eye. It's strange enough to make him pull over.

He gets out of his car, the headlights illuminating the bushes in front beneath a pink sky on the cusp of sunrise. There's an unusual shadow. Instinctively, the man knows something is wrong. As he creeps closer, what he's seen becomes clear. A body hanging from the branch of a huge mango tree. It's Joey.

That happened a decade ago and, as I speak with Kristy, Joey's girlfriend, it's clear the pain is still just as raw.

The boy she fell madly in love with the moment he sat next to her in maths class on the first day of high school has kept all of his demons hidden from her. For the years they're together almost every moment of every day, she gets to know him better than anyone else. There was no inkling that anything was wrong at the time, she tells me. But by relying on hindsight, Kristy tortures herself by discovering what she now thinks of as missed signals. The clues she could've seen – should've seen, she says.

'He was a real larrikin,' she recalls, a deep sadness coating her words. 'The life of the party. Everyone loved him, too. Like, there's dickheads at every party, right, but he got along with everyone. He had that way about him.'

But there, in the limelight of a social setting, a giant, toothy grin plastered on his face, is a broken man trapped just beneath the surface. He's terrified. He knows just how bad he feels but has no idea how to begin to fix himself. It feels like an impossible task.

Within the forum where we meet, for the mothers, partners, and siblings of male survivors, are countless posts seeking advice about how to assist those men who are reluctant to get help for themselves. How to deal with the anger, resentment, secrecy, alcohol or drug abuse, and self-destructive behaviour that they all agree tends to be common.

And there are a few people whose loved ones haven't survived in the end. They seek an outlet for their grief, a place where others will understand the torture their men endured until they couldn't take it any longer.

As well as a shared understanding, there's a shared feeling – or a terror – among those whose men are still alive, that just an angel's hair separates their men from being here, and from being gone.

After he died, Kristy finds a goodbye note from Joey. It's stuck inside her pillowcase. She thinks he must've meant to slide it beneath her pillow, but it got wedged instead. It's there for a week until she realises. She has cried endlessly and hysterically for hours a day, in between restless stretches of sleep, just centimetres from his final words to her.

Across eight pages, front and back, Joey outlines everything that happened to him, beginning with that first weekend and continuing for another year. Eventually, his uncle's drinking becomes so bad that his father kicks him out. He's making a mess and becoming a problem, so enough is enough and he's got to go.

A few times after that, on trips down to Mackay or Brisbane, looking for a job, his uncle stops in at the family home to visit. He only stays a night, maybe two, but when Joey's mum and dad fall asleep, he creeps into Joey's room.

For a while, Joey can push down the feelings of disgust and shame that hang heavy on his heart. But as he grows older, he can't seem to suppress them anymore. They churn around like a cyclonic sea, tearing away at him, bit by bit.

He begins to drink. At fourteen, he's downing a bottle of rum every weekend or so. He doesn't even bother hiding it from his parents, and they don't seem to care. Boys will be boys, they figure. That's how they raise 'em in the country.

In his suicide note, he writes of feeling let down that no one saw his subtle cries for help. No one wondered why a kid so young needed to be drinking quite that much. There was no intervention to see if he was OK. No one stepped up.

Drinking numbs his thoughts enough that he can push through a particularly dark patch. Not unscathed, though.

He falls behind at school and eventually drops out. He wants to be a mechanic, but the seven o'clock starts each morning clash badly with his near-daily hangovers. He sleeps in a few times, misses an hour or two of work. Then he sleeps through the phone calls from his boss entirely and misses a half day, or an entire day. Eventually he's fired.

He just can't quite seem to land on his feet. Everything around him feels unstable, he writes. Moments of contentment are fleeting, and increasingly so. Everything feels precarious and at risk.

Even Kristy, whom he adores and who loves him, is the one good thing in his life that he's certain he'll lose one day. The thought kills him. She'll get the shits with him, he writes. She'll maybe see glimmers of the twisted darkness within and run off. No one will understand, least of all her. Fuck, *he* barely understands.

Joey's words aren't sophisticated or elaborate, but they're brutally real. Kristy shows me the letter in its entirety, but the little bits I'm paraphrasing or quoting here are with her permission.

There's far too much within that tragic goodbye that was Joey's alone while he was alive, and therefore is now hers alone. Things that are too graphic, too personal to share with strangers. Secrets that Kristy is now the keeper of.

But the final few words are ones she insists that I have. They're thoughts she suspects many men like Joey have, probably every day, but which she's certain are never, ever true, in any circumstance.

'You're better off I'm gone,' he writes at the end of his letter. 'It won't feel like it now, but it will one day.'

It still doesn't and it never will, Kristy says. The last thing she is without Joey is better off.

Chapter Five

The more I learn about these men who think and feel like I do, the longer my list of questions grows. I obsessively find and join forums all across the internet to tick them off, one by one.

Are we all scarred in the same way from these exposures to inappropriate behaviour? How do we reconcile those experiences with who we are now? Is it just me who struggles to understand how I fit into the world?

It seems to me that male survivors can have almost nothing in common, in terms of where we come from, what we do, or how old we are, and yet we share so many of the same outcomes. We are broken in very similar ways, despite being made of different materials. We are this way for a reason. If I know what that reason is, can I somehow figure out a way to heal? Is there something constructive that can come out of this?

I write a post on a forum related to men's mental health, asking for men who were sexually abused as children to reach out. That's when I hear from Chris.

Chris isn't sure why he's getting in touch with me, he says. But there was something about my candid introduction in that post, talking about my own fears and struggles, that prompted him to drop me a line.

We arrange a time to speak on the phone. It's an unseasonably cool summer's afternoon and the sound of torrential rain on my roof almost drowns out our voices.

'It's actually lovely today where I am,' Chris says. He's softly spoken and almost painfully polite, but I can hear the trepidation in his voice.

He's in Auckland in New Zealand. He emigrated there a little over a decade ago from London, where he'd spent several years after leaving his small hometown in Britain's north. He's a hypnotherapist and leads a relatively pleasant life, by all accounts. He has great friends, a busy schedule, and considers himself happy and content in most ways.

Or so he thought. The more he thinks about it these past few years, the more Chris realises that there are some deep and dark voids in his soul that he never really noticed before. And the longer he stares into them, the more he finds himself thinking about his early adolescence.

When he's fourteen years old, Chris's class goes into town in the middle of a school day on an excursion of sorts. The students are tasked with writing an essay about the history of the region, interviewing locals about their lives and how they fit in to the area.

Kids dart off in various directions. Chris wanders into a few stores to say hello to the shopkeepers and have a chat, scribbling down notes in his exercise book. He speaks to a woman sitting on a park bench outside the post office. There's a guy waiting in line at the butcher who looks like he's never left this place.

After a few hours, the class reconvenes for lunch together in the park. Chris and his best mate sit and eat their sandwiches beneath the shade of a tree, making plans for what they'll get up to that weekend.

'I've got to go to the toilet,' Chris says, scanning the grassy expanse and spotting a toilet block in the far corner of the field. 'Back in a moment.'

He walks into a cubicle, slides down his trousers and sits on the seat. While he's doing his business, he hears a rustling in the stall next to him. He hadn't realised anyone else was in there. There's a hole in the wall separating the two toilets and he can see someone moving around inside. Suddenly, a man slides his penis through the gap.

Chris leaps up from the seat and hurries to pull his pants up. When he opens the door, there's a man standing there. He's in his mid-twenties. He looks intently at the boy, eyeing him off, with his penis still in his hand.

'I didn't really know anything about anything at that age – I was very sheltered and naive about the world,' Chris recalls. 'But it was obviously a beat.'

For the uninitiated, a beat is a public place – usually a quiet bathroom or a secluded park – where men meet for sex. It's anonymous and a little risky, which probably adds to the allure of it all, but back in the days before broad acceptance of homosexuality, and way before the internet and dating apps like Grindr existed, it was really the only way for gay men to meet for sex in small towns like this.

Chris hasn't yet realised that he's gay. He doesn't really know what that even means, having never been familiar with the notion outside of occasional playground taunts thrown around by other boys. There are few gay characters in television shows or films. There are not really any gay role models to look to for guidance and reassurance.

'I think I always knew I was different,' he tells me. 'I had a lot of friends who were girls growing up, but there wasn't an attraction there, and I knew there probably should be. But I wouldn't have known what "gay" meant, let alone that I was gay. Not for a long time to come.'

At that stage, in the 1990s, all anyone in regional Britain really knew about homosexuality was what a pastor might've uttered in church or what was on the evening news about the AIDS crisis.

'I'm pretty sure it was around that time that *EastEnders* introduced a gay character – but he had AIDS,' Chris sighs.

For days afterwards, all Chris could think about was that man. And when he did, his tummy filled with butterflies in a way it never had before. A curiosity had been unlocked that made him feel nervous but also excited.

'I'd never felt anything like it,' he tells me. 'And so, after a few days, I went back. I shouldn't have. I know that now, obviously. But I was really curious.'

This time, instead of a guy in his mid-twenties, there's a much older man, in his late forties, inside the toilet block. He has a calming presence about him. He's warm and even a little welcoming, sensing Chris's nervousness but also interest. It puts Chris at ease.

The man coaxes him inside a toilet cubicle and abuses him.

That man in his late forties becomes the main offender in a group of several older men who take turns having sex with Chris, almost passing him around like a plaything. They're all brazen and predatory.

One drives around in the morning and afternoon some days looking for him, finding him at the bus stop and picking him up. He takes Chris to a secluded wooded area on the outskirts of town, rapes him, and then drops him off at school.

Another sees him walking through the village and darts out of the shop or the pub he's in to intercept him and lead him off to the toilet block in the park.

One waits in a parked car outside his house on a weekend until Chris ventures out, on his way to hang out with his friends or duck to the shop to get milk for his mum. He beeps the horn or flashes the headlights, ushering the boy to get in the car.

There are gatherings of multiple men in the woods or at someone's house, several adult men at once, where Chris is the main attraction for them. Men in their thirties and forties, most closeted, a few married with children, fixate their attention on a fourteen-year-old schoolboy.

They know how old he is too. He is often in a school uniform when they go hunting for him. He will have to remind them from time to time of the need to be home at a certain hour to look after his younger siblings, before his parents get home from work.

There can be absolutely no doubt at all for those men that they are engaged in what effectively amounts to a paedophile ring.

From time to time, there's another boy at these sordid gatherings who's of a similar age to Chris. The ringleader introduces him as his nephew.

'I'm not sure if it was actually his nephew. It was really weird. But the man would have sex with him, and watch him have sex with other men, or with me.'

It might just be that he's another boy that the older man picked up along the way. Who can tell? Chris vaguely knows of him from around town, but he goes to another school, so their social circles have never overlapped. He was maybe a year older than Chris at most. They've never spoken before, and avoid each other outside of those meetings.

'Funnily enough, I met him years later when we were adults. He was dating a friend of mine in London, a guy I worked with. We never acknowledged each other. It was a bit awkward.

'I think he definitely remembered me and knew who I was, but I tried not to even make eye contact with him.'

The whole thing goes on for three or four years, he thinks. He's not entirely sure about the length of time because it kind of blurs into one big blob of an experience now. He mentally unplugs from the reality of it all when the weight of the shame becomes too heavy.

But it stops for good, finally, around the time that Chris is coming to terms with the fact he is gay, and begins to realise that what has been happening probably isn't in his best interests. So, on the cusp of adulthood, he avoids the places those men are likely to be, ignores them when they find him and tail him, and hides himself away until he can move from the town when he finishes school.

'You're literally the first person I've told about this,' Chris says.

It's a phrase he repeats four or five times more during our long phone conversation. I can't decide if it's his way of apologising for his nervousness or a coping mechanism for whatever emotions must be raging through his veins, saying these things out loud for the first time.

A number of times, he stops and starts sentences, pausing to fully form his thoughts or perhaps to let another surge of shame or guilt or sadness subside.

'I'm sorry,' he whispers at these pauses.

There's such a weight of responsibility on my shoulders all of a sudden. I can't quite fathom that this total stranger is sharing his deepest and darkest secrets with me. I find it difficult to be even one-tenth as vulnerable with my loved ones, with the people who know me better than anyone else.

'It kind of feels good to say it,' he says. I feel relieved. 'I think I should've let it out a lot sooner, told someone about it sooner.'

A few years back, before Covid-19 broke out and put everyone's lives on hold, Chris went to see a therapist. It's something he'd been wanting to do for a long while and, upon turning forty, he bit the bullet and delved into some of the darker parts of his psyche.

'At my grand old age, I've still not managed to be in a proper, meaningful and lasting relationship with a man. And there were some real issues there that I wanted to address, so I went to see someone to talk it through.'

Over the course of several sessions, Chris pours his heart out to a professional therapist. He speaks about his vision of love and what a relationship might look like. His interpretation of that is about as clear as it gets. He knows what he wants.

It's just that he's never really been able to find it, and he's not quite sure why that is.

He speaks of his track record with men. He has no trouble meeting them. He's relatively happy, good-looking, has lots of friends and an interesting job … so he's a catch. And yet, nothing ever seems to last.

'I know myself. I can start dating somebody, anybody, but we get three dates in and I'm done. I don't feel anything. I can't see it going anywhere. I want out.

'Friends of mine tell me that I should give things a better go – you know, probably longer than a few dates at least.

'But I just can't. As soon as somebody shows that they're keen in any way, I feel compelled to back out. In my head I tell myself it's not a right fit, and maybe it's not … but also, maybe the common denominator is me.'

On the other hand, if he was to meet a guy who is standoffish and aloof and distant, but who maybe every now and then throws a few crumbs of interest his way, Chris would be head over heels.

'Oh God, my ideal man is one who completely ignores me,' he laughs. 'I've met some guys and we've gone out on a few dates, but they ghost me, and suddenly I might feel quite keen. It's like, hang on, I want this to go somewhere. But if they did come back, would I then lose interest? Is that just how I'm programmed for whatever reason?'

The therapist gives some good advice about patience and reflection, about getting to know himself a little better and perhaps being a bit kinder when he thinks about who Chris is and what Chris wants, needs and deserves.

'It helped to a certain extent. I think it gave me a bit more clarity on the bad habits I fall back into. It also kind of gave me this resolve to not hook up right away. If I meet someone, don't view them as just someone to have sex with, basically. You know? Take the time to get to know someone first.'

I'm curious about what the therapist had to say about the abuse he was subjected to as an adolescent and how that might be impacting his intimate relationships.

'I didn't tell her,' he whispers.

There's a long pause.

'It was a conscious thing not to say anything. It's kind of stupid to think about now. Like, of course I should've said something. But I just didn't want to.

'I mean, I suppose what happened plays a part in all of that. I've carried that promiscuity from my adolescence through my adult life, and my intimate relationships can have a tendency to be a bit temporary, or disposable I suppose.

'It's not a very healthy way to live life. The borderline joking among friends about Chris being on Grindr and Chris being in love for one night only … it stops being funny at a point.'

I have to hold myself back from playing an armchair psychologist. Well, from playing one *too* much in any case.

I can't completely resist. It's so clear to me that his early experiences with intimacy were so broken, so abusive, so manipulative and so hurtful that he's looking at adult relationships through the same fractured lens.

When he's not being mistreated or used, there's not that same kind of reaction that he might have otherwise felt. The wiring was distorted long ago and never corrected. Of course that makes total sense.

I think back to my own experiences, having seen Dr Rolenstein for so long before I spoke for the first time about what happened to me. I still don't even know why I did – I don't know what inspired me to say it on that day, at that time.

If not for the random combination of factors that made me feel it was the right time to utter those words out loud for the very first time, I don't know if I would've. Ever. Not even to the guy I'm paying $380 an hour.

So, while I'm taken aback by Chris's admission, I'm not overly surprised once I think about it.

How many times have I said the words out loud myself? At this point, right now, as Chris and I speak … how many people have I felt comfortable enough around – or less uncomfortable, I guess – to say those words?

I could maybe put it in an email. Or a book. But to speak it – to let it out of its little box from behind a tall, impenetrable wall, and have it roll out into the open from my mouth – is quite a different thing.

It speaks to the enduring nature of those hastily constructed barriers within men who've experienced something like this. When we build them, we barely know what we're hiding ourselves away from. We can't comprehend the horrors that these haphazard walls are keeping out, but we feverishly layer those bricks and straw and mud, tirelessly, until the wall is complete.

How ironic and depressing is it that for many of us, the only consistent and reliable thing throughout the years has been this shelter borne from hurt and trauma?

It's served a purpose. It's protected us, as designed. But it's a double-edged sword. Chris knew he needed some help and guidance from a professional. He was self-aware enough to recognise his flaws and organise a therapist to begin addressing them.

And yet, when it came to the crunch, he couldn't let her in to see what lay in this darkened recess of himself that no one else has seen.

Until now. Until me.

Maybe he'll go back and give it a go, he tells me, but be completely honest this time.

'It's been going on for years now and I really need somebody to help pay the bills and do the chores, so I better get it sorted.'

We laugh, but then there's another prolonged silence. His voice breaks and he chokes on his words.

'Do I really deserve love, though? Is that kind of partnership, that deep and long-lasting intimacy just not for me? Maybe I'm broken and this is where I'm meant to be.'

There's an enormous amount of conflict raging inside of him still, the better part of thirty years later.

'I do have some anger there, even though I thought I was at peace with it. I mean, I'm much more at peace with it than I was once upon a time. It wasn't right, but also I should've known better ... right?'

He was just a child. Fourteen, but also fourteen in the context of a very different era when adolescents knew very little, were exposed to much less, and had significantly fewer avenues of support and self-education about things like sex, identity and harmful behaviour.

'I was a child, but also I think I kind of enjoyed it,' he says quietly. The guilt and shame reverberates through the phone. 'I'm not sure, looking back on it now, but I must've enjoyed it at the time because I went back, and then I kept going back with these different older men, and let them do those things to me.

'And I can't get to grips with it. I've tried a lot over the years to figure it out in my head but I can't. I kept going back. I kept letting it happen.

'There are children out there who have been literally defenceless and have been attacked or abused. They didn't ask for it. They didn't play a role in it. But I don't think I fit into that category, you know? I was old enough to know better … wasn't I?'

Reflecting on it now, he describes himself as 'slutty' and 'promiscuous'. Fourteen-year-old Chris, not Chris now. He sees that confused and curious and mistreated boy as being the responsible party in a group full of adults, and blames himself for what happened.

He explains what's going through his mind right now, having told me about what happened to him.

'Oh, I should've known better,' he sighs. 'I didn't have to be such a slut. I shouldn't have kept going back again and again. I obviously enjoyed it. It's all my fault.'

But should a fourteen-year-old be held responsible for something so significant? Can a child make those kinds of choices for themselves?

I start to answer, and he laughs: 'That was just a rhetorical question – you don't actually have to answer.'

But I feel compelled to. So much of what he's describing having felt over the years, and right now, strikes a chord with me. Blaming myself. Feeling complicit in the things that happened to me. Wondering how much of what happened was at my urging from time to time.

And there's a great deal of hurt inflicted on my psyche with every internal uttering of those questions to myself. To ourselves.

He tries to put himself in the shoes of younger Chris. He takes himself back to that time in a bid to remember how he might've felt about it all.

He suspects there was an element of excitement – not about the sex, per se, but about having a secret. About being a little bit more grown-up than his peers. He'd never tell them what was going on, of course, but to sit amongst them and know that he was having sex when they almost definitely were not ... well, there was a certain sense of juvenile pride.

There's no such excitement now, obviously. And he's reminded of it from time to time as an adult.

He's been at dinner parties or bars with friends over the years when the inevitable conversation topic comes up – how did everyone lose their virginity? There are tales of school dances and awkward fumbling in car backseats with crushes. There are sheepish admissions of much later first-time experiences at college. Booze is sometimes involved. Everyone agrees their debuts were far from polished. There's raucous laughter and a shared sense of nostalgia.

'I can't remember how I lost my virginity,' Chris tells me. 'Not the very first time, in any case, but I remember having anal sex with one of those men in the woods and him not using a condom or lube, and there being a lot of blood later.'

For the uninitiated, anal sex without lubrication, especially for the first time – or second, or third, or fourth for that matter –

can be extremely unpleasant. And a man who's experienced it would be well aware of that fact.

So, to take a boy who has no clue of what to expect and inflict on him a rough and violent and painful experience, without bothering to consider his needs at that moment, is cruel. Plain cruel. That man must've known how Chris would feel. He must've heard his whimpers, seen the tears streaming down his face, spotted the blood afterward.

He just didn't care.

There's a lingering silence as we both think about those scenarios that Chris the schoolboy found himself in.

Now, as gay men of a certain age, there's a shared horror for what he endured, for what those monsters subjected him to. For me, it's clear cut. He was abused. There was a clear power imbalance. He was manipulated and used by people twenty and thirty years older than him, or more.

But he flip-flops between seeing it that way and then almost instantly returning to blaming himself.

'I guess that situation would never have occurred if those forty-year-old men had never tried to have sex with a child,' he says. 'But then I think, "God, Chris – you were such a slut and a fool."'

There are so many unanswered questions. So many missing pieces of the puzzle that is his make-up. He's tried to find that other boy, the 'nephew', a few times on social media, but there's no trace of him. He wants to know what he remembers and if he has any clearer insight on what the hell that was all about. Who were those men? Was the main guy really his uncle? How did he come to be there?

Sometimes, Chris doesn't think about that time of his life at all. Not consciously and deliberately, anyway.

When he does, occasionally he feels fine about it – at peace with it all, he's sure. But then he'll be hit with that familiar guilt, the foreboding in the pit of his stomach that has haunted him for so long.

'When I last went back to the UK a few years ago, I bumped into the ringleader in the street, just really randomly. He recognised me straight away and stopped, and he was like, "Hey, how are you? How's it going?"

'I felt intense rage. It brought out all of this anger towards him and things I had never really felt about it.'

Chris could've shouted at him. He could've unleashed all the loathing and hatred that had been swirling around inside for years. He could've punched him right in the middle of his wrinkled face. But he didn't. Instead, he swallowed those raging feelings, lowered his head, and quickly walked away.

For days, I replay our conversation in my head. I see so much of myself in Chris – particularly the intense self-judgement. The relentless blame. The utterly toxic notion that we played some part in the things that happened to us.

The way Chris spoke about himself in such harsh terms … I could cry just thinking about it. But then, aren't I exactly the same? Isn't my inner voice just as critical and brutal? It's not just that Chris and I dislike ourselves – in many ways, it's a violent hatred.

We hate the things that happened to us, but also that we couldn't, somehow, stop them from happening. We hate how they shaped us as men. We especially hate how those sharp edges so often catch on just about everything we pass by in life.

Chapter Six

The issue of childhood trauma has become increasingly discussed, debated and dissected in pop culture, the media and modern psychology in recent years.

There are primetime television shows dedicated to parenting styles, with experts watching hidden camera recordings of mums and dads interacting with their kids, offering criticism and advice.

There are countless books based on a given author's self-diagnosis of post-traumatic stress disorder, which is linked – sometimes validly, sometimes fairly tenuously – to the availability of love and the presence of discipline when they were children.

Many therapists might have a tendency to go straight to how someone was raised, to their family structure and parents, when diagnosing a personality disorder.

At the risk of creating a competition out of suffering, or categorising different outcomes of people's experiences growing up, there might be value in putting childhood 'trauma' into perspective. It's a unique kind of trauma that creates a specific psychological profile.

That's the view of the renowned psychiatrist Professor Ian Hickie. He's the co-director of health and policy at the Brain and Mind Centre at the University of Sydney. For six years, he was a commissioner of the National Mental Health Commission. His clinical research in the areas of mood disorders, depression and bipolar disorder is internationally regarded. He was a director of the ground-breaking youth mental health service headspace, and the inaugural chief executive of Beyond Blue – two of Australia's best-known organisations.

We're talking on Zoom as I continue my search for answers about how much of the bad parts of me are perhaps a result of the things I experienced when I was a kid. He has extensive experience in childhood and adolescent mental health conditions and treatment, so I'm hoping he might be able to shed some light.

If there's an answer, it's to be found within trauma and shame, and how those two things are intertwined in my story. I mention my interest in the notion of trauma, and whether there are different grades of traumatic damage.

'There's a tendency for the word "trauma" to cover all experiences these days,' he begins. 'There's a danger that anything that happened in childhood that might be considered adverse gets called trauma, so all trauma becomes the same.

'It's not all the same. Different degrees of trauma are differentially important. Now, it's kind of complicated because in one sense, for each individual, their own life and their own story, their own particular thing, has salience and significance.'

In his view, differentiating types of trauma does matter. It's almost imperative when it comes to discussing the effective treatment of some serious illnesses.

The notion of 'trauma' is so common and so mainstream that young people who see a mental health professional for the first time will probably reference it in some way, Professor Hickie says.

They assume their lack of wellness is the result of some kind of acute trauma, whether they can identify it or not.

'Most people will have an explanation and most people will seek to explain their current circumstances in particular ways.

'There's a thing in mental health, so-called "effort after meaning". People will always have a reason as to why they are seeing a professional and the general kind of dialogue is that people expect there to be a childhood reason as to why they have a problem.'

Sigmund Freud, the famed Austrian founder of psychoanalysis, got some things right, but many things very wrong, the mental health profession generally agrees. The post-Freudian world he shaped tended to assume that the cause of anyone's mental illness is rooted in their childhood.

That approach prevails, not just with some of those working in treatment, but with many of the people seeking help. That's what they've absorbed from films, television shows and books.

They figure it's a valid framework and merely how the world works. And that's what they expect to find when they begin seeing a therapist.

'So, you know, if I'm unwell now, I've got to go back and find the cause in my childhood, I must have been exposed to some pretty bad parenting of some kind,' Professor Hickie says of the common expectations of people who are new to therapy.

'There's even some in the mental health space who will help their patients find an explanation rooted in childhood trauma when there isn't one.'

Or, put more simply, not all negative experiences in childhood are 'trauma' and the answer to why some are the way they are is better explained by their adolescent and adult years.

The point is, by using a catch-all for trauma, for categorising it as one thing instead of many different experiences with various potential outcomes, we risk not seeing the forest for the trees.

And when it comes to victims of child sexual abuse, that type of trauma is very different. It could just be one of the worst things a young person can endure, Professor Hickie says.

'It's clear that child sexual abuse, sexual violence and sexual trauma are more significant than other forms of neglect. It's not the same. It's not just as traumatic. This is true when you look at the longer-term effects, like suicidal behaviour and suicidal thinking or acute mental health problems.'

It's also evident when looking at the shared outcomes for victims of child sexual abuse. The fact there are such similarities in where survivors, particularly men, end up isn't a coincidence. It's the explicit and undeniable consequence of trauma.

'Childhood sexual abuse and violent treatment of children stands out from other forms of less-than-ideal parenting, occasional adverse events, or one-off events of a particular type that may not inevitably be the major cause of difficulties in adolescence or later life, and here's why.

'With some of those less significant but still unpleasant events, not everyone will have a bad outcome. Less toxic things are more mediated by how vulnerable the individual is, or maybe somewhat buffered by other circumstances, like protective factors or social factors.'

So, the individual factors matter, not just the event itself, when the experiences are less severe. But for a really severe traumatic event, like child sexual abuse, the experience matters most, not the individual or otherwise mitigating factors.

'For a large proportion of people who do experience that, there are similarities in the outcomes they have. The more severe an experience, the less the individual factors explain what has happened, and the more that the actual events themselves have affected development. That's why you see these similar outcomes.'

The worse the thing is, the more severe the outcome you're likely to see – and the commonality of outcomes, independent of other individual characteristics, Professor Hickie says.

‘The wiring of normative development is neutral at birth, if you like, and then changes itself including via emotional responsiveness to experiences. The more perverted the experience, the more the wiring goes astray.’

Another uncomfortable but important distinction to make is in the resulting behaviour of male survivors compared to female survivors of child sexual abuse.

For all types of mental health issues, it has long been established that women are significantly more likely to reach out for help when they’re in a dark or dangerous place, and to seek treatment generally for any issues they’re worried about.

On the other hand, men will tend to go it alone. They bristle at the suggestion of seeking help. They certainly aren’t open to preventative care in most cases. When the chips are down, they generally retreat within themselves and hibernate, emotionally and sometimes physically.

And when they’re on the edge and feel they have no other option but to remove themselves from this world, research shows they will turn to much more violent causes of death by suicide to ensure they’re unlikely to survive.

Men are three times more likely to die by suicide in Australia than women, according to the Australian Bureau of Statistics. That statistic is pretty similar across much of the developed world.

For a variety of reasons, men who are mentally unwell or vulnerable to acute disruptions to their wellbeing are at real risk.

'Most men live in much smaller, intimate networks than the women in their lives, whether it's their female partners or their female children or their female parents,' Professor Hickie says.

In all societies, regardless of race, geographic location, economic status or social development, women tend to have broader networks outside of the home and their immediate family, he says. They seek out love and support from a whole range of people, with whom they can share their thoughts and feelings, not just about the bad times, but also the good.

'Women share more of their emotional lives with other people – including the sharing of trauma.'

And while huge progress has been made in recent years to encourage men to feel safe to speak about their problems and be vulnerable without being judged, in some ways, things have gone backwards a little.

'Interestingly, men now don't necessarily participate in some of the social things that their fathers or their grandfathers did. They're probably not members of local football clubs, or part of church communities, or work clubs or unions, in the same way men a few generations back were. So they may not have the same stable network of friends.'

Of course, historically, those men were unlikely to have expressed themselves emotionally within those social circles, but they might have gained some benefit from having a regular and reliable connection. There might've been subtle and accepted ways of debriefing.

That's the view in journalism, the profession I've devoted my life to. In the old days, reporters had a reputation for being drunks who spent more time at the pub than at their desks.

There's one particular watering hole near the News Corp Australia headquarters in Surry Hills that used to have a dedicated phone line direct to the office, with a red handset on the bar that would ring when an editor or layout person had a question about someone's copy.

Journalists, mostly men in those days, would gather to get pissed and talk about the stories they'd covered that day. And many of them were probably traumatic. Death and destruction from the bloke on the police beat. Horrific tales of the worst of humanity from the court reporter. Gore and guts from the general news beat blokes.

I doubt they sat there with arms draped around each other's shoulders, wiping tears from cheeks and offering a gentle squeeze of support and care. Their sharing of traumatic experiences wasn't formalised and deliberate. But there might be something to be said for the debriefing nature of those booze-fuelled late nights.

On top of not seeking treatment for the lifelong and often serious issues that result from the trauma of child sexual abuse, some men remain silent. Forever.

*

Not long after talking to Professor Hickie, I'm in an online forum dedicated to men's mental health and share a little bit of my story in a post. I talk about how I feel the anxiety that's gotten progressively worse in my adult years, or maybe just harder to ignore, must surely be linked to the things that happened to me when I was a boy.

'Maybe it's part of getting older,' I write. 'In my 20s, I could push on through the anxious moments pretty well. I didn't even realise I was anxious a lot of time. These days … I crumble so easily.'

I get a private message from Jack. He's scrolling posts one night when my words catch his eye. It sparks a kind of recognition in him that how he's been feeling lately is quite similar.

He's younger than me and hasn't necessarily had the same increasingly imperative need to look at his behaviour and his wellbeing. But he has also gone through a period of self-reflection. Maybe it's all the extra time to think during Covid.

Jack tells me about growing up in a housing commission home in the Sutherland Shire in Sydney's south. The product of a Greek father and an Anglo-Australian mother, his olive skin and dark hair sees him labelled a 'bloody wog' in the extremely white pocket where he spends the entirety of his childhood.

Apart from the racism, life is pretty good in the grand scheme of things.

His parents separate when he's little but they stay on relatively good terms. His dad owns a huge farm up in Mudgee where he spends chunks of time during the school holidays, mostly unsupervised, tearing through the bush from sunrise until sunset. He hunts, learns to ride a motorbike before a regular pushbike, swims in murky dams, and climbs tall trees. Jack's skin is perpetually covered in a thick layer of mud and that's exactly how he likes it.

Back home in Sydney, he is exposed to some pretty confronting scenes in the public housing block. Wild brawls between drunks. Domestic violence. Drug-taking. A rough guy in his thirties who lives a few doors down has a large collection of guns and lets Jack fire off a few rounds into the back fence.

Jack is fearless, though. Nothing much bothers him. He's confident and outgoing, and loves talking to anyone about anything.

Jack has always been in awe of stories about mediaeval times – Knights of the Round Table, heroes on horseback in armour, King Arthur, chivalry, castles and courts. His mum saves up leftover bits and pieces from her wage to buy him books that tick those boxes and he reads them every night before he goes to sleep.

His modest bedroom often plays host to the most intricate games of make-believe. He doesn't have a whole lot in the way of expensive toys or elaborate props and costumes, but he doesn't really need those things. Jack is happy to grab the pillows from the beds of his mother, brother and sister, then make a fort of his own fashioning. His very own castle, from which he can reign over his vast kingdom.

'I loved castles. I thought castles were indestructible and I loved that idea of ultimate safety. Turrets. Towers. Moats. Drawbridges. I was obsessed.'

One afternoon when Jack is five or six, he's in his bedroom building a pillow fort. He crawls inside it to admire his handiwork when a stranger's voice bellows through the silence. He peers out. It's one of his older brother's friends.

'I'd never met him before,' Jack recalls. 'It was his first time hanging out at the house. I never saw him again either. But he was nice. And while no one else really cared about my pillow fort, seeing it for the childish game it was, this person did. He was cool about it.'

The man is about twenty years old or so. He has a mop of thick red hair, just like Jack's mum. He kneels down next to the mass of pillows and blankets and asks Jack to explain each element of the design. He maintains eye contact the entire time, nodding along enthusiastically.

'He went and quietly closed my door. We mucked around a bit, playing with my fort. He thought my mighty castle of pillows and blankets was just the neatest thing ever. It was fun and normal, until it wasn't.

'He told me to take off my pants and I refused, so to "encourage" me, he took his off.'

The type of abuse that Jack endured is the stuff of parents' nightmares. The monster lurking in the shadows who strikes without warning. The bogeyman who you rarely encounter in life. The reality is that most perpetrators of child sexual abuse are known to the victim. It's a family member, a neighbour, someone at church, or a teacher. They tend to groom a child and offend repeatedly. Jack's abuser appears to have struck in a purely opportunistic fashion.

Dr Michael Davis from the Centre for Forensic Behavioural Science at Monash University wrote about how offenders are often categorised in an article for *InPsych*, the Australian Psychological Society's magazine, in October 2013. There are 'preferential' offenders – those who have a sexual preference for children, such as paedophiles. But there are also a cohort that perpetrate 'situational' offences.

'Those offences towards the situational end of the continuum are thought to reflect basic sexual needs such as lust, or non-sexual needs such as power or anger,' he wrote.

'Such offenders usually do not have a genuine sexual interest in children but may molest them for a number of often complex reasons. Their offending is often impulsive and opportunistic.'

Jack remembers how the abuse started, how it finished, and a couple of details in between. The rest of it is blank. The horror movie that upended his childhood is missing some scenes, but it's a blessing in disguise. He thinks it's better not to remember the particularly awful parts of that day.

Just like Chris, I'm the first person Jack has ever told about what happened to him twenty-five years ago. He's thought about it, but never put into words what that man took from him.

'This is the most active I've ever been with my experience and it's going to force open my Pandora's box, but that's probably a good thing,' he says.

'I've never felt so sad about this experience than I do now and knowing some metaphorical book can never be closed is just salt in the wound.'

Jack started to talk about how his life after that point was 'a lesson in how to bite the bullet – a guide on how to swim in shit while keeping your chin up'. He doesn't think it's a good thing, that there are consequences of running from his painful truth all his life.

Suddenly thinking about that day now, about what it might mean, brings a heavy weight down on him.

'I hate that there is a man out there who got away with doing this to me, a man who could be doing this to other boys. I hate that in order to deal with this I will have to release my ignorance of the experience when thus far it's been easier to forget it ever happened, to never deal or talk about it in a realistic setting.'

I ask Jack if we can speak more about what happened to him, and some of those challenges that he's struggled with since then. He's nervous about talking to me, but also intrigued.

Maybe opening up and letting his guts spill out will be cathartic. Maybe there'll be some deep realisations and those parts of himself that he suspects are a direct result of that attack will make more sense. Maybe there'll be some healing.

Jack and I make a time to chat on the phone, but he reschedules at the last minute. We set a new time a week later, but this time I need to postpone. After that, Jack stops replying to my messages. I try to reach out to him a few times, but I don't hear back.

Perhaps it was too much, too soon. There is comfort in keeping that lid to Pandora's box closed. I don't think it's the easy option like Jack implied, nor cowardly at all. I think for many people it's about survival and self-preservation.

Talking helps. Of course it does. But you've got to be in the right headspace and at a healthy and supported point in your life to rip the band-aid off, especially when it's covering a particularly deep wound.

Letting it rip isn't free of consequences. Perhaps Jack felt that and it was too much. But I'd be lying if I said I wasn't disappointed.

I go in search of more men to speak to. It doesn't go very well.

Chapter Seven

I'm eagerly awaiting the sense that I've found where I'm meant to be. That's what I've come to expect, based on the experiences of so many others who have taken part in support groups for survivors of child sexual abuse.

Men in online forums and social media groups who've gone to these kinds of gatherings that I now find myself attending have later revelled in the feeling of acceptance, of finally being seen.

You can hear the relief through their words on the screen. The sense of excitement that comes with grasping hope after a long period of despair. It's positively palpable. And there's so much comfort that is derived from understanding a lot about yourself, I think.

I want that. Or something like that. It's hard to know exactly what my expectations are, going into the first meeting of the support group I've signed up for. I guess I just desperately hope to no longer feel like I am sick.

I sit here, perched in bed, an ice-cold can of Coke next to me, staring at my laptop. Covid lockdowns have prevented this particular group from meeting in person, as would traditionally be the case, and so it's gone virtual.

As the men file in one by one, I'm feeling hopeful that this could be the ultimate healing breakthrough I need. Dr Rolenstein was my first big step out of the hell I was trapped in. This group could provide a clear roadmap to wellness.

It's quickly pretty clear that it's not going to be like that. From the moment the nine faces pop onto the screen in front of me, to two hours later when they flick back to black once more, I hate this. Every second of it.

It's confronting. It's deeply unsettling. The men range in age from a little younger than me to considerably older than me. They come from different backgrounds and a mix of ethnicities. One wears a fancy suit. A couple are in workwear from their jobs as tradies of some kind. Some are in nice homes; one is in a room in a halfway house. One is even in the back of a moving vehicle, on his way home from a work stint out west.

But they all speak the same language – a shared dialect that only survivors seem to know, without even knowing they know. With lots of words or not many at all, they describe their own living hells – things that are almost impossible to imagine a child enduring.

I hear horrendous tales of sexual and physical abuse of the worst kind. Abuse at the hands of family members. Of a priest. Of a schoolteacher. Of a total stranger who struck opportunistically.

There's talk of negligent parents who looked the other way, who pretended they hadn't heard or seen what was right in front of them. Little boys not being believed. Little boys being told they were lying or imagining things.

There are retellings of the years after the abuse, when men find themselves confronting those first moments of feeling like they were on a slippery slope. Discovering alcohol. Taking drugs. Taking heavier drugs. Cheating on partners. Not showing up for work. Feeling anger boiling over into uncontrollable, blackout rage.

There are a lot of examples of self-destructive tendencies sneaking in when things look to be going well, planting a bomb beneath our own feet – often when those feet are just getting steady for the first time in a long time.

There are quiet, regret-tinged discussions of brushing away helping hands and of running from attempts at intervention.

The men speak about triggers for their trauma. The smell of cigar smoke for one man. Being told to get over it triggers another, just like his mother used to insist he do when he was little. Feeling criticised by a loved one. Feeling like someone is taking the piss.

One of the guys is so broken that he can barely speak. For most of the two-hour session, he sits with his head in his hands, rocking gently from side to side. His body slowly lifts and falls as he takes big, deliberate breaths.

Another shakes with rage when he speaks about the men who abused him. His voice turns cold and venomous when talking about the members of his own family who knew but failed to protect him.

At the end of the night, the facilitators do a quick whip around the virtual room to see how the men are feeling. They agree that they are raw and exposed, but feeling pretty good overall. The shoulders seem a bit lighter. The brow is a little less furrowed. There is a sense of excitement about meeting again next week, to keep going, to push on – together.

Where nervous frowns greeted me two hours earlier, now there are more relaxed faces. Still tired and drawn. But softer.

'And you, Shannon? How do you think it went?'

I nod and give a weak smile. But I don't feel any lighter. There's no sense of relief. Not at all. Instead, I feel like an utter fraud.

The things that happened to me pale in comparison to what these blokes have survived. The brutal, merciless rapes. The floggings. The lit cigarettes stubbed out on bare skin. The taunts and the threats. The lack of belief. The total disregard.

These men have been dragged to hell and made to live there. Really, for some, they haven't yet fully escaped those fiery clutches. They still cop unrelenting torture into adulthood, but this monster doesn't have a face or a name – this torture lives within them.

And me? Some older kid touched me up every other day for a few years and it made me not like being gay. So what? I have hang-ups and don't like myself. Big fucking whoop.

The more I talk to other men, the more I read and the more I absorb, and especially after hearing all of those harrowing stories, I'm unsure if what happened to me is actually abuse. What if I was just some sick and twisted kid? Maybe I was wired wrong and destined to act out in a disgusting way.

Instead of suffering from trauma, maybe I'm just broken. Maybe there's a virus infecting my body. The bits of good that once existed in me have been choked to death. That's why I'm so fucked up. I'm sick.

I'm so angry at myself. I feel like an idiot for having thought this was a good idea. I feel like I'm intruding on this almost sacred space, barging in on a sensitive conversation with a story that doesn't even match. *Wrong place, wrong time*, a voice in my head tells me. *Get out and don't return. You don't deserve to be here.*

'Stick with it,' Luke assures me when I confess how I'm feeling. 'I felt a bit like a fraud too at the beginning but trust me, it's worth it. It's really worth it.'

Going to a support group was Luke's idea in the first place.

He went to one when he was in his early thirties. For him, the group was life changing. He felt seen and heard. He saw himself in others for the very first time and suddenly didn't feel quite so alone.

For several weeks, Luke lapped up every bit of the shared insights, the advice, the comfort and the collective grief. It was a major turning point in his healing journey.

'Give it another go,' he urges me.

I return for the second meeting and throw myself into it head first. I really try. I speak up and share some of my story. I respond to men who tell their truths, offering comfort and encouragement.

But I'm sure I can see looks of disinterest on the men's faces when I detail the things that happened to me. I think I see a roll of the eyes from one of the guys. Paranoia takes over and I'm convinced there's this kind of staggered disbelief that I would even consider myself in the same realm as them.

I have no doubt I'm imagining it. But the irrational part of my brain takes over and I spend much of the two hours peering down, desperate to avoid eye contact with anyone. I clam up and don't want to speak, even when one of the facilitators throws to me.

When the next week rolls around, it's not until the mid-afternoon of an especially busy workday that I realise the meeting is just a few hours away. My stomach drops to my feet. A deep and heavy dread washes over me.

I feel an urgent need to escape – somewhere, anywhere.

Two competing ideas go to war with each other, pushing me into a corner that I know well and desperately hate. The place where my two halves – the rational and the unreasonable – often meet to battle it out.

On one side, the eagerness to do the right thing. The healthy and productive thing. Realistically, I know I should persist with the group and that this thing that makes me anxious will ultimately be good for me. Just like Luke insisted it was for him.

Plus, I've made a commitment. I have taken a spot that was in all likelihood desperately needed by another man who, as a consequence, missed out.

I owe it not just to myself but to him to carry on. I have to keep going. It's shit, but it's the right thing to do.

But on the other side … ah yes, my old frenemy: the easy way out. It ends up being the bad choice almost every single time, but gosh, does it feel good. Like that third tequila shot of the night – something that's right in the moment and then, very quickly after that, not so much.

That side tells me to just run. That's what will make me feel better. The horrible thoughts racing through my head and the physical sensations that they invoke … that will all disappear if I just quit now. It's easy.

The thought of carrying on for six more weeks makes my skin itch. My fight-or-flight response is firmly stuck on the 'get the hell outta there' setting. I'm practically out of breath while sitting perfectly still, waiting for six o'clock to arrive and the Zoom session to begin.

The thought of enduring the pain of smashing through my facade to again expose myself – my true, broken self – is unsettling. The pressure to be broken enough, though, the insecurity that I am unable to truly justify my place in the group – is even scarier.

More than scary. Or not really scary at all, perhaps. Just unpleasant. Sickeningly uncomfortable. I can't do it. Not tonight anyway.

Maybe next week.

Yeah, next week – next week I'll definitely go to the group and really commit to facing my truth, no matter how dark or dull it is. No matter how much it makes me want to tear my own skin off or scream until I swallow my tongue.

I bash out a hastily composed apology to the facilitators and hit send, before slamming shut the lid of my laptop and digitally slinking off into the shadows.

Next week will be different, I tell myself. I'll properly prepare for it and really dig in. I've got seven days to ready myself and then I'll be good to go. I will do this.

But I don't. I never go back to the group. And then, not long after, I spiral.

It's something I've done on countless occasions. I know the warning signs. It starts with negative self-talk – a kind of monologue of all the things wrong with me, all of my terrible flaws. Then it boils over into anxiety that makes my mind race, my hands shake and my heart beat at a million miles an hour. Then it's an exhausting sadness that comes so abruptly that it's terrifying.

Being alone with my thoughts and my feelings is choking when I start to spiral. It's like being locked in a room with the meanest person you've ever encountered. There's no escape and they're relentless. Almost psychopathic in their unbridled hatred of you.

I'm in something of a secret relationship with this raging inner monologue. I hate it and I'm certain it hates me. It longs for my destruction, that much is obvious. I hear it openly rooting for my downfall and cheering at every single misstep I make.

But there's a sick truth about that voice that I can't ignore. I'd be a little lost without my sinister companion.

It's one of the few consistencies in the transience that has been much of my life. When friendships fall away, jobs go to shit, houses stop feeling like homes and lovers leave, it's there, talking through every prodding pain with me from the moment I wake in the morning until I fall asleep at night.

The thought of silence terrifies me. The mere notion of being alone with myself is a horrid thing I can't contemplate.

I have to escape this prison of my own making, and that never involves a healthy intervention. I'm more of a quick-and-easy kind of guy.

I can see myself metaphorically walking into the path of an oncoming train, like I'm having some out-of-body experience, and yet I push on regardless, fully aware of the pain that's about to tear through my body.

I go to my favourite pub for a beer. Just one beer, alone, to decompress, to spend a bit of quiet time with myself on the balcony, and to think. The beer goes down really well. Fast, too – I can smash a pint in five minutes without even really trying.

I get another, and then another. I buy a packet of cigarettes, even if it's been several months since I last lit up. I churn through them, one after the other in quick succession, until my throat burns and my eyes sting and my fingers stink.

I keep drinking, and as I get drunker, my thoughts get darker.

What kind of loser sits at a pub by themselves and gets hammered, I think to myself. *Look at this pathetic excuse of a man*, I silently scoff after catching a glimpse of my reflection in the window. I examine the faces of those around me to see if they've spotted how pitiful I am. But they don't even notice me … and in some small way, isn't that worse?

I lose track of time. The afternoon glow of the sky swirls into a purple-black hue and dusk is here. The volume inside the pub gets higher and happier – laughs and excited chattering from jovial punters sharing good times with friends and colleagues.

Festoon lights that hang on the ceiling above my head switch on, the twinkles almost dancing in the gentle night breeze. I see stars in my eyes when the light hits the faint sheen of tears that have formed. Try as I might to fight off the waterworks, I can feel them coming.

So I order another beer. I stumble downstairs to the pokies lounge, full of bright lights, neon signs, noisy jingles and screeching sirens. It's an assault on the senses and just the kind of onslaught that my mind needs to forget itself.

I slide onto a stool in front of a blaring machine. It's probably got a cartoon Buddha on it making vaguely racist sounds, like some kind of kitschy and now-problematic film from the 1970s.

I slide in a fifty-dollar note and hit the buttons at random. I have no idea how to play. But in the past when I've won, and sometimes I've won really big, I did so by pressing the button on the far right of the top line, and the one on the far left of the bottom line.

It ends up being about fifty cents a spin. It's not much money in the scheme of things, but even now, drunk and spiralling, it feels like a waste of money.

I might strike up a conversation with the person next to me. It's probably a chain-smoking tradie still wearing his reflective orange or yellow workwear from a shift that finished several hours ago. It might be an older woman tearing through her pension. It could be someone who looks like me. Normal-looking, I think, before realising that if I'm so normal, what the fuck am I doing here?

I order another drink. Down here in the pokies lounge, the waitress comes to you. At this pub, for some reason, she's almost always a Thai woman, who has clearly been coached on ways to keep big-spending punters happy. She brings me packets of Pringles and fruit-flavoured Mentos lollies in individual wrappers. Sometimes, she brings around a tray of hot food – battered fish, chicken strips, spring rolls.

It almost makes being here alone on a weeknight, hundreds of dollars down on the pokies, feel worthwhile.

Sometimes I win a little, bet more, then lose it all. Very occasionally, I win a lot. One time I walked out of here with a thousand dollars. No lie. Another time, eight hundred bucks. It's a brilliant feeling and can chase away the darkest of storm clouds that have hung on my day.

Most of the time, I spin and I spin and I spin, until I begin to feel panicked. I haven't had that rush of dopamine that comes from winning. The dark clouds in my head haven't cleared – they've only grown thicker and heavier, and now it looks like there's going to be a downpour. Biblical flooding. I need a win.

Maybe another beer will help. And another packet of cigarettes. Or maybe I should go to another pub with the guy next to me, with whom I've struck up an instant friendship. He seems fun. Yeah, that sounds like a good idea. It's a Wednesday night, but that's all right – I'm used to being hungover and surviving.

I look at my phone to see what time it is. There are four missed calls and nine text messages from my husband. It's midnight and it must be four hours since I said I was having one more beer before heading home. He has no idea where I am. He's probably not overly worried, though. We've been here before.

We both know my spirals.

Eventually, somehow, I get home. I might run out of money, or come very close to it, almost vomiting when I realise I've just funnelled several hundred dollars through those stupid machines. I may get kicked out for being too drunk, as I have once or twice. You know you're shit-faced when the staff at an all-night pokies lounge frequented by desperados, derros and drug addicts thinks you've had too much.

And while rare, from time to time I'll have a brief moment of clarity, looking around and realising that I don't want to be here.

I wake the next morning with a throbbing head and an empty stomach. I don't feel good. In any way, really.

My husband is disappointed in me. His eyes say it, even if he decides to bite his tongue this time. There's pity mixed with fatigue all over his face. We sit in bed and drink coffee, before he tells me that I must get up and confront the day, no matter how horribly hungover I am. That's part of being a responsible adult.

Sometimes I will. Most of the time I won't. I'll build a little fort out of blankets and pillows instead and crawl inside of it, staying there for the next few days.

I can't see people. I can't work. I can't feed or bathe myself. I just wallow in shame and self-loathing for as long as I possibly can.

Chapter Eight

Luke was born while his dad was at theological college. His mum did the odd class there to enrich her own knowledge of her Christian Baptist faith.

'She was in one called "The Imminent Return of Christ" when her waters broke with me,' Luke laughs.

A lot of pastors' kids have difficult experiences at times during their childhood and adolescence, he explains. There's the pressure of expectation. When a parent devotes their life to God and knows every element of their religion and the Bible inside and out, well … that's a lot to live up to.

Any misstep, big or small, is generally much worse for the child of a pastor, too. You're not allowed to push the boundaries. The scrutiny is intense.

'It wasn't like that for me at all, though,' Luke says. 'In fact, Dad did his doctoral thesis on pastors' kids, so I think he knew really well what worked and what didn't in terms of parenting.

'He and Mum were hyper aware of what the job meant for us and so they kind of sought to protect us from the negative sides of it – the potential negatives. There weren't any of those expectations you'd hear about, given that that era of parenting was very much wrapped up in the notion that "if you spare the rod, you spoil the child".'

That phrase actually comes from the Bible. It's from Proverbs 13:24, which says that 'he who spares the rod hates his son, but he who loves him is careful to discipline him'.

I think the 'careful' part is open to interpretation a lot of the time.

And no wonder. The Bible is littered with parables about how children are inherently bad and it's up to fathers to correct that, with whatever means they see fit.

A man of God, who teaches the word of the Lord, who might be inclined to hold especially true to the belief that all children are born with sin and must be guided with a rod to goodness is perhaps more likely to have kids who don't have the best time growing up.

'There was no heavy-handedness with us,' Luke recalls. 'I think they had a more practical view of parenting and how to guide us in the world.'

Take, for example, the time that Luke's younger brother dobbed him in for trying a puff of a cigarette with some other boys down in the bush near their house.

'I came home and expected Mum to lose it, but she calmly explained the dangers of smoking and then said, "Oh well, if you want lung cancer, go for it."'

Neither of his parents grew up especially religious. They each stumbled upon the same church in their teens and met each other there, falling in love and eventually marrying and starting a family.

Religion was their life, but they decided early on that their kids could forge their own paths. As soon as they were old enough, they could decide if they wanted to go to church each Sunday.

Luke loved it, though. Instantly. That passion only grew stronger, not just for his faith but for the other positives church brought to his life.

The entirety of his social life was wrapped up in church. Bible study. Youth group. Special excursions. Even his friends at school were kids who went to his church. The church was a source of comfort when things were difficult and a place for celebration and joy when things went well.

And for the most part, things went well. Life in the Shire – God's country, as locals describe it – was good. After moving there from Sydney's west, where the year of horror had played out, Luke settled in almost overnight.

'I didn't have a lot of hobbies. I didn't play sport or anything like that. I just liked to hang out with my friends. That's all I wanted to do.

'We were always out riding bikes, building forts, digging holes, playing in the bush. I loved that.'

He remembers being a daydreamer. When he had some

quiet time on his own, his mind would drift off and ponder any number of topics. People, places, things. It didn't really matter.

But as he got older, those flights of fancy took him to darker and darker places. Back to the old house he spent the first bit of childhood in. Back to that fence separating his place from the older boy's. Back to that kid's bedroom. Back to all of those horrible things that happened.

It filled him with a toxic shame that permeated through his body, infecting his thoughts and forcing him to question what he thought were solid, unshakable beliefs.

'My belief, my faith, is fairly central to my outlook on life and how I make decisions about how to live. And yet, it comes into conflict with some aspects of who I am.

'I'm not sure that's unique to me, though. I think it's true of anyone who has faith.

'But the things that happened to me contributed to this kind of conflict within me. I never lost faith, but I think I actively tried to distance myself from it.'

There were moments when Luke wondered how God, in all of His glory, He who was so good and loved humanity, could've let something so horrible happen to him at such a tender and vulnerable age.

How could His love for Luke allow this life-altering, scarring thing to take place? How could He not ease the suffering that stretched way beyond that long and painful year?

'I've grappled with it from time to time throughout my life. I guess it's normal. But I always come back to God and the church. I still go to church now. It's a really important part of my life.'

Religious institutions get a bad rap, especially in conversations about child sexual abuse. But religion can often provide important boundaries and frameworks for young people. It offers guidance and support during times of great change and upheaval. The sense of community, like the one Luke was fortunate enough to enjoy, can be crucial when support is needed.

But there's no denying that churches can use those boundaries to punish and exclude those who fall foul of them.

Jason's faith in God was also tested when he was in his mid-teens, only it failed the test. The church, which was right at the centre of his life, and of his family, became something he bitterly resented.

Given how horribly his church let him and his family down, I find it understandable that he drifted away permanently.

I meet Jason on a Reddit forum. I share a post about my quest for answers, about how I've come to be the man I am today, and whether others who've ventured through similar dark forests might be able to relate to my inner turmoil.

He reaches out and we arrange a time to speak over Zoom. When he flashes onto my laptop screen, he fills almost the whole thing. He's tall and toned with a wide frame. The kind of giant of a man who might startle me if we crossed paths on a dark street at a late hour. But he has a soft face and deep, warm eyes. He tells me about his childhood, growing up in a small village in the Hunter Valley wine region in New South Wales. He's a year younger than me.

He was raised in the church and his parents, both working in healthcare, were devoted to not just their faith but the community aspects of worship. They went to mass every Sunday, of course, and also volunteered to run local charity programs, children's recreational activities, fundraisers … basically anything the priest offered up that their busy schedules could accommodate.

'Mum and Dad had their own medical practice. He was a GP and Mum was a nurse. They also worked at the hospital. So they knew everyone in town. But church was the hub of our social life. And it was two blocks away at the end of our street.

'The congregation was huge. Probably a hundred people or so. You knew everyone's names and faces. It was the sort of place that felt a bit like a family, you know? There were very few degrees of separation.'

It's a nice feeling. When he's out and about with his mum or dad, people stop and talk to them. They know what year Jason is in at school. They ask him about his hobbies. It's a very tight-knit, neighbourly place to live.

Life is pretty good for Jason and his younger sister. His mum and dad are present and loving, he enjoys school, he has lots of friends, and he feels a general optimism about what life has in store for him.

On weekends, when he's not busy with Scouts, he rides his bike around the streets with his group of mates. He loves video games but also likes to read.

'I was never in trouble,' he declares proudly.

He's abused for the first time when he's ten. It happens repeatedly – too many times to count – for almost a year.

'He's an older boy who's seventeen,' Jason explains. 'His family and mine knew each other through the church. It started at his house, in his room, while we were playing video games. It was kissing and petting at first, then escalated to more. Much more. And it happened in other places – my house, even inside the church when no one was around.'

On the outside, Jason's abuser is like any other. He's friendly, active in the community, a regular at church. There's no reason for anyone to worry about him or suspect there's a darkness inside of him.

Jason sees the other side. He's manipulative, using gentle coercion at first – the kind you might expect in a grooming situation, where an older person bends the will of a child over time with special attention, gifts, and a sharing of adult wisdom, in a way that creates a feeling of indebtedness. But when that approach loses its effectiveness and Jason tries to pull away, the older boy ups the ante.

He tries to withhold. He won't let Jason play his favourite video game. He lies to his parents about Jason swearing or misbehaving, so he gets in trouble. Then there are violent threats – about what will happen to him, about what will happen to his family.

'He tells me he'll kill my parents if I don't do what he wants. He tells me in quite graphic detail about how he's going to rape my mother. I'm not overly naive at this point about what sex is because Mum and Dad were pretty open and had a healthy perspective on educating children about the body and that kind of thing. So I kind of know what this guy is telling me.'

The older boy tells Jason about his abuse of another child – a boy who's about fifteen. He also goes to their church. In the perpetrator's eyes, they're in some kind of 'relationship', he remembers being told. He boasts about the kinds of things they do together.

Church is no longer a safe space. Jason doesn't enjoy it anymore, given it's where the older boy is. He can't be there without being reminded of the things that are done to him. The terror that haunts him – the fear of his threats, the shame of the abuse, a constant sense of worry about what will happen if anyone finds out – invades this once-special place.

He quits his Sunday role as church acolyte – the child assistant to the priest, carrying candles and crucifixes in, helping the choir, helping the priest with communion. He loved it. But no more.

His faith slips away. It's not even necessarily a conscious thing for Jason. He doesn't remember any specific questioning of it, or blaming God for what's happened to him. One day his love of God and the church is there, the next it's gone. It's as though it's simply died.

'I've never, ever been very comfortable with it since. Being back in a church – I don't like it. It's just, yeah, it's not for me.'

Like a death, he grieved the loss of his faith for a long time. Probably more so the loss of the community aspect, and the familiarity of it – all he'd ever known falling away. There have been times more recently where he especially misses those connections and the grounding they offer. And when he feels lonely, he feels the absence of the religion of his childhood.

'It'd be nice to have. It'd be really nice. And it'd be good for my kids, too, to have what I had. But I don't want to turn up and sit there and pretend, and feel the things I'd probably feel, in exchange. I can't do that. It's not worth it.'

Young Jason changes pretty quickly after the abuse begins – 'and pretty severely'. He's rudderless in the middle of a raging torrent, being thrashed about mercilessly.

It comes to a head one day when he's nearing the end of primary school. At an event at church, he catches the glance of the older boy. There's a menacing look on his face. That look and the emotions it triggers inside of Jason flicks a switch. He's had enough.

That night, when his parents have gone to bed, he switches on the lamp on the desk in the corner of his bedroom and begins writing them a letter. He's meticulous with the detail of what the boy has been doing to him for almost a year. He's almost analytical about it – what's occurred, how it made him feel and the recent consequences.

He leaves it on the kitchen bench and goes to bed.

'They were obviously upset,' he recalls. 'I could tell for them that it was massive. They were shellshocked. Dad swung into action pretty quickly. He called community services, he arranged for me to speak to a psychologist, he called the police … I remember it all happening very fast.'

The police tell his father that it's unlikely to be something that they'll pursue because the prospect of a conviction is slim. No good can come of it, they say. It's better off for everyone if it's just forgotten.

'There was no solid evidence, and it would be my word against his, and given I was so young, you know, it's hard,' he says, having learned from his father later about that conversation with the authorities. 'I do remember quite well after that being very, very disappointed. The fact that there wasn't an outcome was disappointing.

'I have a bit of an issue when there isn't justice for an unjust situation. That's an ingrained part of it.'

There are a handful of times afterwards that Jason has to see his abuser. Given the total lack of consequences, it's unavoidable in some ways. It's a small town. They only live a few minutes from each other. Jason goes to church with his family and the older boy is there with his. But there is never an opportunity for the two of them to be alone. His mum and dad make sure of it.

The priest, who's aware of what has happened, who has sat down for lengthy conversations with Jason's dad, watches him like a hawk.

He is never abused again. But the horror doesn't stop. If anything, it just gets worse.

He goes to boarding school in Armidale in Year Seven. It was always part of his parents' plan. It's just like the regional college his father went to, with a focus on building up young men, mixing academia with recreation and bonding.

Also, the thinking is that a new start might be good for him. It's no coincidence that he's also getting out of town just after telling his parents. There's an urgency to get him as far away from that older boy as possible.

But at his new school, he's surrounded by older boys. Some remind him of his abuser. Some have similar characteristics – domineering, threatening, manipulative and willing to use violence to get what they want. There's no sexual abuse or anything like that, but Jason feels like an outsider. It's a rugby school and the boys are macho and masculine, if not a little homoerotic, wrestling each other and play-fighting.

'I have no interest in that sort of stuff at all and it's hard being away from home and from my parents. I basically hate it.'

The first year of boarding school is manageable because he's in a dormitory room with boys all his own age. But in Year Eight, they're moved into a bigger house with a mix of students right through to senior level.

'I remember that really vividly. It was just very uncomfortable. Near the end of term three, in Year Eight, I was getting really angry. I remember one night absolutely losing it when people were picking on me, and I picked up a cricket bat in this kind of blind rage.

'I mean, looking back now, it's obvious why I was getting so angry and so upset all the time. I could've used some pastoral support, but it just wasn't available. Instead, they'd put me in timeout and so I just became more and more isolated.'

Despite that, he's still fairly studious. Though his grades have begun to slip, especially compared to what they were in primary school when he was placed into advanced classes, they are still good enough to not really be a worry. He's exceptional at mathematics.

'But I can't cope with it for long and I come home for the holidays and refuse to go back. I actually went and walked into the local high school during the holidays and the principal was there in his office. I asked to enrol myself.

'So that's what my parents agreed to let me do and I go to the local high school. It's a really different environment again and I don't have many fond memories of that period of my life.'

When he's back home, around the age of fourteen, he indirectly tells his abuser's family about what has happened. For so long, they'd been kept in the dark. The police knew. The priest knew. Community services knew. But no one did anything, and as a result, no one had thought to tell his family.

'I write him a letter – my abuser,' Jason recalls. 'I've become so angry and torn up inside, and it's not long since I've come back from boarding school, so I'm not in a very good place. And I think I just can't get over the fact that there was no justice. Like, I'm messed up but he's fine, and he's walking around like nothing happened.'

The letter never reaches the older boy.

'His family was this kind of strict, regimented, military family. So when this letter appears in the mailbox, it's intercepted, opened and read.'

A bomb is set off beneath everyone's feet. Jason's parents receive a call from the church, asking them to meet with the priest and officials from the parish. The older boy's family want to meet them, and Jason's parents expect they'll want to search for answers, maybe to offer some kind of apology. Jason's mum and dad take along a friend of theirs, a child psychologist with experience in the area of abuse, as a way to assist everyone to come to terms with it.

They walk into an ambush. The older boy's family demand Jason write a retraction. He's lying, they insist, and the lies have destroyed them. The church is in damage control, with mediators there to pressure Jason's mum and dad into backing down and agreeing the allegations aren't true.

'They had a note that I'd written in school about how angry I felt about everything, about life, which my teacher had raised with the principal and put in my file. Someone high up in the church worked at the school, took the letter and gave it to the mediator.'

Jason can only speculate about why they thought his letter was significant. Maybe it was meant to be some kind of proof that he was unstable. A little disturbed. He wonders if perhaps it was meant to show that his evident issues weren't the result of the abuse, but the reason for his 'invention' of the allegations.

'I got my hands on a summary of the mediation later on. I haven't read it in a while. In it, there's a definite sense that my parents were being intimidated.'

His mum and dad are devastated. The meeting is nothing like what they had imagined. The church, the people they'd spent years – more than a decade – intertwined with, sharing their lives with, had betrayed them. Had betrayed their child. For what? In a bid to make it all go away? To avoid a messy situation, embarrassment, some kind of scandal?

Jason stops going to church. His parents still go, but not quite as often, and they pull back from their broader involvement in the community. They don't donate money anymore. They stop helping with fundraisers and social events.

For Jason, things deteriorate in the years that follow. He loses motivation to do much of anything. He has a few friends but feels like a drifter. He switches off academically and coasts through to his last year of school. He does all right in his final exams, but he knows his results are well below his potential. The realisation that he's performing below his capabilities is depressing.

Jason enrols in university. It never quite sits right, though. He feels directionless, like the path he's on is all wrong. Unlike when he was a kid, when the future felt bright and the world was his to explore, there are few reasons to look forward with optimism.

He changes courses, then changes again. He flunks out. He gets a part-time job, but he doesn't really like it and cuts his hours back, further and further, until he's not really working that much at all.

'I'm around twenty and I find myself getting into things that could sort of swallow me up. I'm playing poker and other card games. I know even during it that there's potential for this to be a slippery slope that I could pretty easily fall down.'

He makes a few friends playing cards, but the relationships never really progress beyond casual acquaintances. He struggles to relate to others, especially men. There's a kind of disconnect that can't be bridged. Most of the time, Jason feels alone.

'I started really drinking when I was about twenty. It was never really destructive – it was more of an enabler to socialise, to meet girls and have fun, and feel really good,' he remembers.

When he's got a few drinks under his belt, he begins to feel things that had been missing for a long time: a sense of relaxation, the tightly wound knot inside of him easing a little. His social inhibitions fall away. He can talk to strangers at parties. There's hope now of some deeper connections.

He meets a girl and falls in love. Suddenly, there's something in Jason's life with high stakes attached. He's got to make a fairly concerted effort not to stuff this up – not to 'phone in' his interactions with her and risk things fizzling out as a result.

He stops drinking. He throws himself into work. He dutifully takes on the role of stepfather to his partner's daughter from a previous relationship. He gets married. He fathers a son.

'The friends I made in my drinking days all disappeared pretty quickly,' he recounts.

He's alone again.

Not long after the birth of his son, when Jason is twenty-nine, his marriage falls apart and he and his wife separate, eventually divorcing.

In hindsight, with a better understanding now of his difficulty navigating intimate relationships, he's not overly surprised by the breakdown of the relationship. He wonders if it was destined to happen. But at the time, it was a crushing blow that coincided with the death of his father. And if that upheaval wasn't hard enough to cope with, Jason finds those letters he had written when he was a teenager about the abuse he'd endured.

'I'd suppressed so much of that, a lot of what had happened to me both during the abuse and afterwards. The stuff about the mediation the church organised, the betrayal of the church and my school, the coercion that was used, the threats … I had forced myself to forget so much of it.'

It all comes flooding back as though Jason is ten years old again and the abuse is happening for the first time. It's as clear as day. Flashes of memories fill his head, jolting him like little electric shocks.

'I have this niggle in my head, like, why did I let it happen? How did all of this come about? Why am I here? It all sort of crystallised in my mind and I started to realise why I was the way I was.'

His tendency to be self-reflective kicks in and Jason makes a lot of personal discoveries about his deep-seated anxiety, and how it has permeated itself through his personality and behaviours. The drinking. Distancing himself from new people. Difficulties being social. Troubles in his intimate relationships.

'I have a pretty good friend through work and I socialise occasionally with other people from there. Outside of that, that's pretty much it for me at the moment.

'I was really good mates with my brother-in-law, but because of my divorce, that's tapered off. It's awkward, you know. And he's busy. So, it's just me a lot. It's definitely something I struggle with, where I have to fight to have multiple relationships at that sort of level. I don't know, it's just draining. But I never felt like that when I was younger. It wasn't hard when I was a kid, so I feel like it's a function of what happened to me.'

More and more pieces fall into place and Jason confronts some of the more potentially damaging aspects of his personality and behaviour. 'I realised I drank because I felt good when I did, and because otherwise it was hard to feel good about much of anything. I realised how much I hate being touched by pretty much anyone. All sorts of things. It made sense after reading those notes from younger me. I had spent such a long time living in the dark.'

These days, Jason works in retail management. It's a job he describes as 'decent', but he's not sure how far it will take him in life. Is there more out there that he could be doing? There doesn't yet feel like much of an urgency to find out.

The benefits of his job are that it requires a lot of backroom management. Working with numbers. Being organised and making plans. Considering the logistics of the operation. That's the kind of thing he's good at and he mostly enjoys it. 'I'm not super good with people and there's not much of that involved, so that's another positive.'

His children are growing up quickly. His stepdaughter is now eleven and his son is five. They're good kids. The intense, extraordinary love he feels for them, not just when they're around but whenever his thoughts drift to them, is something that still takes him by surprise sometimes. 'That kind of love isn't something I've ever felt anywhere else. I think once upon a time I would've been sceptical about whether I could ever feel this kind of love for someone. For anyone really.'

When we start talking, it's mid-2021 and the Covid pandemic has finally made its way to regional New South Wales, where Jason still lives. There are widespread lockdowns as panicked authorities try to contain multiple outbreaks, fearing the devastating impact a spike in hospitalisations would have on the healthcare systems in small towns.

'We're doing the whole home-schooling thing, so that's been fun.' He laughs. 'It's good to spend time with the kids, but it's unusual. I'm not sure how I'm doing as a teacher and I don't really know if they understand why they're stuck inside.

'I think my daughter gets it. She can still talk with her friends. It's pretty hard for my son. He's in kindergarten and misses playing with his friends. It's not like he's at the age where he can be on the computer talking to people. So, it's more challenging.'

The isolation, being forced to stay in, has been quite good

for Jason. He's reconnected with old hobbies that had faded away over the years.

He loves films, so he's been watching old favourites and discovering new ones. He likes photography and has been mucking about with his late father's camera in the backyard, playing with different lighting and shadow techniques.

And he's relished the time with his kids. His ex-wife lives close by, and despite their personal grievances with each other, they co-parent pretty well. So he gets to see his stepdaughter and son a lot.

Each time we speak, Jason is upbeat, but it's clear he's lonely. When the kids are with their mum and it's just him inside the house, he comes home after a long day at work to be greeted by nothing but the sound of the television filling that large space. On those days, a heavy sadness settles in.

He's young. He's a nice guy with a lot to give. There's still a lot of life ahead of him. Maybe one day he'll meet someone with whom he can share a life – with whom he feels comfortable and safe enough to be himself.

But perhaps, knowing that isn't the end point for so many survivors, there's a part of him that fears he'll wind up alone when it's all said and done. I know I worry about it. I'm terrified that my shame and self-destructive tendencies will see me chase off those I love, one by one, until there's no-one left.

Just me, alone in an empty house, with the sound of a TV to keep me company.

Chapter Nine

I'm not sure any of this was a good idea.

It's been a few years now since I first told Dr Rolenstein about what happened to me when I was a boy. Countless conversations followed in our weekly sessions, and on the whole it was helpful. I began to understand more about why I am the way I am.

But lurching off on a major quest to find healing for myself? With the impact it's having on me, and these growing feelings that I'm something of an abuse imposter, what have I actually achieved?

I've been writing about the worst of humanity and the deepest of human suffering since I was twenty, when I began my journalism career. Every cadet gets pushed straight in the deep end of the murky pool of news, where you spend long days listening to a police scanner and chasing the 'action'. You see death and destruction. You sit in court and hear about the most evil kind of people you'd ever dread to encounter. You knock on the front doors of people who've been torn to shreds by tragedy.

There are stories that really stick with me. One or two occasionally keep me up at night years after the fact. There are a couple of particularly traumatic images that flash into the back of my eyelids from time to time. But for the most part, I've learnt to have a thick skin and brush off those confronting experiences.

This is different. I can't quite put my finger on why.

Maybe relating my experiences back to those of the men I've met so far is what's cutting. I hear these horrifying accounts of little boys being abused in the worst ways imaginable and see little flecks of familiarity. When they describe their struggles and their inner-turmoil, a lot of it rings true to what I've felt – and feel. I'm putting myself in their shoes and finding they mostly fit my feet.

In a way, I'm also grieving for them. I find myself on the verge of tears when I think about these men. When I really think about the terror they each felt in those moments and the torment that haunted them long after they were free of their perpetrators, I grieve for the innocent and carefree childhoods they were robbed of.

But perhaps a big part of the struggle I'm feeling now is that I'm grieving for me too. I'm realising how far off course Joshua threw me just as I was emerging into the world.

I wonder what I might've been like if I had been born in a different town, or he'd lived a few streets further away. Might I be more resilient and stronger? Might I be less anxious and sad for no reason? Might I be truly happy?

My husband is a clinical psychologist. He has a special insight into what I'm experiencing on this journey, as well as my own insecurities and faults, that almost any other partner simply wouldn't have.

I wonder if it's more of a blessing or a curse.

We're sitting on the couch, our dog Bard quietly snoring at our feet. It's just past dusk and the house is quiet. I can hear my heart beating rapidly in my chest as I prepare to tear down my internal wall and let him peek inside.

I love Rob. He's my favourite person in the world. My best friend and my biggest supporter. At times in the past when either of us has faced some kind of adversity – a challenge that's shaken our foundations in some way – we'll turn to each other and say: 'It's me and you – we're a team.'

And so, we are. He's been there for me through many ups and downs. I've had many more downs than he has, and yet he never complains or seems to grow tired of being in my corner. But this … this is something altogether different.

I can't look him in the eye. I feel that shame monster inside of me waking from its brief slumber when I try to meet his gaze. Will he think of me differently? Will he be thrown by the things I have to say?

'It's normal for people to worry that their partner is going to think they're crazy or there's something fundamentally broken about them,' he tells me gently.

'The reality is that the partner knows. Obviously, I'm looking at things through the lens of being a psychologist, but if I wasn't and you told me you'd been abused as a child, I think it would all make sense.'

He talks about being on the other side of my tendency to lash out when I feel threatened. And not legitimate threats, but things that for some reason strike me as being scary or overwhelming or infuriating.

'When someone's threat system has been violated by these kinds of experiences, that's very formative,' Rob continues. 'The result is that you're always on the lookout for threats. You see them in things that aren't threatening.

'Sometimes, it feels like you're looking for me to have said or done something to insult or invalidate you.'

It's true. There are days where I feel so tightly wound, so on edge that any tiny straw can break the proverbial camel's back. I'm aware of it. I don't know if I've made much progress in changing my bad habits. Hearing the tinge of sadness in Rob's voice now as he talks about copping those breakdowns … I want to change. I have to change.

He's had patients like me – men who experienced unspeakable things as boys, whose worlds have been upended in adulthood as a result.

'Do you think what happened to me is abuse?' I ask.

'Of course,' he replies instantly.

I tell him about my own doubts. Joshua was only a few years older than me. It was never violent. Wasn't I complicit in it all in some way? We were both kids.

'It's not to do with the perpetrator,' Rob tells me. 'It's about the recipient. The perpetrator's motivation or other factors don't matter unless it's in a forensic sense – to do with the law. It's about how it impacted you. It's about how you felt. And this felt like abuse.'

I tell him about Luke. I talk about the things that happened to him when he was a boy, and how much worse it was compared to what I experienced.

I recount his feelings of guilt and shame. His bruises from battle. The times he's come horribly close to not existing anymore – and the tempting lure of escape that still crops up when things are especially tough.

'I totally get it,' I whisper to Rob as he clutches my hand. 'I get all of it.'

And it's true. I feel like Luke and I are so similar. In fact, I see so much of myself in these men I've met.

I see our shared brokenness that we have masked for years – sometimes convincingly, other times clearly visible through the cracking facades. The glassy eyes when talking about the pain that swirls around inside. The tenseness of shoulders when dragging ourselves back to those dark places to relive the trauma. The angry pursed lips when hearing someone else's account of torment.

I find myself nodding in agreement when they talk about how different they felt to other boys growing up. About how this sickening secret inside of them made them feel like outsiders. It was a secret they had to fight desperately to keep, for fear of being discarded and shunned should it ever see the light of day.

But I also see a determination to make some kind of sense of it all. There must be a way off this path we're stumbling down. There must be another fate for us. Surely who we are isn't set in stone.

Despite all of this, I still can't help but feel a little like my experiences pale in comparison to those I've heard about so far. Should I feel the same as these other men? Do I have the right?

'It's not a competition,' Rob tells me.

'There will always be someone worse off than you. Isn't that true of everything, though? Your experience is your experience, and how you feel is legitimate. You're not in a contest.'

Chapter Ten

Will lives in a rambling old weatherboard house, mostly held together by peeling paint, that sits on top of one of the tallest hills in Sydney's inner west.

From here, he can see almost all of the city: the sparkling skyline of the CBD, which seems to get taller and denser each day, and right now is dotted with dozens of cranes; out across the eastern suburbs and, on a particularly clear day, to the ocean; down over the Cooks River to the south and the expanses of Federation-era homes, Victorian-style cottages, rows of decaying terrace houses, and post-war brick monstrosities; and way out west, where more and more estates are popping up to take in the rapidly growing population.

He spends a lot of afternoons perched on a branch of the massive jacaranda tree in his front yard, watching the world go by below.

The house has been in the family for three generations now, since it was built. It was once in a micro-suburb so tiny that it no longer exists, having long ago been absorbed by the bigger one next door.

Will lives here with his mum and his grandmother. And each day is pretty much the same. He wakes at the crack of dawn and creeps out of bed and into the kitchen, flicking the kettle on and listening carefully to make sure he switches it back off again just before the whistling begins. He tiptoes around, getting a cup, the sugar canister, a tea bag, and some milk from the fridge.

Then, when the brew is complete, he takes it and heads down the long, wide hallway to the front of the house where his nan's bedroom is. He's wearing thick woollen socks so he can slide, rather than walk and risk the easily creaking floorboards coming to life.

He twists the handle and opens the bedroom door, just enough so he can fit through it.

'Nan,' he whispers. She stirs, rolls onto her side and opens her eyes. She smiles her big, toothy grin and sits up.

'Thank you, my wonderful boy,' she croaks, taking the cup.

Will switches on the small television on the dresser in the corner of the room, and it whirs to life. It's almost twice his age but still delivers a picture most of the time, and gets almost all of the channels. He twists the dial to the one that plays cartoons in the morning, making sure the volume is just loud enough for him to make out the characters' words, and clambers into bed with Nan.

He gently rests his head on her shoulder and watches. Nan sips her tea and rests her head on his.

This is their morning ritual. Just the two of them. They watch cartoons together for half an hour until it's time for Will to shower, pull on a clean but tattered school uniform, make his modest lunch of a single jam sandwich, pack his bag and silently slip out of the house.

He makes the precarious journey down his steep street to the bus stop at the bottom. School isn't too far away. He has a couple of friends, but they're not close. They chat, they sit together at lunch, but that's about it.

Will would never invite anyone to his house. The distance he ensures is maintained, a barrier between the outside world and the one inside his home, stops anyone from becoming a really good mate.

In the afternoon, he climbs back up the hill, his shins aching by the time he's at the front door. He pauses and listens, as he does each day, to see if he can hear Mum. Sometimes she's awake, sitting in the lounge room watching TV, the volume blaring, while other times she's still asleep. It's fifty-fifty really.

Today, she's awake and she's in a rare good mood.

'Will!' she squeals as he pushes his way inside, slipping off his backpack and kicking off his tattered black leather shoes. 'Will's home, Mum!'

'Hello, my wonderful boy!' Nan calls from the kitchen.

Will smiles. It's been a long time since he's had a greeting like this. Mum's been in one of her down patches for much longer than usual. Since December, and it's now April.

She stays up all night, listening to records on the old player in her bedroom, drinking cheap wine from the bottle and crying loudly. Her sobs radiate through the house, piercing the paper-thin walls, long after Will and Nan have gone to sleep.

He checks in on her from time to time when she's like this. He'll peer through the door, open just a crack. Sometimes Mum is curled up on the floor, tightly hugging her knees to her chest. Other times, she's propped up in bed, staring aimlessly out the window.

The down periods last two weeks usually, sometimes a month. This one has been the longest by far. It began on Boxing Day.

Mum grew up in this house with her two older brothers, Paul and Johnny. Her dad died suddenly of a heart attack when the kids were still young, so Nan was left to raise them alone. Paul and Johnny were both creative and musical, and after their father's death, they took dance and singing lessons as a way of helping them cope with their grief.

They excelled. Their dance teacher introduced them to a television executive who cast them in a commercial, where the boys garnered further attention, leading to another TV advertisement, and then another.

Paul auditioned to be a dancer on the Saturday-night music variety show *Bandstand* and landed the role. Each week, he'd travel over the Harbour Bridge to Channel Nine's studio in Willoughby, and for hours he'd dance along to the singers and bands who were starring in that episode.

He became a minor celebrity and the dribs and drabs of money he earned helped keep the family afloat.

The first chance he got, Paul took off overseas. He got jobs in the chorus lines of theatre productions in London, performed in a show in Paris, and worked on a cruise ship for a while in America. Eventually, he returned home to Australia, but he was not alone.

Francesco was an Italian photographer who shot moody street scenes in Rome, which he developed at his friend's camera shop and blew up to sell to tourists at a hefty premium. It was boring work and a waste of his immense talent, but it funded his penchant for expensive clothes and weekends in Paris.

One overcast afternoon in Rome, Paul wandered by the handsome European. He was on a long weekend break from work – a production in London he was starring in – and out to explore the city. He suddenly realised he'd walked straight into the dark-haired stranger's shot, and held up his hand in apology.

'Pose for me,' Franco, as he insisted everyone call him, yelled. A blushing Paul obliged, leaning against a lamp-post and looking off into the distance. It began to rain heavily and within seconds, they were both drenched. They ran together, Franco dragging Paul by the cuff of his shirt, to underneath the awning of a nearby cafe. The Italian smiled. Paul blushed again.

'Love at first sight,' Paul would declare whenever he was retelling that story for decades to come.

Nan had known Paul was gay from the moment he could start walking. She did not fully understand it, but she accepted him unconditionally. Whenever he and Franco decided to visit Australia, she was thrilled and insisted they stay in the house when they were in Sydney.

And so they did – and continued to do right up until Will was born, meaning his two uncles have been frequent fixtures in his life for as long as he can remember. Paul is his surrogate father, given he never really had one. Will's dad died after he was born, his mum told him, but he knows nothing else about him.

Paul is warm and kind and deeply attentive. Franco is the fun one who always has a chocolate in his pocket and is ready at a moment's notice to pluck the youngster from the confines of his ordinary life to take him on an adventure.

During one trip back to Australia, Paul met up with some old friends from *Bandstand*, one of whom was producing a new comedy variety show. He invited Paul to help him make it.

'What do I know about making television?' Paul gasped.

‘I don’t know. What do I know?’ his friend laughed in reply.

And so, Paul and Franco called it quits on Europe and settled in Melbourne. Paul’s small-screen career was born. He worked on a string of big hits, climbing further and further up the ladder of Australia’s entertainment industry. Eventually, he made his own program – a music-themed show – and it was a ratings hit. He went to work for a major producer, devising new concepts and bringing them to life.

Franco was always by his side as his faithful ‘assistant’, although he didn’t tend to do much more than chain-smoke and ogle the handsome young men on set.

Their relationship was close but extremely fiery, with both men drinking heavily and fighting often, usually over trivial things. They always reconciled and were drawn closer to each other in the glow of forgiveness. Will grew up basking in their love for each other.

It’s the lead-up to Christmas, and Paul and Franco are coming to town. Mum is thrilled – she loves it when her brother and brother-in-law come, bringing with them a cyclonic force of energy, and a suitcase full of expensive presents and high-quality wine. She adores them.

Will also loves their visits – not just because his uncles are fun and let him tag along to whatever set they’re working on or to their television industry parties, but because of their ability to instantly lift Mum out of a funk.

Now, on reflection, Will can't remember much of Christmas Day itself. That memory has been swamped and totally consumed by the events of the next afternoon.

It's Boxing Day and the morning begins slowly, with Mum, Paul and Franco having stayed up drinking until the early hours. They sleep until noon, wake with horrid hangovers, and start boozing again with Bloody Marys.

'Hair of the dog!' Paul screeches as the trio clink their glasses.

By the late afternoon, Will is playing outside, sheltering from the scorching heat in the shade underneath the house. There's nothing else down here but an old laundry tub and a wheelbarrow filled with pieces of junk. He's tinkering in the dirt with the action figures Paul and Franco bought him as a Christmas gift.

'Willy!' Franco calls as he stumbles down the rickety stairs. 'This is where you've been hiding.'

His words are slurred. Will looks up and sees *that* look in his eyes. He sighs and stands. Franco pulls him close, wrapping him in a tight hug.

'I've missed you,' he whispers.

Will knows what is coming next. And he loathes it. He's loathed it from the moment it first happened. As Franco pushes the boy onto his knees, he's filled with dread. Neither of them hear Mum coming down the stairs a few minutes later. They hear her shriek, though.

She's just seen them doing the things that started several months earlier when Will was in Melbourne on a trip to see his uncles. It's school holidays and Paul paid for a plane ticket so his beloved nephew can escape the mundanity of the house. It ends with the young boy being wracked with guilt, despair and shame that dulls over the coming months but never entirely goes away.

Franco gasps, pulls up his pants, and pushes a kneeling Will away. He falls backwards with a thud onto the hard dirt. Franco rushes after Mum.

Will is left alone, distraught and filled with shame. He's terrified to go upstairs, where he can hear the murmurs of adult voices. They're raised, but only slightly. Eventually he hears a pair of heavy footsteps heading down the hallway, the opening and closing of car doors, and the roar of a car engine.

It's pitch black when he crawls out and slinks inside. The house is completely silent. He makes his way to the front of the house. Mum's door is closed and he can hear her heavy snores. Nan is in her room, sitting in bed and reading a book.

'There's my wonderful boy,' she smiles. 'Where have you been?'

She doesn't know. Relief washes over Will.

His uncles are gone. Mum stays in her room for two days and when she emerges, she glances at her son briefly, nods, and doesn't say a word. She never says a word about what she saw. She doesn't do anything. She carries on like it never happened.

The only hint of the shock and horror is her deep depression. The deepest by far. She's stuck in the depths of her despair for months, past the New Year, past the start of Will's schooling, and well into April, until the phone rings one day and Paul announces he and Franco are coming to visit.

She's out. She's out of the funk. The boys and their infectious energy are coming and she couldn't be happier, clearly having forgotten Boxing Day.

Will's happiness is tinged by guilt. He's torn between his love for his uncles, especially for Paul, and his excitement at the presents and adventures their trip will bring. But he knows that inevitably Franco will want to do those things to him again – those horrible, shameful things that often keep him up at night.

I start talking to Will after we exchange a few messages on a forum on Reddit after I share a post about how childhood trauma haunts you into adulthood.

'It feels like I can't escape it,' I write. 'It has warped my relationships and how I view sex. It has made me feel like I'm a freak. I feel angry for no reason ... or sad or scared. Just when I think I've got a handle on it and that the therapy is working, it sneaks up on me out of nowhere and sucks me back in.'

Will tells me he can relate. I'm struck immediately by his gregarious and open nature. Initially, I tiptoe around our shared elephant in the room. That's what you do with one as big, scary and unpredictable as this. But he's not fazed at all.

He's almost matter-of-fact about what happened to him, as though it happened to someone else and he's a subject-matter expert. He's a philosophy scholar and knows more about Kant than anyone else.

Will relays the most horrific and gruelling stories about his childhood with the same upbeat tempo as he might the plot to a *Batman* film. His temperament never changes the whole time we speak – several times over the course of months. Will is Will – what you see is what you get.

It wasn't always this way. Will used to get very mad, very suddenly. Oftentimes there were warning signs about the rage that was about to be unleashed, only he didn't know how to spot them.

And so, to him, he was merely this person who was prone to snapping at absolutely nothing, at the drop of a hat, engulfing any good times or good people around him.

The triggers are hard to spot and to intercept, but Will isn't clueless about the sources of his pain and anger. He's self-aware enough to recognise them well. As he puts it, they're demons he got to know a long time ago. He's named them and catalogued them.

There's Franco, the instigator of so much of his hurt. The

demon for whom he reserves the most raw hatred. There is no doubt about Will's feelings for the man who broke him at such a young age.

He was seven the first time Franco abused him, during that school holiday trip to Melbourne. Will camped on a pull-out sofa in their hotel room – a big, grand hotel in the middle of the city that felt a million miles away from his falling-down house.

Back then, before the horror started, Will adored Franco. He had been a fixture in his life since he returned from overseas with his uncle – this loud and larger than life European man who oozed glamour and sophistication. He was like a friendly alien.

And for a kid with few people in his life who loved him, he was like a king.

'He was such a major part of my life and I kind of admired him,' he recalls, his voice now tinged with bitterness.

Every time we talk about Franco, the jovial edge in Will's voice fades . 'I loved my uncle and spending time with him, but he slept all day, hungover, whereas Franco was up early with me, hanging out and playing, taking me to the movies or shopping.

'He was a fun escape from life. No one really paid attention to me or did much with me, but he did.'

The first time he was abused, Will essentially disassociated. He remembers lying back on the bed in the master suite of the hotel room and watching himself in the mirror. Franco was doing something to him that felt so wrong and so shameful. But he did it with his typically reassuring and encouraging manner.

Will can't remember much of it. He was in shock. It was like his soul left his body that afternoon and took itself somewhere else, for his own protection. But it was a one-time salvation and the instances of abuse that followed are scarred into his psyche.

'He groomed me after that first time. I think he knew that I was quite affected by it and that he'd have to work hard to have it continue without me making a fuss.

'He was coaxing and manipulative in the beginning, almost playful in some ways, but it got progressively worse and worse, and by the end it was quite violent and aggressive. He pushed the boundaries a lot.

'He would almost barter. He would buy me a video game or take me to the movies and then say, it's yours if you do this. Or if I needed clothes, he would get them for me but on the condition that I do what he wanted. It was like a transaction.

'He showered me with attention and affection and gifts, but there was a price. There was always a price.'

To Franco, this was a secretive arrangement, but he didn't seem to see anything wrong with it. He never apologised. He never seemed to feel bad about what he was doing to Will. The more it went on, the more he treated the youngster like an adult – sickeningly, almost like a romantic partner.

In the darkness of a movie theatre, he would grab Will's

hand and hold it tenderly. When he could, he would steal a kiss and caress his cheek.

'He would say all the time, "Come on, Will. You'll love it. It feels good. You'll like it."

'I can hear it in my head now. His accent, his inflection. It haunts me. Now, if someone says to me, "You'll like it," I could almost vomit.

'But he was very clear that it had to be a secret. If I ever told anyone, he'd punish me. If anyone ever found out, it would be bad for both of us. Not just him, but for me too. And so I stayed quiet.'

The abuse occurred almost every single time that Will was alone with Franco. When his uncle would fly him to Melbourne for a visit and was at work or sleeping, it would happen. If the men were in Sydney to see his mum and nan, Franco would make his move the moment they were alone.

'It got to the point where people would be in the other room and he would do it. It was brazen.'

The older Will got, the more Franco would treat him like someone well beyond his years. It was sinister, he recalls now. It was as though his entry into adolescence normalised the abuse even more for Franco, and he became even more daring with the things he would do to him.

When he was thirteen, he was in Melbourne during the school holidays on one of his frequent visits. His uncle was away on a shoot, and so he left Will alone with Franco.

'He ran out of cigarettes and took me with him to get some more. We got the tram up to Chapel Street. There's a big park there and he dragged me in. It was night time. We sat down on a bench outside a public toilet. This younger guy came out and approached us.

'I obviously didn't know it then, but the toilet block was a gay beat where men would meet for sex. It was pre-Grindr and pre-Tinder, so that was just how things were done, I guess. I'm a kid and I've been taken to this place in the middle of the night. It was nearing midnight.

'Franco had dragged me here to find someone to have sex with me. This young guy was in front of me and Franco was urging me to go into the toilet with him. I remember him saying, "You like it with me, so you must be gay. Go with him."'

Will flung himself off the park bench and ran. He kept running, through the park and out the gate, onto the street that was bustling with revellers and late-night diners finishing their meals. He kept running, dodging cars and trams, and only stopped when he was completely out of breath.

He barely knew Melbourne. He was especially unfamiliar with the city in the dark. He had no idea where he was or how to get back to the hotel.

Eventually, after hours, he recognised enough landmarks and familiar streetscapes to be able to make his way back. He was exhausted and his little legs were numb.

'I walked in and he was sitting there on the couch, drinking and smoking a cigarette. He looked up and said hello. That was it. He showed no remorse at all.'

Will also harbours plenty of anger for his mum, with whom he still shares a fraught relationship. They hold each other at arm's length, or perhaps even further apart. They share few words about what happened to him but there's an unspoken acknowledgment of the horror, and of what she knew about it then.

He flip-flops on how he feels about her. On the one hand, she was deeply broken herself and had been sucked into a hollow void long before he could walk or talk. Nothing had ever gone very right in her life and the more the wrongs piled up, the less she could cope with the burden.

So, she drank. She withdrew into herself and numbed her turmoil with cheap wine by the bottle. Over the years, her self-medicating destroyed not just her ability to cope with fairly basic responsibilities as a parent, like cooking and cleaning, holding down a job, and keeping a secure roof over Will's head, but more importantly the things he really needed most. Love. Empathy. Presence.

Mum never took him anywhere. Hell, she barely left her room let alone the house, but with no car and little desire to play a part in life, there were no normal outings that mother and son would ordinarily enjoy.

'She never took me to the movies. We never went to the park. We didn't go on family holidays. She didn't even take me to the dentist – I had never gone to a dentist until I was sixteen and chipped a tooth and took myself.'

Nan filled the gaping holes in Will's care left by his mother. She was, as he puts it now, 'a peaceful and stabilising presence in the middle of utter chaos'. For most of the time, it was like the two of them existed in a parallel universe – an alternate timeline to the one his mother was hopelessly stumbling through.

But Nan was protective of Will. Extremely protective. She was terrified of him coming upon some kind of evil outside the four walls of their ramshackle home. She hated the idea of him going out, unless it was to school. The worry was constant and suffocating, and Will began to absorb elements of it that warped his own view of the world and his place in it.

Hanging out at a mate's house was fraught. Merely asking Nan if he could go was enough to bring her to panicked tears. School camps were no-go zones. Going into the city after school to hang out at the shops with friends or go to the movies or the arcade were notions that she considered too dangerous, and so she'd entreat him not to go. If he was especially pleading, she'd become harsh and flat-out forbid him from leaving the house.

'I don't really know why she was like that,' he says. 'I didn't understand it then and I don't now. I'm not sure if there was something that happened in her earlier life that made her like that, and whether she was projecting her own personal fears about life onto me. It's a mystery.'

Maybe she recognised a vulnerability in Will that Franco had seen and exploited. A yearning to be loved and to be nurtured, especially by a male role model. A desperation to be seen for who he was, for all of the good and for the overflowing potential and hope that bubbled away inside of him. All things his mum couldn't or wouldn't see.

Perhaps Nan sensed something going on with Franco. Maybe she didn't fully understand what it was, but saw a blurring of the lines and feared that if there was a danger inside the home, the dangers outside it were bound to seduce and swallow up her beloved Will.

'Across the road was another young family. They had two kids who were around my age. I'd sometimes be allowed to go to their house to hang out with them and play in the front yard, because Nan could see me from the window.'

Apart from that, for much of his childhood, it was just the two of them, chatting endlessly about everything and nothing at all.

Nan died when Will was fourteen, and life for him and his mum imploded.

'Mum lost her best friend a few months before, then when Nan died, she had a nervous breakdown. She couldn't work anymore, so we had no money coming in apart from the disability pension.

'Each night became a recurring pattern of her getting very drunk and either getting mad or becoming hysterical. She would have panic attacks. She'd curl up into a ball and cry or scream.'

Sometimes, Will can still hear those screams. Long, guttural howls that bounced off the thin walls and the hardwood floors, echoing throughout the house, like an animal in pain.

The crying would exhaust her and then, when she was completely spent of energy, she would scream in agony.

'At the start, the neighbours would come over and help by trying to calm her down, but it became so frequent that eventually it was just me taking care of her most nights, from age fourteen onwards.'

There was little appreciation for the heavy burden Will was carrying. Quite the opposite sometimes, he recalls now. It was as though she was bitter about how weakened she was and how strong he was being in the face of it; so bitter that she'd lash out.

When backed against the wall, she would spit venom at him. She still does it now from time to time, especially whenever Will tries to bring up Franco and what she knew, and why she didn't do more to protect him.

But it was especially bad then, when her demons were in full control of her strings and pulled them mercilessly.

'On one of these drunken nights she spoke about my father for the first and only time. Basically, she didn't really know him well or have a relationship with him, but slept with him so she could have a child.

'He found out she was pregnant but she insisted it wasn't his. And so, he disappeared.'

He wasn't dead, as he'd been led to believe. Instead, Mum had deliberately kept Will from him or any knowledge of how he came to be an equal contributor to his creation. The poor bastard didn't know Will was his.

In that moment, in the midst of crushing grief from the death of Nan and beneath the heavy weight of his desperate loneliness, coupled with sheer exhaustion from babysitting his drunken mother, Will was totally spent. He felt utterly devastated.

'She had one photo of him, just a snapshot of him holding a beer. Very casual. A moment of time captured when he wouldn't have possibly imagined fifteen years later some kid would be looking at it thinking, oh, that's my dad.'

He still has the photo somewhere. He hasn't looked at it in years. Will worries that if he does, if he stares at it for too long and lets himself ponder what might've been, he'll explode.

Thinking about it now makes him angry. A frothing, violent rage threatens to overtake him if he lets himself sit with the feelings about his mother's unspeakable decision to deceive him for all those years.

Now, all this time later, and being a father himself, Will spends a great deal of energy not thinking about the mystery man in his life. He can't. It's too horrible to consider.

'I agonise over whether I should meet him or not. The ultimate decision is that I'd go and ruin this guy's life. Right? That's the reality of it. What do I do to him by bursting through the door and being like, "Hi Dad"?

'What if he wants nothing to do with me? There's no scenario in my head where that goes well. For me or for him.'

He feels angry now talking to me about this painful part of his upbringing. How could she do that to him? How could she see the things he was lacking and desperately wanted and deprive him of the person who might be able to give them? Even if his father wasn't willing or able to be part of his life, that was a journey Will should've been able to decide to take, if he wanted. It was a choice his dad should've been offered an opportunity to make. Both were robbed of it.

There's also plenty of anger for his uncle, Paul, but these emotions are perhaps the most complex of all the feelings he has.

He was an enormous figure who had stepped in, when he could and to the best of his ability, to play the role of father figure in Will's life. When he was in Sydney, Paul would buy his nephew gifts. Elaborate and expensive toys, but more than that, the essentials he needed that Mum neglected to get him. Clothes to replace the worn and tattered ones he had made do with for too long. New shoes, when Paul noticed the current ones were crumbling and filled with holes that Will's socks would poke out of. His arrival would also herald the sudden stocking of a fridge full of food and a pantry full of staples.

He was caring and loving, but caught in the ramifications of his battle with alcoholism. And so, while he was present, it was only in the afternoon when he would wake from a nasty hangover, and until the late evening when he would be drunk again.

Paul scooped up Will and brought him into his glitzy and fabulous world of entertainment. There were tales of socialising with the rich and the famous, and even royalty – of dancing with Princess Diana at some gala fundraiser on one of her trips to Australia.

'Paul took me to a movie premiere one night and I remember just being in awe of all the famous people I recognised coming up to talk to him. Everyone in the room knew him and loved him. Lots of air kisses and toasts. We shared a cab with Geoffrey Rush afterwards and he told me about the plot of *Pirates of the Caribbean III* before it was released.

'I met Sir Ian McKellen at another premiere and I pestered him at the after party talking about *Lord of the Rings* and Shakespeare.

'I grew up living vicariously through Paul and his very glamorous life and incredible escapades.'

Paul's growing success in the entertainment industry allowed Will to flitter around the edges of a world he would've otherwise only been able to dream of taking a peek at. It was an escape from the loneliness of his own existence – from its choking banality.

'It was such a juxtaposition to have this kind of poor and chaotic homelife, going to school in shoes that were held together with Band-Aids, that kind of thing, but then go to the premiere of some glitzy show. I got to live this whole other life periodically.'

Paul's love and affection let Will live an almost Cinderella life. He would swoop in and whisk the boy away from the pain he knew and plop him down into a world that seemed perfect. It was fun and exciting.

'I'd go into this insane and enthralling existence, but then at midnight, the clock struck and the carriage turned back into a pumpkin, or a taxi home to our house on top of the hill.'

After high school, while studying broadcast production at college, Will was tasked with creating a three-minute segment with an interview subject who could speak about the year 1975. Someone with insight into a different era who could give context to a year the students knew almost nothing about.

'I asked Paul, "What do you remember about 1975?" He laughed and jokingly said, "Absolutely nothing," and then spoke for almost two hours. It was incredible. I couldn't cut it down to anything less than twenty minutes and insisted my teacher accept it, even though it didn't fit the assignment criteria, because it was so fascinating.'

When Paul died, the final cut of that interview was played at his funeral. They were almost the last words he had spoken about an extraordinary life.

Paul died penniless, a tragic end for a man who achieved so much acclaim in difficult circumstances – coming from a problem-plagued family with a difficult upbringing, and being an openly gay man at a time when it was dangerous to be one, even in entertainment.

But he lived a life of relentless excess, blowing his money on booze, drugs and gambling, and bizarre whims that he perhaps hoped would satisfy a worsening void inside him.

'He'd fly to Paris or Singapore spontaneously and come back with a new wardrobe and expensive colognes and bottles of champagne. He never owned property and instead paid a fortune on rent for these fantastic apartments, or on living in five-star hotels.'

He was an entirely live-in-the-moment person, and it became a real problem for him in his final years. Paul would turn up at work still drunk from the night before. He was erratic and unpredictable. His focus shifted from the job he was born to do, which had made him a star in the industry. His perfection slipped.

'People lost patience with him. If he hadn't died soon after, I think he would've been fired for sure.'

When Will was fifteen, he went to Melbourne during the school holidays to visit his uncle as he normally would. But Paul and Franco were on a break. Something serious had happened and it didn't seem like there would be a resolution.

Will was grateful to not have to be around Franco and to be subjected to the inevitable abuse that their time alone would lead to.

He bunkered down with Paul at the Westin in the city. It was a sleek and modern place where the guests were well-dressed and the staff almost floated around the grand lobby, ready to attend to any need or want.

The pair went out for dinner and Paul got tanked. He talked and talked and talked, jumping from one outrageous tale to another, so much so that Will could barely keep up. His uncle wasn't like how he normally was – drunk, but happy drunk. He was heavy with dread.

'We wound up in the bar in the lobby of the hotel. It was a quarter to two in the morning and I was sitting next to him having a Coke while he drank God knows what. It's kind of amazing that no one queried why a child was in a bar so late at night.'

The entertaining stories stopped and Paul sat quietly, staring straight ahead. After a long while, he took a deep breath and dropped a bomb.

'He looked at me with these empty eyes and said, "I know". That's it. I don't know what I thought at the time. Maybe I didn't let myself think much of anything about it. Or I didn't realise the significance. I can't remember. But a few years after he died, I remember thinking back to that moment and it dawning on me. Like, fuck, he *knew*.'

That's probably why he and Franco were on a break, he suspects now. His uncle somehow found out what was going on and walked out.

Franco had a digital camera, which was the height of technology in those days. He would often take photos of Will while he was in various stages of undress, or entirely naked, and once or twice used the video function to record himself abusing the boy. Maybe Paul had seen them. Franco had become increasingly sloppy with hiding his offending.

But with all the love his uncle had for him, and for the obvious anger and concern he felt for the boy after seemingly discovering his partner's abuse of him, it wasn't enough. Paul and Franco reconciled and stayed together until he died.

'They got back together,' Will says now. 'Knowing that in the context of what dawned on me in my twenties, that he knew but went back to Franco anyway, absolutely destroyed me. I tried to kill myself. I felt so betrayed. It was just sickening.

'This person I loved and trusted knew what was being done to me but did nothing about it. And worse, stayed with the person doing it to me. I was not good for a long time. It completely upended my life. I withdrew and started lashing out. I was angry and hurt and disgusted.

'This person I'd looked up to my entire life, who formed so much of who I thought I was, he knew and did nothing. And by doing nothing, he enabled it.'

Will speaks about his uncle with such fondness, but it's a bittersweet recollection of the man who in some ways saved him. His upbringing was miserable and fraught with difficulty, the kinds of which no child should see, but Paul's regular interventions – providing for him, offering an escape, letting him into his fabulous world – softened the blow. They were perhaps enough to drag him off a path that might've put him somewhere much more disastrous than where he ended up instead.

'It's a real struggle,' he tells me. For the first and only time in our lengthy conversations, he pauses, holding back tears.

'I love him and I'm so grateful for all that he did for me, but at the same time I also wish I'd never met him in some ways. I hold him responsible for a lot of what happened to me.'

Franco last abused Will when he was sixteen. Three years later, on the day of Paul's funeral, at a booze-fuelled wake at someone's house, Franco lured him to the laundry and tried to rape him.

'I was old enough then to fight him off. He never tried it again.'

Those are Will's three main demons – his mother, his uncle and Franco. They come to him less frequently than they once did. Sometimes they emerge individually to toy with him on their own, and occasionally all three gang up to really do a number on his mental health.

But there are other demons that don't have recognisable faces or distinguishable features like that trio do. Shame. Guilt. Self-loathing.

Those are less predictable and easy to manage because they're not separate entities who torment him, but rather parts of himself. They're cancers that have infected his body and attached themselves to his vital organs. How do you begin to cut those growths out when their removal could do more harm than good?

'I blamed myself a lot. How could I let myself be in this situation? How could I let it happen? Why didn't I say or do something?

'There's a huge amount of shame. There's shame that it happened. There's a lot of shame about specific things that happened. There's shame about how I sometimes felt in those moments.'

Those dark thoughts are ones he keeps to himself. The full details of them, in any case. He's allowed himself to reveal the full gory extent of that trauma to his doctor, a therapist, and now me. But mostly, he carried them on his own in secret.

He's used to shouldering more than he should. That's what his childhood and adolescence set him up for in some ways – taking on unimaginable difficulties and just carrying on, mostly because there's no other choice.

'You step up or you fold. I've seen what folding looks like. I've seen what it looks like when you give in or give up.'

Carrying on, pushing on against the tidal wave, is motivated by not wanting to fail, because failure – admitting defeat – is something that leads to fates lived by his mother and his uncle.

'I think I'm motivated by not wanting to be like that ... like them,' he says.

The anger has subsided over the years and his handle on it has firmed. For the most part, there's an acceptance of the scars that Franco inflicted – 'maybe 80 per cent of the time,' he says.

But that's during waking hours. When he sleeps, when he has no control over how he regulates the shame and the anger and the regret, all of his demons come out to play.

'The nightmares are bad. They're so vivid and so realistic. I wake up feeling like I was just right there, back when it happened.

'It's kind of every night. I don't always remember them but I wake up knowing I've had one because of how I feel. Sometimes I feel totally destroyed and like I've been hit by a bus.

'Working out what my demons are and giving them names – this trauma or that trauma – it's empowering. You get to understand it and come up with a plan to cope. I can mitigate it.

'Dreams are a different thing. You can't really stop them.

This thing in my head does what it wants and it doesn't care what I think. It's very invasive and inescapable.'

Sometimes in the night, he'll wake up and he's able to just hear the tail-end of the echo of a scream. Sometimes it sounds like his mother's – that haunting sound he knows so well from his teenage years.

The loss of control in his subconscious is frustrating. He feels a different kind of anger about not being able to keep a lid on that anger.

'Ironic, huh?' he laughs.

I feel much of the anger that Will feels. I used to have a pretty good handle on it, but the grip seems to be harder to maintain as I get older.

Sometimes I'll be consumed by a blinding rage over nothing. A rude taxi driver. A well-laid plan not going exactly as I imagined.

Most of the time, I keep it bottled up inside. Except for maybe a furrowed brow or a downturned lip, no one might suspect that my blood is boiling as it courses through my veins. But sometimes, and more and more in these past few years, it ruptures out and makes itself known.

Recently, I yelled at a woman who shoved in front of me at the cinema. She physically shoved me out of the way to get to the ticketing counter first, just as I was about to step forward. When I gestured and shot her a filthy look, she told me to fuck off. I exploded. I made the kind of scene that I once would've been horrified to be part of. But I could barely control myself, a deep red masking my vision.

I've taken it out on those I love, too. They've been collateral damage to my uncontrollable anger. My husband, who I've shouted at and blamed for a bad situation. Mum, who I've snapped at when I'm in a foul mood.

I hate being this person. I'm scared to be this person. I have to get off this destructive course.

Chapter Eleven

One of the common struggling points I've noticed many of these men have relates to the lack of justice they feel. They've been sentenced to a life of hurt and struggle, while most of their perpetrators have been allowed to carry on exactly as they like.

I think that's where a lot of the anger comes from. We've been left on the floor in crumpled heaps. They've run off into the sunset. Fuck that.

Of all the men I've met so far, Luke is the only one who sought to make his abuser accountable for what he did. And even though it didn't turn out how he initially hoped, there was still some kind of healing that came from being able to stand up and tell his story.

And it erased a lot of the rage that had been bubbling away beneath the surface for a long time.

It's a Monday morning and Luke has just arrived at the courthouse in Parramatta. He's an hour early, although he doesn't really know why. Maybe it's just a chance to be by himself, alone with his thoughts, before the circus begins.

He takes the elevator six floors up and emerges into an expanse of natural light that almost takes his breath away. There's a courtroom on either side of him – one to the left, one to the right. In the middle is a breezy foyer.

He sits on an uncomfortable wooden bench and opens a book. He's not really absorbing the words on the page. Instead, his mind wanders.

'Luke?' a familiar voice calls.

He looks up, somewhat startled, to see the face of a childhood friend from the Shire. A lanky lad who became a policeman before taking on a law degree and eventually becoming a barrister. They smile at each other and Luke stands, extending a hand.

'I hadn't seen him for years,' Luke recalls. 'I didn't know he had made the transition from cop to lawyer, so there was this real kind of weird shock, like, what are you doing here?'

'He goes, what are you here for? Kind of chuckling a little, I explained why. I think he maybe knew a little bit of what had happened.'

They chat for a moment before parting ways. His friend is due in the courtroom to the right. Not long after, Luke's supporters arrive. Mum and Dad. His sister-in-law, who'd only recently married his brother but embraced with full force the role of loving surrogate sibling. His aunt. They huddle around him in a strange sort of football scrum, taking turns to pat his shoulder or give a quiet, knowing nod.

The 'bing' of the elevator sounds and they each casually turn their gazes towards it, almost out of instinct. And out *he* walks.

It's been such a long time, but Luke recognises him instantly. He's changed – he's older, his face is lined, his posture is a little more hunched. His once-vibrant mahogany hair has faded to a muted, ashy brown and he's greying fairly significantly at his temples. And yet, he still looks so familiar.

'I feel quite threatened,' Luke recalls. 'The hairs on the back of my neck stand up, I feel the blood rush to my feet, that kind of thing. Mum can see it. Maybe I'm pale or clammy or something. She puts her arms around my shoulder and forces me to walk, even though I can't feel my legs.'

The family moves to the furthest end of the corridor, outside the other courtroom. There's a room there. A kind of holding pen for those associated with the case. They shelter in there so no one has to see his face.

Luke's mum is being called as a witness, so she can't be in the courtroom until it's her turn. She sits outside, occasionally getting up to pace the full length of the corridor, up and down, until her ankles tire. His dad pops out occasionally to check on her, to make sure she's holding up alright.

Inside, the perpetrator's family is on one side, Luke and his supporters are on the other, including a friend – a kind of mentor – from a support group. Proceedings begin.

It's a blur. Luke doesn't remember a great deal of specifics. Little flashes of vivid memory here and there, amidst a sea of blurry echoes. The judge leaning back in his chair, pondering a particular piece of testimony. Someone in the jury having a brief coughing fit. The man's wife peering over her right shoulder and sneering.

The most vivid recollection is of his abuser's testimony. Luke was determined to remember every single detail of it, so he could replay it in his mind later. The creases in his shirt. The little beads of sweat forming at his hairline. The way his eyes darted around the room, desperate to find an object to settle and fixate on, anything, except Luke, who stared with an intensity he'd never felt before.

'The guilt was written all over his face,' he tells me. 'Like, it was just so clear – he's guilty. And he knew he was guilty. I could tell. And I could sense that almost everyone in the room knew it too.'

Eventually, towards the end of the week, it is Luke's turn to speak. He stands, a little shaky on his feet at first, and moves slowly to the front of the room, stepping up into the witness box. The view from here is so different. Being a little elevated, he feels ever so slightly at ease. As though he's now the one in charge.

'I felt quite empowered giving my evidence. I was quite confident. I knew he'd done it, so I wasn't nervous to get up and say it.'

The defence is ruthless. His barrister is good at his job, and almost immediately, he's trying to trip Luke up. He's messing with him, trying to poke holes in his recollection.

He's coaxing him towards inconsistencies and posing really specific questions that are difficult to answer.

'I'm not tied up in knots, necessarily, but it's still hard. Remembering absolutely everything is impossible. Your memory is so pliable and prone to lapses. That's normal, right? I think most people understand that.

'But so many 'not guilty' verdicts, rightly or wrongly, come down to little seeds of doubt that are sown when a victim isn't absolutely emphatic, totally certain about something. But how could you be?'

The defence barrister suggests it wasn't his client who abused Luke, but someone else. Maybe it was the man's older brother? Maybe it was his father? Maybe it was one of Luke's father's colleagues.

'At one point he says, didn't his nice father show you around the aviary in their backyard one day? I was like, well, yeah, but he showed me the birds because I wanted to see the birds. He didn't abuse me.'

The barrister didn't suggest Luke was lying. He knew that would be trial suicide. He was suggesting Luke was confused. The totality of their argument was that, sure, he was probably abused, but it was someone else.

'They were basically saying that it could have been the guy's brother, his dad, maybe my dad's boss, someone else … you know, all these people who had access to me. But definitely not him.'

With each suggestion of an alternative perpetrator, Luke was dealt a blow. A wave of shock. Almost total disbelief that his abuser would be willing – no, comfortable and content – to throw his own brother and father under the bus in order to create just a little bit of doubt in the minds of the jury members.

Doesn't that say it all?

Luke endures the intense examination. He says his piece and he feels good about it. Then, at the end of that Wednesday, it's all over.

On the Thursday morning, the jury is sent out to deliberate on a verdict, and the family retreats back to the furthest end of the corridor to wait. The man and his supporters wait at the other end. It's like the corners of a boxing ring.

By midday on Friday, it's clear the jury is stuck. All but two of them are satisfied he is guilty. They believe Luke. They believe his account of the abuse. They could see the lies and guilt on the defendant's face. But there are two people who aren't convinced. Not convinced at all.

They're sent away again by the judge to think some more and re-examine the evidence. But eventually, they return. There's no convincing two members. And so, it's a hung jury. He's not guilty, but he's also *not* not guilty. The guy is nothing. The prosecution could always try again in the future if they felt there was a reasonable prospect of conviction.

For now, it's all over. The jury is dismissed.

That's it. One full week and it's all done. In the eyes of the law, Luke is some kid who made a mistake. There is no justice.

He's lifted to his feet and whisked outside. There are tears and hugs and looks of disbelief. The courtroom doors swing open and there *he* is. His wife is by his side, absolutely seething, and locks eyes with Luke.

'Go to hell,' she spits at him.

The thing that strikes Luke is that she's not necessarily angry. She just seems to be totally consumed by denial. She's drunk on the desperate belief that the man she married, who she committed to spending her life with, with whom she'd had a child, isn't a monster.

'It's understandable, if you think about it,' Luke says.

'If the reality is that I'm a kid who made a mistake, a terrible mistake, and it wasn't her husband who did these things, maybe it was someone else … there's perhaps some sympathy for me, right? But if she's got to use anger to cover up the faint realisation that she married a peadophile … I think that'd be much more potent.'

Luke's mum touches his elbow gently and suggests they wait in the small room to their right – the little holding pen – until he's gone. But he doesn't want to. Luke wants to stand right here, his feet firmly planted, and get one final look at him.

'So, I stood and stared at him until they got too uncomfortable that they wanted to leave. For me, it was a line in the sand for myself. At that moment, I felt it wasn't my problem anymore. It was now their problem, and I was determined to transfer every last drop of the anger and confusion and shame to them.

'I think that's a big part of why I haven't gone back to the court case to try again. Sure, I think it'd be great if he went to gaol. But the reality is … what is justice? Him going to gaol wouldn't take away what he did to me.

'Maybe the justice for me was him having to get up in front of his loved ones and hear him answer questions about what he'd done to me for so long. I shifted the responsibility to him. Finally, it wasn't all about me.

'I know he's guilty. Almost all of the jury knew he was guilty. I reckon there was suddenly a question about whether he was for at least some of his family members. And that's that.'

A security guard lurches forward, standing in front of the wife, who's still standing there with that look on her face. He blocks her view of Luke and his distraught family. He tells her to back off and she does, slinking into the waiting elevator with her husband.

A few seconds later, they're gone.

For a long while, Luke and his family sit in almost total silence. They're each absorbing what had just happened. They're devastated. His mother's breath is shallow as she tries not to sob. His brother and sister stare out the oversized window onto the street below, lost in their thoughts, occasionally shaking their heads in disbelief.

'Let's go,' Luke sighs.

Downstairs, outside the courthouse in the forecourt, stands a woman from the jury. She was the one tasked with telling the judge that a verdict couldn't be reached. It's the last person Luke expected to see. She steps forward and opens her mouth, expectantly. She's been waiting there for hours.

She and Luke move to a quiet corner of the courtyard alone, beneath the shade of a tree, to talk. She tells him that everyone in the jury except for those two people believed Luke. Completely believed him, well beyond a reasonable doubt. And she was sorry. She was so sorry it hadn't gone like he'd hoped.

With her eyes welling with tears, she says she can't imagine how Luke must be feeling. Crushed, she guesses. Inconsolable, perhaps?

But he doesn't. He figures he probably should, given the days and days of preparation for the trial, the work he'd done with his therapist for what he was going to endure. The time with his family, taking on their angst and dread about the process, trying to reassure and comfort them. The week of his life spent in or just outside that courtroom. And then, nothing.

He feels fine. He feels empowered. He feels like finally, it's over, and even though he didn't get what he thought he wanted, he got what he needed. And that's OK. He's OK.

That is, until he's not. Some five years later, it all comes to a very messy head at a bachelor party.

A mate from work is getting married. He and Luke are friendly. Not super close friends, but he's a work buddy and they hang out outside of the office a bit. So, he scores an invite to his bachelor party.

He doesn't want to go. It's an all-day thing, starting with several hours on a boat on Sydney Harbour, and then kicking on at someone's apartment, maybe a bar and a club.

'Everyone's going to be smashed, there'll probably be drugs, I'm sure there'll be strippers and that sort of thing,' he tells me, groaning just thinking about it now.

'No judgement. I don't mind the idea of drinking on a boat. But I don't like the idea of strippers. I struggle with that kind of macho, toxic, objectifying thing.'

He makes a compromise. He'll skip the boat part and meet up with the guys when they're back on dry land, at whoever's apartment having drinks. That way, he could leave whenever he wanted, rather than being stuck in the middle of a body of water with no escape.

'It was a pretty cool apartment. An architect's apartment. And what do you get when you throw architects into a cool space? Lots of shop talk. We're checking out the space, talking about it, and then we end up in one of the bathrooms, looking at it.'

There are three others crammed inside, taking turns hoovering up lines of coke that are racked up on the marble top of the vanity.

'I'd tried it once years and years before and hated it. It's not for me and I had no desire to do it again, but this guy is like, "here, one for you".'

Luke shakes his head and holds up his hand. He's good, he tells them. But they should go for gold. Have a good time. He'll stick with beer.

But they're insistent. *Go on!* He should have one. They're shouting after all. So, he does. Only, he doesn't know why. He can't understand why his will is bent so easily with so little pressure applied.

'And then I had a complete breakdown,' he recalls.

He's texting with another mate and it's clear to him that Luke is not OK at all. His words are erratic. He's emotional and obviously in a bad place. The mate is coming to pick him up, he says. Mid-meltdown, his heart rate climbing thanks to the drugs, his vision beginning to get shaky, he can still agree that it's a good idea.

'I got in his car and I just fell apart. I think I realised that there was this chink in my armour that had been hidden, but which was a major defensive flaw. Like, I was somehow just peer-pressured into doing drugs, but as a thirty-two-year-old man.

'I wasn't a kid. I was an adult who'd been looking after himself and living as an adult for ages now. I wasn't a drug-taker. I didn't want to do drugs. But they didn't even have to push hard and I folded.

'They weren't being mean. If I'd said no again, they would have been like, yeah, alright, whatever. And it would have been fine. It would've been so fine.

'But in an instant, I gave up my agency as a person. I did something I didn't want to do, which I knew wouldn't be good for me. I ran full force into the brick wall, knowing it would hurt, with almost no encouragement to do so.'

For days, Luke sits with those thoughts. Locked away in his darkened bedroom, he relives those few minutes in the bathroom. He plays them out again and again, saying no, then saying yes when asked a second time, then regretting it and hating himself.

And he notices a pattern. He realises that this kind of succumbing, giving big chunks of himself away for free – then paying the price – isn't new. It is a trait that runs very, very deep.

'So much agency had been stolen from me as a kid. Here I was, as an adult, giving so much more of my agency away without even really realising it.'

Much of Luke's sex life in his twenties wasn't healthy. He did things he didn't want to do with people he wasn't overly interested in, just because the other person wanted to do it. Regularly.

There were moments when he'd be in the midst of an encounter and had a sudden, sickening realisation that he didn't want to be there. It wasn't right. It was unpleasant or uncomfortable and awkward. And yet, he couldn't get up and leave.

'Somehow, time and time again, I would put myself in these positions. It was looking for affirmation. It was wanting to be wanted, to be loved. It was needing affection or comfort or something. I don't know. But it was never good.

'I'd go through a cycle of guilt and shame afterwards. I didn't really understand it and I knew no one else would, so I kind of just carried on.'

Frankly, it doesn't sound too dissimilar to what other guys in their twenties get up to. One-night stands. Friends with benefits. Nothing overly scandalous. But as Luke explains it, it was the way he felt that was different. It was especially the horrible way he felt, and that he kept going back for more despite it.

'It was so damaging for me. I brought it up in counselling one day. I talked through what was going on and how it was making me feel and she was like, you've got to stop. You can't keep going like this and think things are going to improve. So, you've got to stop.'

Chapter Twelve

Talking so candidly with Luke is refreshing. It's not something men tend to do that much. Not in a deep and meaningful way, in any case. But while we're open and honest with each other, there are still times when one of us will physically cringe with awkwardness, as though stung by the uncomfortable nature of bearing our hearts.

We each feel so much shame about these things that live inside of us. That shame is potent and choking.

It's much more than just shame on its own, though. It's as though shame has been stitched to shame, then welded to some more shame, some kind of Frankenstein-like monstrous creation.

My shame is complex, confusing, and confronting. I know it inside out and back to front. We've been acquaintances for most of my life now. But even still, there are parts of it that have the power to surprise me – to really rattle me after all this time.

One such chilling confrontation came after a session of my failed group therapy experience. We'd been talking about shame and what it meant for us. It was only hours later that a stomach-churning realisation popped into my head.

One of the guys had spoken about how for years he had struggled to reconcile with himself the fact that during some of his abuse, he would get an erection. He hated himself for it. While he didn't consider himself gay – and he's not, as it turns out – that reaction to him meant that he must've enjoyed elements of his rape, and therefore, was complicit in it.

Years later, in therapy, the man was reassured at length that an erection doesn't equal enjoyment. It's a purely physiological response that is often outside of a man's control. Or, to paraphrase his memory of what his therapist said, some guys get a boner on the bus because of the rocking and vibrations – it doesn't mean they suddenly want to fuck a bus.

When I was a boy and Joshua was doing those things to me … there were times when I suspect I didn't entirely hate it.

The guilt and the fear aside, there was something validating about being sought like that. There was a small sensation of being special for having this secret with an older boy, a boy who wanted to be my friend.

Before he was going to do it, his demeanour would often turn especially friendly. He would praise me and compliment me. He'd give me his best toy to play with.

In hindsight, he was wooing me. Perhaps he sensed that I was reluctant to be a party to his abuse most of the time. And so, he had to work a little to ease me in. He would coax me, closer and closer, until he had what he wanted.

And then, when he was done, probably feeling a certain amount of shame himself, he would throw me aside. I was no longer needed. He was done with me for now and I should get out of his sight.

To be lured in and then tossed away again and again, a cycle of use and rejection, does something to the wiring of the brain. Things that don't really go together suddenly do, even though you absolutely know they shouldn't. Signals get crossed. Parts of your psyche that would do well not to interact now merge together with ease.

Maybe that's why there was a small part of what he did to me – what we did – that was a little enjoyable. I knew it was wrong. The need for secrecy told me as much, as young and naive as I was. But it was also interesting and exciting.

That's quite a torrid mix of sensations to have gurgling away deep inside of you when you're five and six.

'Shame can be defined as a feeling of embarrassment or humiliation that arises in relation to the perception of having done something dishonourable, immoral, or improper,' Arlin Cuncic, a psychologist and author of *The Anxiety Workbook*, explained in an article for the website Verywell Mind.

'People who experience shame usually try to hide the thing that they feel ashamed of. When shame is chronic it can involve the feeling that you are fundamentally flawed. Shame can often be hard to identify in oneself.'

Shame isn't always a bad thing, though. As she explains,

shame played an important role in the development of the human species, and without it, we might not be able to follow laws, social customs, and accepted behaviour.

But when it's internalised and allowed to fester, sparking destructive self-evaluation that muddies how we view ourselves, shame becomes harmful.

'This critic might tell you that you are a bad person, that you are worthless, or that you have no value,' she writes. 'However, the truth is that how deeply you feel ashamed often has little to do with your worth or what you have done wrong.'

In his book *Guilt, Shame and Anxiety*, the psychiatrist Peter R. Breggin described some of the feelings that shame can induce. They include: feeling rejected, being afraid to look stupid, wanting to shut people out, feeling inadequate, being consumed by regret, and feeling dishonourable.

Chronic shame, as Cuncic dubs it, describes a sensation that is always present. It doesn't subside and it becomes almost crippling. It makes you feel as though you're never quite good enough. The impact this can have on mental health and wellbeing is significant.

When Will and I are speaking one evening, the sound of his family life echoing in the background – his child chattering away while his partner prepares dinner, clanging pots and pans in the kitchen – he tells me that he can relate to a lot of what I've felt.

The embarrassment of what happened. The guilt that we somehow let it happen, or even encouraged it. The immense shame that erupts from those thoughts.

'The rational part of you knows there's nothing to be ashamed of. If someone else told you about an identical situation, your heart would break for them, and you wouldn't see them as being to blame at all. But when it's yourself, the rational part dies off. The emotive part is plagued by shame.

'I feel embarrassment that it happened. I also feel guilt that I let it happen. I do feel like in some ways I let it happen.

'Even saying it now, the rational part of me knows that's ridiculous. Like, I was a fucking kid. You don't let this sort of thing happen. This happens to you. But I hold myself accountable for it. I didn't stop it. I didn't fight. Maybe I was even promiscuous at times. I can find ways to blame myself for some of it.'

As he got older and started to become more acutely aware of how wrong the situation was and started to push back a little, Franco would barter with him. The later parts of Will's abuse contained a transactional element that haunts him.

'The things that he forced me to do to him, they were in exchange for a new video game or an outing or something. That shifted things. It was no longer something he was doing to me – it was something I was doing to him.

'And that is very difficult to reconcile with myself.'

This part of his story is the only detail he really struggles to talk about. As he hit his teens, Franco wanted more and more things from Will than he had before. And he wanted Will to do them to him.

It was an upping of the ante that was totally inconceivable for him, even with all of the manipulation and coaxing and guilting that he'd been conditioned with. And so, Franco became more forceful. He was aggressive in a way that he hadn't been before.

'He tried to rape me but it didn't "work" because of the size dynamics. I remember the pain so well. That was kind of the limit for him – not because he didn't want to do it to me, because he wanted to stop there, but because he physically couldn't.'

Franco flipped the script instead and offered inducements to make Will agreeable.

'And I did. I hate myself for that. I let him buy me. I really struggle to get my head around that even now.'

Like me, so much of the shame he feels is wrapped up in acknowledging that there were moments, however brief, when there was something resembling ... I don't know. Enjoyment doesn't feel like the right word.

'Something along those lines,' Will says.

'I mean, speaking physically, in a pure biological response sense, it did feel good at times, whether I wanted it to or not. This bad thing happening in some ways felt good.

'That's a really hard bridge to cross. Once you start thinking about it, it's kind of haunting because if you accept that it felt good, then it must mean you let it happen or you wanted it to happen. A lot of the shame comes from that.'

Like Chris and like Will, I've always had something of an insecurity about being loved. It sounds almost nonsensical. Who wouldn't want to be loved? And of course, I love being loved – in many ways, it's what I've spent much of my life searching for.

But as I've become older and with the benefit of acquired wisdom and hindsight, I've come to learn that what I was looking for wasn't love. It was tricked up to look like it, sure, but it wasn't really pure, tender love.

Whatever it was – validation, needing to be needed or wanted, a submissive surrendering to someone more powerful, a self-loathing, raw self-destruction – I went looking for it too often.

I'm fifteen and I'm sitting on a bright yellow park bench outside an ice cream shop in the main square of Cherry Grove, an especially gay community on the famed Fire Island in New York.

This isn't the only homosexually charged enclave to call this narrow stretch of high-priced land home. The next township up, the Pines, is just on the other side of a forest. It's where you'll find cashed-up men of a certain age taking their first facelift out to an endless stream of cocaine-fuelled parties at jaw-dropping beach houses attended by the rich and the fabulous.

Cherry Grove isn't quite like that. It's charming and family friendly, with just the slightest edge. Drag shows at brunch.

Crude jokes about fisting traded in the fruit aisle at the convenience store. That kind of thing.

It's a warm summer afternoon and I'm waiting for my friend Christine to finish work at the gift store across the way. I used to work there. It's how we met. But after a month, I throw in the towel because the shifts are too long and the money is terrible. Five dollars an hour! Fuck that. I get a job upstairs at a fancy restaurant overlooking the bay. I'm a bus boy and when it's busy I take home one hundred dollars in tips a night.

I'm halfway through a year of student exchange in America. I've left the confines of my hellish hometown, where I wasn't much more than a sideshow spectacle as the only suspected gay in the village. My only way of surviving is to get out, and so here I am.

My host mum, Barbara, has called Connecticut home for about a decade, but she still maintains all of her New Yorker roots. She was born and raised in Flushing, Queens. She loves Manhattan. She adores Fire Island. As a progressive bisexual woman, she spends every single summer here.

And so this year, I do too.

It's a wild ride. I work locally and I'm here every single day, so I get to know most people. On my second weekend, someone at the gift shop invites me out for a drink. I open my mouth to explain that I'm underage, but I get swept up in the crowd of excited revellers and straight into the door of the Ice Palace. It's the most popular bar-slash-nightclub on the island.

Fat Boy Slim did a set here last summer, everybody reminds me at least once a week.

I sit nervously on a stool and the bartender saunters up to me. He's a handsome college student with perfect hair and big brown eyes. He smiles. He recognises me from the store. What do I want to drink?

'A rum and Coke?'

He nods and brings me one. And another. Then another. I have an amazing night with my new work friends, drinking and dancing. That kind of sets the scene for me on the island, as just one of the seasonal workers like everybody else.

I mention I'm a student and from Australia, and it gets misinterpreted as me being at college – not high school – and that, coupled with me being here for three months … well, it's just assumed I'm twenty-one at least.

I don't look remotely close to twenty-one. No one seems to care.

This Saturday afternoon, it's quieter in town than it usually is. There are storms forecast so the crowds who come for the weekend have obviously decided to stay home. Christine and I are going to grab a pizza, have a swim at the beach and then get a few drinks at the Ice Palace. I'll crash at her place. Barbara gives me her blessing.

I light a cigarette while I wait for six o'clock to roll around and Christine to get off work. I take a seat on a bench on the main thoroughfare just as a ferry pulls in with a load of passengers from the mainland. It's not busy. A few groups of younger people, a family, an older couple, and a guy on his own.

The solo traveller clocks me straight away and makes a beeline. I can see him coming. I feel a little flurry of butterflies in my stomach.

Being young and a little more outgoing than I should be has earnt me a fair amount of attention these past several weeks. I've got big blue eyes, pale skin and, as of recently, bright red hair. I wear tight T-shirts. I'm easygoing and friendly.

I'm kind of a novelty. A classic twink, my boss at the restaurant informs me, before adding that I should be careful.

I've never had attention of the positive kind before. This time last year, I was running from bullies in Yeppoon, spending every lunch time hiding out, using my older brother as a kind of bodyguard. I spent my free time praying that I could disappear – just instantly vanish.

Now, men are looking at me. They're talking to me. They're buying me drinks. Sure, many of them are old or a bit creepy, but it's still kind of flattering. My ego is enormous.

This guy isn't especially attractive. He's fit but short and has a receding hairline. But his smile is really nice. He has those big, typically American teeth. The ones that look like sculpted marble. He's walking towards me and he's got a bit of swagger. I like confidence.

‘Hey,’ he says smoothly. I smile sheepishly.

We talk for a little while. He’s here for the night from Manhattan. Some friends were coming too but they bailed at the last minute. So, he’ll see where the night takes him.

He asks about my accent. I tell him that I’m from Australia and I’m here studying. He asks me point blank how old I am. I tell him the truth. I always do if someone asks me directly.

‘I’m thirty-eight,’ he replies. ‘Is that alright?’

I shrug.

I’m not instantly drawn to him. He’s fine. He seems nice. But it’s not as though I’ve developed a deep crush and find myself lusting over this guy. I’ve even forgotten his name and it’s probably too late to ask.

Christine wanders out, sees me and squeals. She’s a larger-than-life lesbian from Long Island who comes from a big Italian family. I’m almost certain they’re mobsters, the way she talks about them. But she’s funny and friendly, and we hang out most days.

‘Well, well, well,’ she smirks, pointing at my new friend. ‘Who’s this then?’

He introduces himself and I’m not paying good enough attention to listen for his name, so I still don’t know it. But he re-tells Christine his story about being here for one night only. She has an expectant look on her face and keeps glancing at me, eyes wide.

I shoot her a pleading look and she gets the message, telling the guy that we're off for dinner but maybe we'll see him out later.

By the time we scoff down a pepperoni pizza, float around in the ocean while the sun sets and then shower and change at Christine's apartment, I've forgotten all about what's-his-name. Those kinds of interactions aren't uncommon. This is a time before Tinder. It's almost an archaic and real-life version of swiping left or right.

When we strut into the Ice Palace at nine o'clock, it's almost dead. There are a few people perched at the bar and a couple of occupied tables out on the deck. And there's the guy, sitting at a high table just inside the front door.

He pounces on us as we enter and follows us to a table. The three of us sit and make small talk. He works in retail in the city. He grew up in Brooklyn. He's just out of a long-term relationship.

It's fine. He's fine. There's nothing overly remarkable about him or the situation, and no reason to think this will be anything other than a fairly ordinary night, until I get back from a trip to the bathroom and find Christine has gone.

'She insisted we stay and have fun!' he beams.

I'm instantly on guard. I'm staying at her place. Why would she abruptly leave? The next day, she tells me that the guy insisted that I was giving him signals and he wanted to have a crack, but was worried she was being a third wheel. Sweetly, but naively, she believed him and made an escape.

'I should go,' I say, leaning down to pick up my wallet and cigarettes. He grabs my arm gently and pulls me into the chair.

'Stay,' he says. 'At least for one more drink.'

That's the last coherent thought I have from that night. That was my second drink but it completely smashed me. I have flashes of memory of me swaying on the chair. I think a glass was knocked over. Then it's bright and I'm propped up on the reception desk of the hotel that adjoins the Ice Palace.

'Is your friend OK?' I hear someone ask.

I remember the guy taking my wallet out of my shorts pocket and pulling out a fifty dollar note, to help pay for the room.

Then I remember falling onto the bed. Or being thrown onto the bed, I guess, given I didn't have use of my legs.

Mercifully, I don't remember much else, except for being propped up with pillows that he shoved under my waist while I was face down. And I recall hearing the echo of me yelling. Then nothing until the next morning when the sun is screeching at me through a gap in the curtain.

I lift my head. It's hot as hell and it stinks of stale sweat. The room is tiny, barely fitting much more than the single bed we're on and a bar fridge in the corner. There's a sliding door that leads to the bathroom, and I stumble in. My face looks so drawn in the mirror. My hair is matted and my eyes are bloodshot. I'm dizzy and I have a pain in my stomach.

I splash my face and try not to cry. I find my clothes and get dressed, but wake up the guy in the process.

'Good morning, handsome,' he slurs at me.

I want to vomit. I smile politely, still unwilling to be rude even in circumstances like these. I dress as quickly as I can, stumbling and bashing my shoulder into the wall in the process. I mumble a goodbye and leave.

As I speed walk down the stairs and through the entrance, there's a pulsating pain coming from my bottom.

I've never had sex before, but it doesn't take a genius to recognise the signs of what it probably feels like the next day. I'm almost distraught but can't decide what to do. If I go home in this state, Barbara will panic. I don't want to upset her. She's entrusted me to behave responsibly. So, I go to Christine's.

Her jaw drops when she opens the door. She was expecting me to be beaming, here to celebrate a saucy conquest. Instead, I fall into her arms, sobbing uncontrollably.

She strips my clothes off and puts me in her shower. We sit all morning drinking coffee and holding hands, and she gets snippets from me of what happened. She explains her disappearance. We both cry.

Later that day, arriving for my shift at the restaurant, I see him. He's walking down the dock to the departing ferry, on his way back to the mainland. I hide out of sight until the boat pulls away, and then I stand and watch it until I can't see it anymore.

*

For a long time, I beat myself up about that night. Shit, I still find myself doing it now. What was I doing there? Who did I think I was, trying to navigate such an adult setting with absolutely no idea what I was doing?

And how desperate must I have been for attention and affection – of any kind, from anyone – that I wouldn't run at the first of those many red flags?

Him pouncing on us as we got inside. Him scaring off Christine. Him insisting on getting the drinks. Jesus, I mean, him brushing aside the fact I was only fifteen?

I shouldn't have been there. And though I was, I should've run at the obvious signs of danger. Instead, I stayed. Why?

Because he was nice to me? Because it would've been awkward if I'd wanted to leave? I might've offended him if I made a fuss? Honestly.

I put myself in a stupid position and paid a horrible price. I guess I'm lucky I wasn't murdered too.

That wasn't the last intimate moment I found myself in that was far from ideal. Throughout my teens and twenties, I routinely stumbled into situations that were unhealthy, dangerous and demoralising. Sometimes I even realised it midway through, but still stayed. I would be somewhere, with someone, and desperately want to leave … but not.

Those instances with Joshua sexualised me far too early. A button in my head was prematurely pressed. While I had this topline knowledge about something, I was deeply naive about what to do with it and woefully unprepared for the consequences.

It's like being plonked in the driver's seat of a powerful vehicle. I had a key to start it, but no clue how to control the thing once it was going. As hard as I tried to keep it steady, I'd more often than not veer wildly out of control.

Those shameful and guilt-infested experiences nudged me into the path of an intimacy minefield. I wandered haplessly across it for years, hopeful but clueless and with a clouded judgement.

I rolled from one toxic relationship, if you could even call them 'relationships', to another. I allowed myself to be used and abused. Belittled. Taken advantage of. Promised affection, care and respect that never eventuated.

When I've found the real deal – love without conditions, love that's fair and equal, love built on a foundation of trust and empathy – I've done my best to shoo it away.

Because I have something of an insecurity about being loved. It's nonsensical. But inside, I'm so broken when it comes to love – or what I think it should look and feel like – that anything overly nice must surely be a trick. And those lovely people are delicate concepts held together by fraying seams that threaten to wear and snap at a moment's notice.

I'm paranoid just thinking about the real deal. It's going to go away as quickly as it's come. I'm going to be discovered as a fraud and a shameful deviant who's unworthy of it.

For most of my adult life, it was just easier to steer clear of that and instead throw myself head first at the fake love. The unhealthy version, whatever it is, wearing a fairly convincing disguise. In the past when I sought out a dalliance, needing and wanting intimacy of some kind, they usually left me feeling dirty and degraded, not fulfilled.

I knew it was shit. That it wasn't acceptable. But I didn't really know anything else, or that I was deserving of more. And so, shame coated all that I did with partners. I deeply disliked myself during and after each and every instance of sex.

Literally. Every single intimate moment in my life, in some respect, has been shrouded in guilt.

I can't help but trace that back to Joshua.

I'm not entirely off the mark, Professor Hickie tells me. The way young people develop intimate relationships – the way they take their first forays into heady scenarios of love and sexuality – is based on experience. Or, in the case of boys like me, a lack thereof.

A child who comes from a caring background, or one without an early sexual experience borne from abuse, tends to get to the onset of adolescence, around fifteen or sixteen years old, and find themselves wanting to form relationships outside of the family structure.

'And they're likely to be sexualised – they're going to develop gender expression, sexuality, whatever else,' Professor Hickie says.

'And if you've come from a quality experience of care and of trust, then you kind of have an expectation of what that might look like. You know, this is what will happen next if I do this. It's far from perfect and it's probably ham-fisted at times, it's not sophisticated, but those young people tend to form relationships with other young people who have a similarly strong background of care and of trust. There are emotional characteristics that they share.'

Or, as I put it, non-fucked up kids are probably drawn to other non-fucked up kids and scenarios. Why wouldn't they be? They know healthy love and affection and trust, so that's what they gravitate towards.

Professor Hickie probably doesn't condone my simplistic and dark way of looking at it, but I'm largely on the money.

'Sadly, in contrast, kids who've had a lot of corrupted relationships, untrusting relationships, may be drawn into more risky relationships. They may have low expectations and be drawn into the sorts of scenarios where it's more likely that they will again be abused. Placing their trust in untrustworthy people, getting into much more risky situations, having a poor sense of themselves as being undeserving of affection, undeserving of trust within the transaction.

'And it's complicated and interesting, because this is all something you have to develop as an adolescent and young adult. It's an evolving concept.

'I'm not saying the kids who've grown up in healthy environments simply have it, or the capacity for it, but they've got a better chance of finding it. They're better along the path of how to develop the appropriate reciprocal relationship with another. They have a stronger set of expectations that the person will trust and care for them in a reciprocal way, just as they invest, trust, and care in the other person.

'They're more likely to pull away from situations that are risky, from an emotional point of view. They recognise if someone is not a good person. Or if they're in a situation that is abusive or has the potential to be abusive, they have a stronger sense of "I deserve more than this". If there's something not right in the nature of this particular transaction, they are more likely to recognise it.'

And they're much more likely to not view those unhealthy, abusive or dangerous scenarios as ones they deserve. Or ones that they're destined to be in – that are as good as they're likely to find.

In 2020, two researchers sought to examine just how prevalent sexual assault later in life is for survivors of child sexual abuse.

Nina Papalia, a postdoctoral research fellow at the Centre for Forensic Behavioural Science at the Victorian Institute of Forensic Mental Health at Swinburne University, and Professor James Ogloff, the director of the Centre for Forensic Behavioural Science, wrote about their findings in an article for *The Conversation.*

They re-analysed the cases of 2759 children who were medically confirmed to have been sexually abused in Australia between 1964 and 1995. The study noted where survivors had contact with the police, having been victims of further crime as adults. The findings were compared to a sample from the general population.

They found that child sexual abuse survivors were much more likely to be re-victimised later in life than the control group, and to suffer what criminologists consider to be medium- to high-harm personal injury offences.

'For instance, they were five times more likely to have been victims of sexual assault later in life, twice as likely to be victims of physical assault, four times as likely to be threatened with violence and twice as likely to be stalked,' they write.

'We also found the increased risk of re-victimisation was not just experienced by women. For example, male survivors of child sexual abuse were seven times more likely to be the victims of a further sexual assault than the men in the control group.'

Why? The reasons are complex and interconnected. Professor Hickie's observations are on the mark. The

Swinburne researchers also note that gender and the survivor's age when they were sexually abused likely play a role.

But overwhelmingly, child sexual abuse survivors with mental illnesses are much more likely to be re-victimised later in life.

'The links between mental illness and re-victimisation, however, were complex,' the Swinburne researchers write.

'Child sexual abuse survivors who developed personality disorders or anxiety disorders, for example, were roughly twice as likely to be victims of all types of crimes as adults compared to survivors who did not develop these conditions.

'Other mental illnesses were linked to some forms of re-victimisation, but not others. Post-traumatic stress disorders, for example, were linked with higher rates of sexual re-victimisation. Mood disorders were linked to violent re-victimisation.

'And survivors who developed substance abuse issues were more likely to become victims of both violent and non-violent crimes later in life.'

It's likely, as Professor Hickie noted, that the symptoms of mental illness impair a survivor's capacity to spot risky situations or dangerous people and to respond accordingly. In addition, perpetrators are likely to recognise vulnerabilities that a survivor of child sexual abuse might have and be able to target and exploit them. And those perpetrators often exploit people who appear unstable or could be painted as emotionally troubled, so as to defend against any future allegations.

'Second, survivors who suffer re-victimisation later in life may be more prone to serious mental health problems due to the cumulative impacts of repeat abuse,' the Swinburne researchers write. 'That is, mental illness may be a consequence of, not a contributor to, this continuous cycle of abuse.

'The truth is that both explanations likely contribute to the relationship between mental illness and re-victimisation.'

Chapter Thirteen

Like Chris's experience of talking with mates about their early sexual encounters – of sharing war stories of awkward dates as teenagers and first loves on the cusp of adulthood – Will has encountered some of these painful conversations.

'Hearing the way people speak about relationships and intimacy has always been a weird experience for me,' Will says.

'You know, guys talking about their first sexual experiences or whatever, and me sitting there thinking about how fucked mine was. It feels like you're on the outside looking in, normal people having normal conversations, pretending what happened to you didn't happen at all.

'I mean, that's not something you bring up in conversation. You don't just talk about it with anyone.'

Not for the first time, he has felt excluded from normalcy in those circumstances. He's reminded, suddenly, that a large chunk of his childhood was abnormal. It was wrong. If people knew, they'd be aghast. Maybe for him, maybe at him – it's hard to be sure.

Whatever the scenario, whether it's mates talking about losing their virginity or a crude conversation about some sex act that he became familiar with when his age was in the single digits, the feelings of being on the outer stick with him for a long time. He ruminates on them.

'There's a certain level of feeling like a bit of a freak. You've got this past, these scars, and you have to mask them so others don't see and feel uncomfortable or shocked or horrified.'

He too had a difficult path with adult intimate relationships. Being hypersexualised from a young age has landed him in some tricky situations.

'It distorts how you think about things, or I guess the age you think about them. Things that would be in my head felt normal to me, but in hindsight, they're not. The frequency with which I thought about them too, probably more than others.'

At an age when he should've been thinking about Pokémon or action films or video games, or whatever young boys of ten and eleven think about, his mind would often drift to the things being done to him. Those unwelcome daydreams would be heavily coated with confusion and shame and occasionally excitement, the latter of which would inevitably plunge him into a storm of guilt and self-loathing.

There was a certain level of awareness too that what was going through his head wasn't normal. Other boys weren't thinking about those things.

'The first time being with a girl wasn't great. There was a lot about it that was hard to enjoy because similar previous experiences had been unenjoyable and wrapped up in a lot of really heavy and difficult emotions. And shame. The worst one, I think.

'Things that he used to do to me … it took a while to be able to do that with a girl and think about it in the context of a nice and healthy interaction.'

There are still times when those intimate encounters with his partner throw up a long-hidden memory flash of Franco and he has to stop, feeling instantly sick to the stomach.

I have often felt much the same as Will does about how he sometimes viewed his abuse when he was a child. Having a physical response like that, however infrequent and fleeting, planted a seed in my mind very early on that I was different. I wasn't like other boys. I wasn't sure how, but I knew it deep down.

As I grew older and came to understand what it meant to be gay, and that I almost certainly was, it didn't take me long to conclude how I'd ended up that way.

Joshua.

It had to have been him and what he did to me … the things we did, that I sometimes didn't entirely loathe … that made me gay.

Of course, it's not. I know it's not! I'm a rational adult with a fair degree of intelligence and an open-minded worldview.

Of course I know I'm not gay because of what Joshua did to me.

But am I?

There's maybe two or three per cent of me that wonders. I know it's stupid and it doesn't make any sense at all. But it's there, and all of the logic in my bones can't wish it away. Small as it may be, there's a part of me that can't help drawing a line between those two parts of myself.

I had repeated sexual experiences with another boy for several years during my childhood, on the cusp of adolescence, and then I wound up being attracted to other boys. That can't be entirely a coincidence, right?

The coincidence would be if I was born gay *and* happened to encounter a kid like Joshua. What are the odds of that? Probably lower than the cause-and-effect belief that a small part of me holds.

In an article published in the scientific journal *Psychological Science In The Public Interest* in 2016, J Michael Bailey from Northwestern University in the United States and others examined the latest research about sexual orientation.

The paper drew several conclusions, including observations about the cause and prevalence of homosexuality. Among them, the paper notes that 'various biological factors' are likely to contribute to a person's sexual orientation, such as prenatal hormones and specific genetic profiles.

Although, those factors are not the sole cause.

'Scientific evidence suggests that biological and non-social environmental factors jointly influence sexual orientation,' the article states.

'Scientific findings do not support the notion that sexual orientation can be taught or learned through social means. And there is little evidence to suggest that non-heterosexual orientations become more common with increased social tolerance.'

But what about child sexual abuse? Can that have some kind of impact on whether a person ends up being homosexual?

The organisation PFLAG – Parents and Friends of Lesbians and Gays – has chapters all around the world, including here in Australia. It's a movement that was born from the need to support the parents of young people coming to terms with their sexuality in environments that are unsafe or unaccepting.

Basically, someone whose kid comes out can head to PFLAG for advice, insight and support with just about anything. And their children can also benefit from the group's inclusive model.

There's a great article put together by PFLAG in Atlanta in the American state of Georgia – an east coast city about halfway down the country that's conservative with a dash of liberal. It's a little bit 'Southern' but not too much, if you know what I mean.

As they point out, there's no definitive and conclusive explanation for why people are gay, lesbian or bisexual. The same goes for the causal link between child sexual abuse and sexual orientation. Some studies in the 90s established a connection between the two, while other more contemporary work has emphatically ruled it out.

That just makes the whole question of whether being abused as a kid can make you gay murkier and more uncomfortable to sit with.

But, as PFLAG Atlanta's article demonstrates, the numbers simply don't stack up. In the United States, reliable data indicates that about 16 per cent of males and 27 per cent of females in America have been sexually abused in childhood.

And yet, studies on the number of people who identify as gay, lesbian, bisexual or transgender in the United States vary wildly from 1.5 per cent to as high as 8 per cent. It's generally accepted that the latter is probably close to the mark.

'Therefore, if there is a causal link between childhood sexual abuse and identifying as GLBT later in life, then why aren't the figures for the number of GLBT people in the population reflected by the abuse statistics?' the article asks.

There are significantly more cases of child sexual abuse than people who identify as being gay, lesbian, bisexual or transgender. And furthermore, the majority of people who were sexually abused as children identify as heterosexual.

'Claims that [sexual orientation] can be caused by child sexual abuse are troublesome because this implicitly implies that being GLBT is not a positive thing, but something that has occurred as a result of serious trauma,' the article continues.

'Therefore, are we not comparing being GLBT to suffering from PTSD … or depression? Being GLBT is not an illness!

'Of course, sexual abuse can interfere with a survivor's sexual development, sexual enjoyment, the way they engage in sexual behaviours, the ability to know and voice what they want – but it seems unlikely that it would play a role in creating passion, attraction and love for another person.'

I ask Carol Ronken from Bravehearts about my gay chicken-and-egg dilemma. I can almost hear her nodding through the phone, as though she's heard this question countless times before.

'Your sexuality is not something that's determined by those types of experiences,' Carol tells me.

I'm quite determined when I broach this topic to be as measured with my speech as possible. I hope that it's a question that others have had. I'm an impartial player and not asking for myself. That's what I want her to believe.

'It's really sad, but there are a number of men who are gay and who were abused as children who do wonder if their sexuality was determined by those kinds of awful experiences,' Carol says.

'We are who we are. We're made the way we are. But it's absolutely heart-breaking that there are so many kids, so many young people, who feel that their abuse is somehow going to have a long-term impact on their sexuality. It certainly doesn't.'

*

There's no doubt that a significant part of my question is tied up with my own struggles with being gay throughout the entirety of my adolescence.

I went to an all-boys, rugby league-mad Catholic school in central Queensland at the cusp of the new millennium. It was a time before social media and the popularisation of the internet. There were no online communities for confused young people wanting information and support about the things they might be feeling. There were few, if any, positive role models in popular culture for a little gay boy in a shithole small town to look up to for reassurance.

I was horrifically bullied. It was brutal and relentless, and almost every single day of those two years at that school was a living hell. Constant taunts. Physical violence. Ostracisation. Social exclusion.

Being gay was disgusting and wrong and sinful. Some of the teachers even perpetuated that view and egged on the boys' mistreatment of me. There were religion classes on the horrors of homosexuality and how gays would absolutely end up in hell. There were smirks from trusted adults when I was shoved over, spat on, or called a faggot and a poofter.

I remember going on a week-long camp during the first year of high school. The entire class of Year Eight kids went to a secluded creek an hour or so out of town and spent several days doing activities designed to make us men, I guess, and foster bonding and mateship. I hated every single second of it.

I vividly remember being grabbed from behind by someone and dragged to a tree, where a group quickly wrapped rope around my torso to tie me up, then took turns beating me with kayak oars.

But by far the most humiliating moment was on the final night, when the class gathered around a massive campfire and took part in a talent show. A few kids played guitar and sang, one did some kind of ball dribbling skills thing, I don't know – something with a football – but the majority stood up and told jokes.

Literally every single one of them was about gay people or being gay. And most of the amateur comedians would include me in their routines in some way – either by naming me or pointing at me. It was horrid.

That was the kind of stuff my high school years were full of. It was never-ending. Is it any wonder that I hated myself?

But while I didn't really, truly realise what it meant to be gay, and certainly couldn't identify any of the positive or non-horrid elements of my sexuality, I knew that it was an inevitability. It just kind of 'clicked' that this was who I was going to be. I didn't feel anything for girls, except a kind of discomfort about trying to force myself to have a girlfriend or kiss. It felt like a lie and I was overcome with guilt at trying to be something I clearly wasn't.

At the same time, it was very clear to me that being gay was just about the worst thing you could be. My treatment at school told me as much. But more than that, the indifference of adults who witnessed it cemented the realisation that many people – perhaps even the majority of people – didn't especially like 'the gays' either.

It wasn't a fear, as the term 'homophobia' implies, but a raw and unbridled hatred. I felt that at thirteen and fourteen. And that set me up for a very lengthy period of trying to undo all of the negative notions I held about myself.

Will never considered himself gay. Neither did Jason. It was never much of a consideration for them. Luke tells me he felt a certain element of confusion from time to time in his late adolescence and early adulthood, but he is heterosexual.

I'm not 100 per cent convinced. I still can't quite settle on the conclusion that I'm gay because I'm gay, and not because of what Joshua and I did when we were kids.

Verbalising that among some of my gay friends would be like social suicide. After accepting our sexuality and coming out, gay men are meant to be unquestionably proud and totally sure of themselves and their identity.

There is no room for doubt or insecurity about why we are the way we are – at a surface level, in any case. We're just homos, and we're fabulous. We're here, we're queer – get used to it!

And while I can have that attitude most of the time, I still harbour difficult views of myself and my homosexuality.

*

I imagine sometimes what kind of man I would be if I'd never met Joshua. If our paths had never crossed and we'd never been friends, and he'd never touched me that way in his bedroom, and all of those other times hadn't followed, who might Shannon Molloy be?

Might I be a blokey bloke? Might I work in some kind of tough and physically gruelling job where your hands become calloused and your nail beds are perpetually dirty? Or where you don't ever for one second think nor care about the condition of your nails, for fuck's sake?

Might I be more stoic in the face of adversity? Might I be better equipped to brush off the world's woes that so heavily drag me down from time to time? Might I cry less, especially during emotive dog food commercials, like I did for an embarrassingly long period of time a few years back?

Might I be more mentally stable? Or, more accurately, let's face it, just as prone to mental ill health but better able to mask it and carry on?

Might I be able to kick a ball in a straight line, or to catch a ball without looking like I'm using my hands for the first time?

Might I be heterosexual? Might the years of hell I endured at school, being relentlessly bullied for being the town faggot, have never happened? Might I have never had hang-ups about my intimate relationships? Might I have had *normal* intimate relationships that don't occasionally make me feel disgusted with myself?

How much of who I am now was inherited from those shameful and wrong childhood experiences? How many of my faults, whether unfairly perceived or real, were imprinted on me?

It's a source of great shame, but this kind of thinking is a big part of the reason that I was desperate for my child to be a girl. It's something I felt the moment my husband and I first began discussing starting a family together. The fear I felt about being the father of a boy never dimmed.

I figured that I would raise a daughter well. My penchant for the dramatic and inherently feminine nature would suit a little girl who might stereotypically like dance and make-up and singalongs in the car. We'd go out for lunch or go shopping and have so much in common. She'd gravitate towards me and my energy. I'd see her longing to absorb every drop of my personality like a sponge.

I'd be a great dad to a girl. I've always thought that, without any hesitation or doubt. But me having a boy? It would be a recipe for disaster, I feared.

I'd raise the kind of little man that I was. Camp, weak and overly emotional. He would flit around the place, prancing instead of walking, and be ostracised by his male peers. He wouldn't play sports or like girls, and would be destined for the same type of life of being ostracised that I endured. He would be miserable and it would be all my fault.

I couldn't do that to the person I was hoping to bring into the world. The enormous relief that came with having a girl is something that troubles me as a supposedly proud gay man.

It's the type of internalised homophobia that my community won't or can't accept. Perhaps because it raises some uncomfortable questions for many of us, about how we still see ourselves. Perhaps inside, a little bit, we are all still scared little boys who don't fit in.

Chapter Fourteen

A ground-breaking study by Margaret Cutajar, Paul Mullen and others from Monash University, published in the international academic journal *Child Abuse & Neglect* in 2010, showed just how significant the mental health implications of severe trauma can be.

The researchers examined the forensic medical records of 2759 children who had been sexually abused between 1964 and 1995. Those cases were linked with a public psychiatric database between twelve and forty-three years later. The team analysed the outcomes of those children and compared them with control subjects matched on age and gender, drawn from the general population through a random sample.

They found that a lifetime of recorded contact with mental health services was evident in 23 per cent of cases. In the control group, this was just 7 per cent.

The survivors of child sexual abuse accessed mental health services at a rate that was three-and-a-half times higher than the general population.

‘Exposure to sexual abuse increased risks for the majority of outcomes including psychosis, affective, anxiety, substance abuse, and personality disorders,’ the study notes.

Child sexual abuse survivors had ‘significantly higher’ rates of clinical psychiatric disorders.

I’ve never had a formal mental health diagnosis. In my view, it’s kind of obvious enough that it doesn’t really need a label or a stamp on a piece of paper. Is that how psychiatric diagnoses are recorded? With a giant red stamp on a document that’s slid inside your medical history?

The consensus is that I have depression and anxiety with a bit of post-traumatic stress thrown in. The stuff that Joshua did. The extreme bullying I endured at school. The date rape. Various instances of betrayal and loss. It has all played a part in bringing me to the precarious mental state I find myself in now.

For a long time, I did nothing about it. My husband gently encouraged me to start addressing the things that I hadn’t really seen at first, but which were beginning to upend my life.

I saw Dr Rolenstein for a long time. In addition to psychotherapy every single week, and sometimes twice a week, he prescribed me an antidepressant that did a fairly good job of bringing my baseline back to a moderate level for a while.

I look at my baseline as being the middle of my emotions. Above it is the good and below it is the bad. The baseline shifts depending on the state of my mental health. The lower the threshold is, the easier it is for me to slump to the very depths of despair. The higher it is, the further away that rock bottom is.

Without the pills, that baseline was so low that even the slightest upset in my normal rhythm and routine would plunge me into a deep hole.

A disagreement with a colleague could lead me to want to quit my job. On one occasion, I did – I threw in the towel and walked away from a place I loved working, doing something I loved doing, over an intense but fairly brief brouhaha with a boss. I burnt a lot of bridges in the process and lost a few friends. I deeply offended a mentor who'd championed my career and backed me without question every single day I was there. We mended the bridge but things were never the same.

When my baseline is low, a disruption in my personal life could prompt me to walk away from a relationship. A good relationship too. Feeling like I've been slighted or unfairly criticised or taken for granted is my kryptonite. It's absolutely crushing, and in the moment, I've simply got to get as far away from the scenario as possible.

I'm often irrational when my baseline is low. I can't see the forest for the trees. Everything feels hopeless and pointless.

'Oh yeah.' Will laughs when I explain the tendency for my baseline to creep below an optimal level without me noticing. 'I hear you.'

He's been diagnosed with rapid cycling bipolar. In a nutshell and generally speaking, bipolar causes people to have episodes, either depressive or manic, that can last for days and sometimes weeks. Will's last for a matter of minutes.

'It's up and down, up and down, very rapidly,' he says. 'It's absolutely exhausting. I'm tired a lot and often feel totally zapped of energy and can't do anything.

'If I'm allowed to, I can sleep for twelve hours at a time or more. I still wake up feeling exhausted, like total shit. It's like I haven't slept at all.'

That's how I feel too. I sometimes sleep for twelve hours and don't feel refreshed at all. I nap most days, almost unable to stay awake. I never wake in the morning feeling bright – it's always a struggle to get out of bed and I've got to be really firm with myself to get up. Sometimes it's too hard, and so I stay there until I absolutely can't stay any longer.

I always figured it was my nose. I broke it at some point and it healed horribly. A surgeon shoved a camera up there a few years back and almost fell off his chair. I need it corrected, but who has seven weeks to spare for the long and painful recovery such an operation requires?

So, instead, I annoy the shit out of my husband with my chainsaw-like snoring and don't allow myself to have a proper sleep.

But maybe there's something linked to the trauma that also keeps my brain awake more than it should be when I fall into a slumber? A kind of hypervigilance, where my brain is constantly assessing potential threats. Maybe, like Will, my nervous system is running at such a frantic pace during the day that it depletes me in a way that others aren't being drained of their energy.'

'I have a very clear memory of the last time I had a good night's sleep and woke up feeling refreshed.' Will says. 'I remember so much about it, like it was a singular instance.'

Will has also been diagnosed with depression, he tells me, but adds, 'Who isn't depressed?'

Anxiety is by far his biggest struggle. It's like carrying an invisible 170-kilogram gorilla around, piggyback. Beneath the reassuring smile and beyond the masking of his dry wit and gregarious nature is a near-constant fear. It's a sense of being unsettled – of feeling unnerved in situations that don't warrant such a buzz.

If someone comes up behind him too suddenly or too quietly, he'll leap out of his skin when he realises their presence. Sometimes he'll yelp in surprised pain. He's tightly wound and constantly on edge.

I'm much the same. It's like I'm always on high alert for something – or someone – to attack. The feeling is heightened in some situations, like being in a loud public place, such as a shopping centre or on a bus or train. Then there are situations where strangers are more likely to be perceived by my broken flight-or-fight system as threats, like seeing orange workwear-clad tradies in a pub, probably harking back to my experiences with violent homophobes who tended to be very blokey blokes.

Some of the time I have a handle on it. In other cases, I don't. Again, when my baseline is low, these kinds of experiences go from being somewhat disruptive to downright destabilising.

Like many of the men I've met through this process of trying to understand more about myself, Will has also been diagnosed with complex post-traumatic stress disorder. It's like PTSD plus – some bonus features of an already difficult condition. It's usually the result of repeated exposure to trauma or traumas, and comes with a range of added symptoms, such as anger, distrust of the world, difficulty regulating emotions, persistent negative thoughts, avoidance and guilt.

He is prone to pangs of paranoia. He can shift from feeling fairly secure in his surroundings to being absolutely convinced that everyone around him is talking about him. They hate him and they want to bring him down. They're eyeing him off like the prize bull at the stockyards.

And like many other survivors, he is prone to suicidal feelings from time to time, when things get especially tough. There have been a few suicide attempts – once after he discovered that his uncle knew about Franco's abuse, and another that seemed to come out of the blue.

'I was on my way to work one day when I was twenty-three. I was at Flinders Street Station in Melbourne when I felt this intense urge to step in front of a train. It was like I wanted nothing more than to jump in front of this train. It scared me.'

Of course, it hadn't come entirely out of the blue. It was the culmination of weeks, if not months of the ramifications of his unresolved trauma building up and up, until he didn't believe he could carry the weight anymore.

Something inside him fought back against the darkness. A small sliver of light broke through. He heard a voice urging him to step back from the edge of the platform and to leave the train station. And so, he did.

'I went straight to my doctor and told him what had happened and he put me on medication. It was way too strong and really disorienting, totally unsuitable for what I was struggling with. It gave me really trippy dreams.

'I transitioned to another medication but it didn't work for me. Finally, I landed on this one and it has been love ever since. I can't do without it.'

Some of Will's current condition can be explained by the category that his abuser falls into, Professor Hickie explains.

There's obviously no 'ideal' perpetrator. All abuse is horrid and every abuser is evil, but there are some instances in which the damage done can be more severe.

'If it's happened within a trusted network where fundamental relationships, be they family or close family friend, are degraded or distorted, or entirely broken,' he tells me. 'As a result of that, the development of other relationships can become extremely problematic.'

It kind of makes sense when you think about it.

If someone deeply trusted by you as a child betrays you in such a destructive way, how can you view any other significant relationship in the same way again?

'For all children, the model or the template for future relationships is built around those classic notions of attachment. Children mimic what they see. If you look within particular societies, the degree of care experienced as a child through parents, adult siblings, other adults within the family circle, grandparents, whoever – all those key figures within trusted family networks provide the template for relationships for the rest of their life.'

At the same time, on top of that view of a trusted adult being upended, not having other similarly close people within your family network is disastrous, Professor Hickie says.

A child who is abused faces a multitude of challenges. But a child who is abused and remains within the love and care of family within a network has more of a buffer against the worst consequences.

'And you see it with people who live through war, such as refugees who've fled really terrible places. If that trusted network remains intact, generally the kids do OK in life despite all sorts of stuff going on, and do OK in their relationships in life. It's with a lot of support, of course, but the outcomes aren't quite as catastrophic in a lot of cases.

'By contrast, if that fundamental set of relationships is broken down, or in the case of child sexual abuse, it is corrupted by behaviour within that network, this has enduring effects throughout life.'

Not only was Will sexually abused by a trusted figure within his family network, but except for his grandmother before she died, he had no one else to fall back on. His mother found out and did nothing, offering another significant betrayal. For years after, she refused to acknowledge her role in his pain, once more dealing a heavy blow to Will's sense of security and trust.

And then there was the heaviest blow of all in the discovery that his beloved uncle also knew and not only didn't do anything, but by all appearances forgave Will's abuser and took him back as his life companion.

Chapter Fifteen

Craig Hughes-Cashmore was sexually abused when he was a teenager by three men in his life who he should've been able to trust – a family friend who worked with his adoptive father, one of his teachers at high school, and an academic.

A podcast series called *Stronger*, produced by the organisation SAMSN – Survivors and Mates Support Network – features the story of his pursuit of criminal justice. It makes for extremely difficult listening and his experience, which is not dissimilar to many endured by surivors of child sexual abuse, paints a picture of why there are so few successful prosecutions of perpetrators.

'Ten years or so ago, I went to the police and reported my three perpetrators,' Craig recalls in the podcast. 'Two of those ended up in charges and ultimately, two cases, two trials. And my experience, through that experience of the legal system, was such that I walked away thinking there's a lot of room for improvement, to put it mildly.'

At the other end of the long and gruelling process, Craig was left feeling absolutely battered. It's still difficult to talk about now. The trauma of going to the police, of going to court, and of feeling utterly humiliated took years to come to terms with.

'As it turned out, my two trials were scheduled a month apart. The first trial was my first time in court, I had no knowledge of the legal system. I was terrified. I felt very alone, very isolated, very exposed, and vulnerable.

'All of those things mirror the experience and the dynamics of childhood sexual abuse, right? So it was really challenging, and I felt as though I didn't really have any support. I didn't feel like anyone had my back.'

In the podcast, he describes the cross-examination by the defence as being the most humiliating experience of his life. Craig sat there with the eyes of every single person in the room fixated on him. The twelve jurors, the judge, the court personnel, the lawyers ... all staring at him, trying to read whether he was telling the truth or making it all up.

Sordid details of his life were dragged out and paraded in front of those strangers and used to try to paint him as a liar, as a drug addict, as a sex worker. The difficulties he'd faced as a result of his horrific abuse, the things he fell into for comfort, as a crutch, as some kind of validation, or merely as a result of the pain he felt, were now being used against him for the benefit of one of the men who'd driven him to them.

'The jury never got to hear the context around my story because really, I fell victim to the tactics and strategies that defence lawyers use in cases like these every day. I didn't know what to expect, I didn't really know what my rights were. My lawyer didn't interject. It was a terrible experience.'

The jury found the man not guilty. It was a crushing blow for Craig. The deep shame he grappled with had been exploited as a legal tactic. He now feared having to go through the entire experience all over again in just a few weeks.

But rather than crumble, Craig decided to fight back. He decided that he would defend himself, in a sense, and represent himself. If no one else was going to, if there was zero support for victims like him, then he'd do it himself.

'I had to go to battle. And I got my hands on a book called *Surviving the Legal System*, which has been written by an amazing woman, Caroline Taylor. And in it she described those tactics and strategies that defence lawyers use. And I recognised instantly that that's what I had been through. And I was now a survivor of the legal system.'

The second case was fairly high profile. There were television crews camped outside the court each day. There had been a great deal of attention. As a result, it was a judge-only trial without a jury.

Craig went in with a fierce determination. He knew his rights – that he could ask for a break, that he could turn to the judge if the defence cut him off and ask that he be allowed to finish his answer. And he could have people in court to support him.

'I'd come to understand that it would be important for me to have people in there, not just personally, but also to show the court that there were people that loved and supported me and believed me. And so they were there. And that made a huge difference.

'And little things like just having my iPod with a playlist of music. That would help ground me during that whole process. So the result, personally, was incredibly different, but the outcome was [also] different.'

The perpetrator was found guilty.

The way the first trial played out was almost a textbook case of the very worst experiences of survivors who pursue justice. The lack of preparation for what to expect, the lack of information about what he was entitled to in the courtroom, the absence of support, the poor handling of the case ... all of it was deeply flawed.

Craig's situation was a little unique in that there was a second trial, and he was determined to take control of the situation and arm himself with as much knowledge as he could, so he could defend himself.

Not many survivors have that opportunity. Far too many face the same appalling experience in the justice system that Craig did the first time around.

'We really owe it to the survivors who choose to do that to improve the system, because I don't think it's okay to put people through a system that we know is going to be harrowing and traumatic when it doesn't necessarily need to be.

'That to me just seems incredibly dishonest and unfair. And I don't think most survivors, like me, have [any] understanding what it's really going to look like, what it's really going to be like.'

The burden shouldn't be on survivors to merely cope with the broken system. They shouldn't feel obligated to come forward and get paedophiles and abusers off the street. Those who come forward deserve better.

'Putting them through a system that routinely re-traumatises and actually adds to people's trauma is just plain unjust, and negligent, I would suggest.'

I caught up with Craig to hear about how he got to the point of wanting to go to the police after keeping secret for so long what had happened to him. And weirdly, it all essentially manifested itself on a train one bright Sydney morning.

At this stage of his life, in his mid-thirties, Craig was working as a talent agent in the entertainment industry, looking after actors, directors and screenwriters. His job was important and he was good at it. But he was also an alcoholic whose drinking was getting wildly out of control.

'I'd done the whole alcohol addiction thing quite well for a while and then at some point, I came across ice and decided I'd try it. And try it. And try it. That got me into a drug and alcohol clinic where I spoke to a counsellor, who referred me to a shrink, and I got clean and sober.'

At the start of his recovery, he was on the train to work in the middle of his usual ritual of reading the *Sydney Morning Herald* newspaper. On the front page was a story ahead of the sentencing of New South Wales Labor Minister Milton Orkopoulos, who had been convicted of sexually abusing three teenage boys.

One of his victims had chosen to identify himself. Ben Blackburn gave an interview to the newspaper to speak about how Orkopoulos targeted him and groomed him, showing interest in the boy's ambitions and offering him a job in his electorate office. He used that access to harass and assault the teenager.

'I started reading this story about Ben and I just started crying. I had my sunglasses on, thank God, because this grief just came up through my body in waves and I was sobbing. It was very much my story. There was so much in how he was treated, how all those boys were treated, that suddenly I went, "Oh fuck, I was abused". It hit me like a ton of bricks.'

He could suddenly see as plain as day that the things he endured as a teenager were abuse. He could see all of the impacts the abuse had on him throughout his adult life.

Craig got off the train and walked to his office. Once there, he couldn't go inside. He was absolutely distraught. The newspaper story had mentioned the support group Bravehearts, and so Craig looked up their number and called.

'This guy picked up the phone and I was blabbering down the line about what had happened to me. I just decided that

I would go to the police now. I'd never considered it before. I never forgot what happened to me – it's not that I was in denial, but I just did everything I could not to think about it for too long. But now, it was there – it was out there.'

He was put in touch with the sex crimes unit of New South Wales Police, who were in touch with their counterparts in South Australia. Within two weeks, Craig was sitting in front of a detective giving a statement over the course of three days.

After both of the trials, Craig decided to sue the perpetrator who'd been found guilty, as well as the Department of Education in South Australia. He was successful and suddenly, for the first time in his life, he had money.

'But I was conflicted. No one wants to think that you're doing it for the money. And of course I wasn't. But it felt dirty taking the money, so I thought, I'm going to use this for something good.'

Several months earlier, as he was navigating his way through the criminal justice system, a support worker put Craig in touch with a fellow survivor named Shane. He too had multiple perpetrators and was preparing for court. He was hesitant. What would they possibly talk about? He'd never really spoken to anyone about what happened to him, apart from the police and lawyers. But eventually, he decided to grab dinner with this guy.

'We couldn't have been more different. He's this straight guy who's madly into sports and has three kids. Chalk and cheese. But it was incredible. It was a huge relief for both of us. We're different and our stories are different, but it was like the similarities we shared in terms of our trauma and our emotional responses is what mattered.'

One of the big realisations to come from that meeting was how woeful they'd both found the level of support offered to men in the health system.

There were few, if any, avenues for male survivors to go down. What services did exist were predominantly geared towards women. Some were even explicit in their exclusion of men. It was 2010, and yet it still seemed that male survivors were doomed to live in silence – and worse, to be at risk of dying in silence.

'I'd had three suicide attempts that landed me in a mental health ward – twenty-one, thirty, and thirty-five. I had lived with suicidal ideation almost daily for twenty or so years. I knew what it was like to be in a dark place, and to think that there was nowhere for men like me to turn … it was mind-boggling.'

He spent hours researching every single service that existed. He was sure he and Shane had to have missed one or two. He got on the phone and rang every single organisation, government and non-government, in the state to see what was on offer. He was looking for a dedicated support group of some kind for men.

There was nothing. Not a single, solitary crumb of help or hope.

‘Shane and I were talking and we were like, someone should do something. That’s how the conversation started.’

The pair went to an all-day workshop devoted to dealing with trauma and met another bloke there who was a survivor. They roped him in to form their own support circle. Three became four and then four became five, and suddenly, the group was meeting every week in Shane’s kitchen. They eventually moved to a community hall in Erskineville, and through word of mouth, a few more survivors joined the catch-ups.

It was mostly just chatting, Shane recalls. But there was something so powerful about being heard for the very first time. There’s something freeing about not feeling judged, about sharing an understanding about something so unimaginable. About being believed.

More and more men came along. Craig met a psychologist who introduced him to a support worker at a sexual assault clinic, and the idea was struck to pay them to run a more formal and structured support group for survivors.

When the money from his lawsuit ran out, Craig sold chocolates, Shane ran charity poker nights, and together they scraped together enough money for the social worker’s time. The very first formal support group was held at the end of 2011.

‘That’s how we started,’ Craig says, speaking of the founding of SAMSN. It’s the only dedicated support network for male survivors of child sexual abuse.

‘We’ve run 83 eight-week support groups since then. We’ve got a waitlist of more than one hundred guys for those groups.’

The support groups are a vital source of healing for the men who attend them. Over eight weeks, they join with other survivors in a safe and welcoming environment, guided by specially trained experts, to unpack what happened to them and how it’s shaped their lives.

SAMSN does a hell of a lot more in the space. There’s crisis counselling, awareness, advocacy and government lobbying. Craig and the group played a major role in the Royal Commission into Institutional Responses To Child Abuse – a ground-breaking examination of more than 42,000 cases, which heard from survivors in more than 8000 private sessions, and made more than 2500 referrals to authorities, including the police.

Of the private sessions held with survivors by the Commission, two-thirds were the testimonies of men. Of all the people who came forward, one in ten were disclosing their abuse for the very first time.

‘Many survivors face a complex set of challenges throughout their lives,’ the Commission noted in its final report.

‘At various times, depending on the circumstances, victims and survivors seek support from a range of mainstream and specialist services to help manage the detrimental impacts of abuse on their mental health. They may also need support for legal, education, housing, health, employment and financial issues, and for assistance with reporting abuse.

'The services used by victims and survivors span several sectors and can be difficult to navigate. The need for support often extends to secondary victims, such as family members, carers and friends and others in the institution where the abuse occurred.'

The Commission found that the support services that do exist are in various ways lacking in their abilities to meet the needs of survivors who reach out to them for help. It found:

'Currently, service systems across Australia do not have the capacity to meet victims' and survivors' needs. Inadequacies are most apparent when a victim or survivor is experiencing multiple and complex impacts from the trauma of child sexual abuse, particularly for those deemed as not fitting within the remit of a single service. In many cases, one individual will be in multiple systems, moving in and out of services over many years.'

Information is difficult to find and services are often prohibitively expensive, the report noted. Survivors spoke of the multiple systemic and structural barriers they encountered in the pursuit of healing, from a lack of coordination and collaboration between services, chronic under-resourcing, and an inconsistent standard of service across different jurisdictions.

The type of support someone might get in Sydney is vastly different to what a survivor can expect in Melbourne or Brisbane, for example, and those in regional or rural areas are likely to find very limited options.

The Commission also noted that there are particular gaps in service offerings for men – mirroring what Craig found when he initially set out to find help.

'Inadequate service responses can re-traumatise survivors of child sexual abuse,' the report noted.

'Poor therapeutic treatment can leave a victim with chronic symptoms that follow them into adulthood. Ineffective treatment may cause victims to lose hope and disengage from treatment altogether.'

The comprehensive report, tens of thousands of pages long, included a staggering 409 recommendations in total, 189 of which were new. Some of the reforms have been adopted with gusto by state and territory and federal authorities. Many are still awaiting meaningful action.

One of the major recommendations was for the removal of stringent limitation periods of pursuing civil litigation. Previously, a victim of child sexual abuse had three years after turning eighteen to bring forward an action. After that, their chances of successful compensation were slim.

The Royal Commission sparked a firestorm in the legal world, and major firms have taken abuse out of their broader personal injury practices and established dedicated teams to help service the flood of victims.

Slater and Gordon Lawyers is one such firm. Their abuse practice is headed by Jacqui Eager, who has worked in the personal injury space for more than fifteen years.

'Now, most of the states and territories have finalised the removal of limitation for sexual abuse, and the legislation was also amended so that we can, on behalf of our clients, apply to have previous deeds set aside,' Eager says. 'So, if they've settled their claim commercially in the past and settled commercially because of existing limitations or whatnot, and it's an unfair result, we can now apply that to be set aside.'

Across the firm's three offices in New South Wales, Victoria, and Queensland is now a team of thirty lawyers working exclusively on abuse cases. There's more work than they can handle, with hundreds of potential clients waiting to be assessed.

'We can't find enough skilled lawyers,' Eager says. 'We have more clients than we can get to – we could act for so many more than we are at the moment. We're trying to get to them but dealing with the volume is challenging.

'We have clients in the thousands. There are so many stories. No wonder the mental health system is in crisis. We have thousands, but we're one firm. Imagine how many claims the other top firms might have. These aren't numbers – they're individuals. We're dealing with a crisis. Are these people being adequately supported and cared for in the mental health system? I highly doubt it.'

The majority of their clients are men. They come from all walks of life and their stories of abuse vary, from horrific experiences in institutionalised settings to perpetrators who were in trusted roles, such as teachers.

Female survivors who come to Slater and Gordon have usually disclosed to someone in the past, but Eager says she was struck by how many men she meets who have never told anyone before.

'A lot of our women have had some type of treatment, they've had some sort of support structure, whereas a lot of the men we see, we're the first people they will ever tell. They will reach out and disclose to a lawyer for the first time. I think that comes from a place of shame.'

One of the first conversations she'll have with a new client is to set the expectations of what's going to result from a civil action. Or rather, what the process is *not* going to give them. A criminal process will often deliver a form of vindication – justice, or someone being held accountable in the eyes of the law.

'One thing I'm very clear on with clients is that this is not going to give them that. Civil doesn't give them that because ultimately, who pays the compensation is not the perpetrator. Very rarely, anyway.'

Interestingly, assigning blame is often a deeply personal and very individual process. If a survivor's perpetrator is a priest, they might also hold blame for the church. Likewise, if it's a teacher, the school or the broader education system might be seen as being complicit.

The failure to protect a child in the first instance, and often to take care of them afterwards, can in many cases go beyond the individual abuser.

'It's the people that fail to look after them in the scenario they experienced,' Eager explains.

'So what the civil process does is it gives an acknowledgement from those bodies that something horrible happened, and that they've got to pay compensation.'

Part of the process fostered by Slater and Gordon is that the survivor will often receive a verbal or written apology from someone on behalf of the defendant. That element is extremely powerful, in her experience.

'The ones I've sat in have been absolute tear-jerkers. It's a hugely moving moment. Often, that means more to the client than the compensation itself. They've finally been heard, they've finally been believed. It's a big moment.'

Ciara White is a lawyer who works in Slater and Gordon's abuse practice and has handled a number of cases involving predominantly men.

'I think in this modern age, it's a lot more common for women to be able to move forward and share their story, and to identify themselves as survivors in this space,' White says.

'But I don't think that space has been carved out for men,

and I'm finding that the men who do come forward – it's taken them a very, very long time to feel safe to share their stories. The time it takes for them to get to a point where they feel open to talking about it can be a very long time.'

As someone working day in, day out with survivors, helping them navigate the process, helping them to get to the point they want to reach, and often *need* to reach, White has come to be in awe of the apology element.

Being able to face those who symbolise responsibility for what happened to them in some way, big or small, and to be told that someone is sorry, that someone knows the things they endured were hurtful and harmful and wrong, is hugely important, she says.

'One thing I like to do in my mediation, my informal settlement conferences, is to make sure that the [defendant's] representatives and their lawyers are sitting in the room with the client, because I want them to see my client.

'I had one recently. He's a man who was basically tortured for fifty-five days straight in a government institution. Just absolutely horrific. He came in and sat there, and he's a big man, and the apology was read to him. He just fell apart. Nobody on the other side of the table could make eye contact. But it was the very first time that there had been some acknowledgement.

'It was an acknowledgement that he should've been cared for. That someone should've cared for him. It was confirmation that they had done something wrong and they knew it.'

*

Clients are also now being offered the opportunity to make a statement to the defendant or their representatives. It gives survivors who have been largely voiceless, sometimes for most of their lives, the chance to speak.

White sees it as a way for her clients to take back some of the power that was robbed from them when they were children. It's their chance to regain control of the narrative, to claw back some of their agency.

'I tell the clients that we're their narrator. This is their story. We're here to help them write it. It's their chance to take back their voice and to say their piece and have people really listen.'

An experience in 2021 that has stuck with Eager involved the settlement of an action for forty-two claimants, all First Nations people, who had been abused in a mission in the Northern Territory, where many had been forcibly relocated as members of the Stolen Generation. The apology that was organised was a public one. There was a representative from the Commonwealth and from three church institutions.

'They showed up and apologised in front of a crowd of survivors and their family members. There were about one hundred people to hear this apology. It was one of the most powerful things I've ever participated in over the course of my career. There wasn't a dry eye there. It was taking back power, it was about people taking accountability. Three survivors stood up and told their stories, in front of the representatives of the plaintiffs and in front of their community.'

When a survivor comes to White, her job in bringing a claim is to assess what's called 'heads of damages'. Put simply, these are different categories of damages or loss suffered by the claimant.

The first is pain and suffering, or non-economic damage. To measure this in an abuse context, a psychiatrist assesses a client to determine what their whole-of-person impairment is, or to what extent the abuse they were subjected to has caused damages.

'There's usually a psychiatric injury, like PTSD, or some mix of cluster B personality traits. There's a plethora of them. In my experience, it's typically a 40 per cent whole-of-person impairment, so it's a significant impact on many aspects of their lives.'

Personality disorders are a group of mental health conditions, in which inflexible and atypical emotional and behavioural patterns cause the sufferer distress. People who experience cluster B traits have trouble with impulse control and emotional regulation, appearing erratic or histrionic, and tend to be characterised by unpredictable thinking or behaviour that's disproportionately emotional, irrational or dramatic.

'Most of these people don't have stable relationships with family, friends, or intimate partners. They've isolated themselves.

They struggle to maintain meaningful relationships and they might be estranged from children.

'Many of them just want to block out the pain altogether, so you're dealing with substance abuse issues as well. They might've had violent outbursts. They are likely to have done anything that they can do to not feel what they're feeling. So it just goes through all their lives. A lot of them live like hermits. Many that I've worked with have had periods of incarceration.'

Then there's the economic loss incurred by survivors. Some may struggle to hold down a job. Many will try to study at university or try to learn a trade, but struggle with the stressful environment or the fear of failure. Some may self-sabotage. Many will find it hard to hold down employment.

'We deal with people that have been so broken so very early on in their lives, and they generally don't function well in society.'

Some clients are men who were sexually abused while they were in state care, such as juvenile detention or foster care. The disadvantage they were already dealing with was compounded significantly by the abuse they were subjected to, setting them up for a significantly poorer outcome.

Many of those survivors have brushes with the law and some can spend much of their adult life in and out of prison settings. In other cases, the survivors could be from more secure childhood environments – well-off parents who sent them to top schools.

'But what's common is they've all got recurring mental health issues that interfere with their ability to live a normal life, have a normal relationship, to have regulated emotional responses to stressors, to gain and maintain employment,' Eager says.

'A lot of the men who were abused as boys by men will second-guess whether they're heterosexual or homosexual, going through really difficult cycles of shame and loss of identity. There are heavy impacts in all facets of their lives.'

The work that's done at Slater and Gordon can sometimes extend beyond the purely legal. There have been clients who have spent a great deal of time in prison and don't know how to use a computer or have never laid their hands on a mobile phone, and so need additional support to be able to play a role in their own case. There are some who have insecure housing and need to be linked with community organisations.

Even with that extraordinary level of care, there's no denying that the entire process can be gruelling for survivors who take it on.

When White begins working with a client, the type of timeframe they're looking at depends entirely on the defendant. If the defendant is open and engaged, and willing to sit down and hear the survivor's story and the kind of damages they've incurred throughout their lives, the process could be about six months from start to finish.

If the defendant is obstructive or resistant, it can take anywhere between twelve months to twenty-four months. And even in the post-Royal Commission era, amid community outcry and bad press, certain organisations – even government authorities – are usually resistant.

'When you look at litigation as a lawyer, you want to try and run your file as soon as the evidence is fresh. So traditionally, in a litigation space, you've got three years from the date of injury to bring your claim and the reason for that is the evidence is fresh in everybody's mind, no one is prejudiced.

'The advantage for [a defendant] in this space is that they can drag their heels. A survivor has waited years, sometimes twenty years or more, to get in front of them. What's the rush? The evidence is only going to get harder for a client to corroborate. Also, they're dealing with someone who has serious psychological injuries and they might not have the staying power. They know that. So, the longer it's been, great, and the sicker someone is, perfect – they'll take whatever money they're offered, they figure.'

For survivors who want to explore some kind of legal justice, the criminal route is fraught with dangers, as Craig discovered. His experience in the first court case isn't uncommon. The successful prosecution in the second instance is.

Landmark research into the criminal justice system response to child sexual abuse reports to police in New

South Wales over a fourteen-year period makes for sobering reading.

It's obviously difficult to know what proportion of child sexual abuse instances are reported to the police. Those who work in the field fear that the vast majority aren't disclosed to authorities. But what is known is how many of those complaints result in a successful prosecution.

And it's not many.

In their report 'Fourteen-Year Trends in the Criminal Justice Response to Child Sexual Abuse Reports in New South Wales', published in 2019, University of Sydney researchers Judith Cashmore, Alan Taylor and Patrick Parkinson examined the outcomes of the 63,008 reports to police between 2003 and 2016.

Of those, legal action commenced for one fifth. That is, just 21 per cent of reports went beyond the investigation phase. All charges were dismissed in about a quarter of those cases across local courts, the children's court and higher courts. Overall, a conviction was successful in just 12 per cent of cases.

Those numbers are consistent with past analysis of the criminal justice system's response to child sexual abuse reports in other jurisdictions and over varying lengths of time.

'Research over several decades in Australia, Canada, England and Wales, Scotland, and the United States indicates that when complaints of child sexual abuse are reported to the police, only a small proportion result in prosecution and conviction, with a substantial drop-off at each stage of the criminal justice process,' the report notes.

The researchers delivered their finding with the important caveat that not all reports will involve criminal offences that should result in charges and be prosecuted. Some are the result of mandatory reporting frameworks. Some may involve offenders under the age of eighteen where the criminality is more of a grey area.

'The system clearly fails, however, when poor interviewing and investigation by police fail to elicit relevant evidence and leave that child and others at risk,' the report states.

'It also fails when stressful prosecution and court processes intimidate complainants, making children and families unwilling to be involved, and making it difficult or impossible for the victims of child sexual abuse – as child witnesses or as adults in delayed reporting matters – to provide reliable evidence. It is not clear, however, exactly how police and prosecutors decide which cases should proceed – and to what extent the cases that do not reach the courts are matters that would and should have resulted in an appropriate plea or conviction. Those are the attrition "failures".'

Associate Professor Salter, whom I mentioned earlier – the academic from the University of New South Wales who has studied child sexual abuse and the response to it by the justice system – offered his thoughts in the wake of the Royal Commission. Of its many important findings, the recommendations relating to the critically important role of police were of particular interest.

In an article for *The Conversation* published in 2017 he noted that as gatekeepers of the criminal justice system, police have the power to obstruct child sexual abuse survivors from pursuing complaints against their perpetrators.

It's direct and indirect. It's malicious and it's not. It's a cultural matter and merely a case of deeply ingrained ignorance. Whatever the cause of these barriers, the ones to truly suffer are survivors who, yet again, have encountered someone who seemingly doesn't believe them, doesn't take their story seriously, or doesn't care.

'Submissions to the Commission suggested there has been a general reluctance within police to investigate historical complaints of child sexual abuse,' Salter writes.

'Survivors described police discouraging them from making a formal statement, telling them it was unlikely their allegations could be proven in court. Survivors flagged issues with policing culture, and described situations in which police told survivors they were culpable for their abuse and should "get over it". Survivors felt that some abuse complaints were not investigated due to disbelief, while others were only investigated after sustained pressure and repeated inquiries from survivors.'

While there have been improvements in policing over recent times, especially in the past decade or so as awareness of the issue has grown and demands for better outcomes have become louder, there is still a lot of room for improvement.

The Commission recommended that forces work to devise standards that clearly outline what survivors, no matter how old they are or when the abuse occurred, should expect when they are dealing with police. Those standards should be built on a foundation of respect and consideration.

Aside from Craig, all of the men I've spoken to have had largely unsuccessful experiences with authorities, either police or the courts. Some were fobbed off in the very first instance when they went to police.

In Will's case, he was essentially laughed out of a police station when he summoned the courage to speak to authorities about what happened to him.

In Jason's case, officers discouraged his father from making a formal complaint, apparently out of concern for the arduous legal process that would follow.

For Luke, while there were positives in his experience – in being able to say his piece and to face his perpetrator – the man walked free.

And so, for those who are successful in a civil law sense, it might be a case of 'better than nothing'. They can come to terms with the deep flaws in the criminal justice system and the pain they've endured by being let down yet again by the very people tasked with protecting them.

*

But what about broader society? Are we collectively content that the system should remain broken?

If not for the survivors who deserve justice, and for the moral imperative of someone doing something horribly wrong being punished for it … then what about just the basic protection of other vulnerable children?

A perpetrator not put behind bars is a perpetrator walking around freely in the community. Maybe they won't offend again. Maybe they will. Is that really a situation we're willing to accept?

Chapter Sixteen

Will and I get into a long and detailed conversation about how good things never last while talking about an old, run-down funeral parlour.

As he so often does, he's regaling me with an equal-parts hilarious and tragic tale from his adolescence. It's the kind of story that has me cringing so much that I'll need to see a physiotherapist in two or three days' time.

'After Nan died, Mum went into a deep depressive spiral and stopped leaving the house entirely. She would just drink all night, sleep all day, and repeat the process. The bits and pieces of work she had been able to do stopped entirely. There was no money coming in.'

She was at risk of losing the family home – the one that generations had lived in, which had never been owned by anyone else. But the bank came knocking and there were few options.

Desperate, his mum struck a deal with a cousin that they would buy the house and let her and Will keep living there.

They'd pay rent, but a fairly nominal amount. But even that was too much and eventually, they were kicked to the curb.

'We'd lost the family home that I'd grown up in, my mother grew up in, her mother grew up in … it was the second-oldest house in the neighbourhood. It was a hundred and something years old when I lived there.

'It messed me up pretty bad. There weren't exactly only good memories in that place, but it was home. You know?'

It startled her and sobered her up just enough that she realised the gravity of the situation. They couldn't just be homeless. They couldn't sleep in the car. So, she found a job that came with discounted accommodation: a tiny two-bedroom cottage at the rear of a funeral parlour in western Sydney.

'It used to be a brothel before it was a funeral home, just to make the story even more fucked up,' Will laughs.

He's in his final year of high school when they move in. For three years, he's been trying to take care of his mum the best he can, while dealing with the mounting turmoil inside of him about what Franco had been doing to him. Even though it's been a little while since he was able to get at him, the nightmares come almost every night.

He's exhausted. He's totally dropped the ball at school. And now, to add to the pressure, he's got to drive an hour or so every morning to school back near their old house, then an hour or so back in the afternoon.

Plus, he lives in a shitty old house at the back of a funeral parlour. In the middle of the night he can hear the screeching of the roller door on the garage across from his bedroom window. He lays there and listens as the hearse roars to life and then rumbles down the long driveway, off somewhere to retrieve a dead body and bring it back to the morgue freezer.

'I'm seventeen, I'm going through changes that other kids are, the emotional rollercoaster kind of stuff, plus I'm a bit fucked about what's been happening to me. Then I wind up living in a funeral parlour. Friends didn't really want to come over to hang out that much.'

His mental health declines and Will withdraws from life almost entirely. He makes a friend who isn't the kind of kid who's good to hang around with when you're in the depths of your despair. Pretty soon, Will is sneaking out most nights to meet him and go drinking. They'll head to some random person's place and get on the piss. Or they'll go anywhere really. Parks, underpasses, railway tracks, bus stops … whatever.

The guy smokes a lot of meth. He's always offering it to Will. The chemical smell makes his stomach turn though and so he says no every time. Thank God.

'He's dodgy as fuck,' Will recalls. 'I remember one night he wanted me to come with him to rob this house. Another time, he comes over to my house and my mum is sleeping in the next room, and he pulls out a gun. I freak out. That's probably the point where I realise we shouldn't be friends anymore.'

His mum starts drinking again. It's kind of a given – Will was waiting for her to slump back into the darkness again. She hasn't been showing up to work, even though it's fifteen steps away from their front door, and so they're about to get kicked out again.

'Mum's cousin sells the house around this time, so she gets a little bit of money from it. We decide that she's not going to waste it – she's going to use it to set herself up somewhere for a fresh start.

'I help her find a place she likes down in regional Victoria. My uncle and Franco are back down in Melbourne at this stage and so they help her get settled. It was a nice old weatherboard place, like our house, and there's lots of space.'

Will stays with her for a bit, then moves back to Sydney and crashes on a friend's couch for a little while, before finding a sharehouse. Then back to his mum's, then back to Sydney again.

'It was a very disjointed and unstable part of my life for a couple of years, and it came at just the worst possible time.'

There's a precariousness that infects life when your foundations are as wobbly as they tend to be when you've experienced trauma.

Will still feels it. He's clawed his way out of misery and managed to head off an outcome that many others who've experienced his kind of extensive trauma might face. He's fallen in love, started a family, started to build a good career, bought a house, and found for himself a lot of the stability and certainty that he never had as a child.

And yet, he can't quite ever allow himself to enjoy his life – a life achieved against all odds.

The good times feel like they won't last. He's suspicious of them, in fact. Something really wonderful bursts into his life and his first reaction tends to be: Who sent you and why?

That's how I am too. I'm always waiting for the other shoe to drop.

Conversely, when the bad times arrive, it can feel like they're going to last forever. In the midst of it, he can't remember a moment in his life when things weren't this awful. It's insufferable. The pain sucks all of the oxygen out of his lungs and leaves him gasping, heart racing, legs shaking.

Being constantly engaged in fight or flight mode is exhausting. The engine never stops running at full speed. As it turns out, that's quite damaging.

Significant trauma doesn't just impact someone's mental health, but it can physiologically change them also.

There are the psychological outcomes you might expect to see: anxiety, depression, distress, self-harm, suicidal ideation or behaviour.

'We also see abnormal risk-taking behaviour,' Professor Hickie explains.

'We can also see people leaving themselves open to further physical abuse, to further sexual abuse. There is other extreme risk-taking via drugs and alcohol and other things. Degrees of that declare themselves in different ways.'

But the other consequence of trauma that isn't often considered is the physiological impact. It's clouded by the dominant focus on the behavioural and emotional implications of abuse's enduring trauma. But there can be just as significant an effect on someone's physical health.

'And it must be emphasised and recognised in the treatment of trauma that there's often a physiology of abnormal arousals affecting the physical aspects of health and its representation. I think we've become very psychologically minded, which is great, but that other bit, that there's a whole-body disturbance, has gotten a bit lost along the way.'

The focus can often be entirely on the psychological impacts and how to address them. Many health professionals look at the behavioural outcomes of the trauma, not recognising that people are quite physically sick too – or at risk of becoming so.

I've read bits and pieces about this on my journey so far, but I have to admit that I considered it a pretty abstract notion. Some sort of New Age hypothesis that's interesting but not really my thing, so I skirted over it.

It's not new at all. It was a pretty well-established theory back in the pre-Freud era of psychology. But then Sigmund came along and turned the whole game on its head, and the link between physical and mental health was kind of discarded for a long time.

But the science now is clear and unequivocal. The clinical profession is taking a little bit of time to catch up in its whole-of-body thinking, Professor Hickie says.

'We have stress arousal systems – we're wired to run away from fear, or to cope with it if we can, but not to be aroused all the time. You know, you should be protected. You should be comforted. You should be aroused and do those particular things which have a whole lot of hormonal, immunological and physiological effects. But it should only be for short periods of time. Not for long periods of time.'

Living life in a constant state of prolonged stress – feeling as though you're at threat and being consumed by the distress of that all or most of the time – is dangerous for the body, not just the mind.

There can be a range of physiological impacts as a result of the nervous system running at full steam for extended periods of time.

'It might be a super-sensitivity to arousal or to stress. There are impacts on the hypothalamic–pituitary–adrenal axis, which drives cortisol, the adrenaline response through the sympathetic nervous system, or impacts on the body's immune response, which is responding to all sorts of infections.

'There could be metabolic responses in a particular way.

Some of these most fundamental are our so-called homeostatic mechanisms, or things that allow us to respond to the external world.

'Think of it as your arousal level – which is, your body's response to things – being set at a permanently high level. Now when that happens, the body's systems can wear themselves out. You're constantly running at such a high capacity that the system is exhausted. That can lead to premature ageing. It puts you at risk of other chronic diseases. And it likely will lead to a chronic over-response to minor stuff.

'You want a system that has a low setpoint and a high capacity to react, and then turns itself off again to recover. Any body systems won't cope well with having a high setpoint because it then can't react and will also tend to exhaust itself and wear out.

'There tend to be bad health consequences of chronic, prolonged stress. It's very bad for your health.'

Holy shit. That's me down to the ground. The inability to respond in a reasonable manner to pretty minor stressors – ones that a normal person would be better equipped to take on or brush off without a total meltdown.

I have shoddy blood pressure. I'm prone to exhaustion. My teeth are fucked from constant grinding. I have an endless stream of gut issues that come and go without rhyme or reason. I have horrendous nightmares.

Are these isolated issues that have nothing to do with each other or with the trauma I've carried with me for thirty-odd years? Or are they the result of it? It's hard to say.

Trauma is a complex beast that has a close relationship with mental illness. For all of the advances healthcare systems have made in acknowledging and treating psychiatric issues, appropriately tackling trauma is still a work in progress.

'The whole dialogue I think in neuroscience is changing the way we consider how those systems react to the environment, when they have been perverted during their development. There's a lot of work still to do though,' Professor Hickie says.

Trauma-informed mental health treatment is very much an emerging focus. A system that provides a coordinated and integrated approach for those suffering trauma will deliver better outcomes. It will also avoid people being re-traumatised by a shonky system.

The state of Australia's mental health system is, to put it bluntly, absolutely shit. It's no well-kept secret – countless inquiries and reviews have come to the same conclusion, albeit using more polished language.

The Royal Commission into Victoria's Mental Health System in 2021 is the most recent, and while it's state-specific, the observations and the identified flaws are hardly unique.

'Despite the goodwill and hard work of many people, Victoria's mental health system has deteriorated for a multitude of reasons and over the course of many years,' the Commission's summary states.

It found that the system had 'catastrophically failed to live up to expectations and was underprepared for current and future challenges' facing Victorians, and that good mental health and wellbeing had for too long been a low priority for governments at all levels.

Those failings mean the system is forced to operate at a crisis level all of the time. There's no room for intervention and prevention, but merely for reactionary measures that at best keep people's heads just enough above the water, and at worst, leaves them to drown.

The Commission's report states: 'The system is overwhelmed and cannot keep up with the number of people who seek treatment, care and support. This is evident at all levels, from individual mental health professionals to acute and emergency services.'

Too many people are unable to access treatment, care, and support. There's either no capacity for patient needs or the services aren't close to their homes or in their communities.

And so, while awareness days and fundraisers and celebrity ambassadors and campaigning politicians tell us all to 'reach out' when we need help, a lot of the time, there's no one to reach out to. This is especially the case for those with complex needs, the Commission notes in its report.

‘A large and growing group of people have needs that are too ‘complex’, too ‘severe’ and/or too ‘enduring’ to be supported through primary care alone, but not ‘severe’ enough to meet the strict criteria for entry into specialist mental health services. As a result, people receive inadequate treatment, care and support, or none at all.’

And among the Commission’s many recommendations was a focus on trauma. In its recommendation for a new approach to mental health and wellbeing, one that offers different types of treatment, it singled out trauma as a key area requiring specialist care.

‘A statewide trauma centre will help in delivering the best possible mental health outcomes for people who have experienced trauma,’ the report notes.

Recommendations are all well and good, but they’re not worth the paper they’re printed on if governments don’t act on them.

Right now in this country, if you’re struggling with your mental health and want to get support, you best be prepared to wait for months. In early 2022, estimates were that one in three psychologists had closed books due to unprecedented demand. It’s a perfect storm of factors – the significant impact of Covid-19 on mental health and wellbeing, an exacerbation of symptoms in people who were already mentally unwell, existing structural issues in the healthcare system that were put under intense strain, and burnout in the medical and healing professions, to name a few.

For those seeking help from a mental health professional, they're likely to have struggled to find any. Psychologists were forced to close their books. That is, no waiting list, no room for new appointments – absolutely no room at the inn.

If you can get an appointment to see someone, you're likely to pay a couple of hundred bucks per session. At least three to four hundred bucks if it's a psychiatrist. A mental healthcare plan from your doctor will cover some of the psychologist's bill by subsidising a certain number of visits, and the odd clinician here and there might bulk bill.

But by and large, to engage in meaningful treatment over an extended period of time with a suitable professional who understands your needs and issues, and with whom you gel enough to feel safe and comfortable to speak openly with, requires a lot of time and a lot of money.

What happens if you're really struggling? What happens if you're battling complex issues like trauma or a personality disorder? What happens if you're in a dark place?

Sure, you can head to an emergency room, but they're likely to patch you up, make sure you're OK, and then send you home to keep waiting. And they're so overrun, used as an entry point to the health system for a variety of conditions these days, that expecting people to turn to a hospital for an illness is unsustainable and unfair for all involved.

For people who are in dire distress, crisis assessment and treatment teams are based at major hospitals. They can and should be utilised by those in need. But these services weren't meant to be relied upon by people who are well enough to access support in the community, like a psychologist, but who have nowhere to go due to chronic shortages.

How, in one of the wealthiest countries in the world, with a healthcare system we're told is first-class and totally sufficient for our needs, are people who need urgent help expected to simply … wait? And then pay a small fortune for it?

For anyone struggling, not being able to find help when you need it is an atrocious position to be in. But for those with acute and specialist needs, like many of the men I've met – and like me at certain points in the past – it can feel like it's just you against the world.

Chapter Seventeen

The American not-for-profit Defend Innocence, which exists with the mission of eradicating child sexual abuse, calls it 'child-on-child sexual abuse'.

They say that in the US, one-third of all instances of child sexual abuse falls into this category, where the person carrying out the behaviour and the one on the receiving end are under the age of eighteen.

'While the trauma for the victim is the same as if it had been perpetrated by an adult, this type of abuse often goes unreported – either because it's dismissed by adults as "kids being kids" or for the fear of what will happen to one or both of the children to have the abuse known,' they say.

'The truth is that both children need help in a situation like this. The child being abused certainly needs the appropriate care to avoid the weight of lifelong trauma that so many survivors of child sexual abuse experience, as well as the symptoms that go with it.

'The child who has engaged in the harmful sexual behaviour needs help as well. If they are able to see a licensed medical/

mental health professional to help them work through these age-inappropriate sexual behaviours, then they are less likely to engage in harmful sexual behaviour again.'

Age-inappropriate sexual behaviours. It's a term that kind of speaks for itself ... but is it clear cut what an appropriate behaviour might be?

Not necessarily, another not-for-profit called Stop It Now! believes. An uncomfortable truth is that children are sexual beings, pretty much from birth, and like other areas of development, it's normal for kids to be curious, to feel things, sometimes intensely, and to have a changing awareness about themselves.

'Each child is an individual and will develop in his or her own way,' they say in their resource on on preventing sexual abuse among children and youth.

'However, there is a generally accepted range of behaviours linked to children's changing age and developmental stages. These behaviours may include exploration with other children of similar power or stature – by virtue of age, size, ability or social status.

'Sometimes, it can be difficult to tell the difference between sexual exploration that is appropriate to a developmental stage and interactions that are warning signs of harmful behaviour.'

Stop It Now! breaks down various age groups and defines what might be appropriate or expected developmental behaviour.

In the preschool age, between birth and five years old, which I was right on the cusp of outgrowing when Joshua began molesting me, talking about private body parts is common. So too are occasions of self-stimulation. What's uncommon is the discussion of specific sexual or intimate acts, as well as any adult-like intentional sexual contact with other children.

That remains uncommon, and is a warning sign of harmful sexual behaviour in the next age bracket, between the ages of six and twelve. But more common then is experimentation with same-age children, like kissing or touching and role-playing.

'Sexually harmful behaviour by children and young people may range from experimentation that has gone too far to serious sexual assault,' Stop It Now! says.

'It is important for adults to recognise that many children will engage in some forms of sexual exploration with children of a similar age, size, social status or power. Sometimes a child or young person may engage in sexual play with a much younger or more vulnerable child, or use force, tricks or bribery to involve someone in sexual activity.

'While such manipulation may be a cause for concern, it is critical to realise that manipulation may not, in itself, indicate a tendency toward sexual aggression. Professional help and advice is needed to determine the best way to support a child in managing any concerning impulses.'

In many instances, neither of the children understands that the behaviour they're engaging in is harmful. The one being harmed is likely feeling uncomfortable or confused, but may believe that he or she is a willing participant, and therefore to blame for being in the situation.

It's refreshing to find such a frank overview of what's a really taboo topic, even in child abuse prevention circles. Still, it seems difficult to know when to worry and when not to. And what if you miss the signs of behaviour that's potentially harmful?

Our parents didn't know that anything untoward was going on. My mum says she wishes she had known, because she would've throttled Joshua. But at his age, in that bracket, is he deserving of punishment?

There's a section in Queensland's Child Safety Protection Manual about when a child is sexually abused by another child. I come across it while scouring the internet for information and insight about what Joshua and I did.

'If it is determined that one child or young person in the dynamic used coercion, or if the dynamic is inequitable due to a significant age gap or developmental difference (i.e. if one child has an intellectual impairment), this provides a strong indicator that the behaviour was sexually abusive,' the manual reads.

An age gap of two years or more between peers 'found engaging in sexual behaviour' would indicate inequality in power dynamics, it continues. So too could acts of coercion or aggression.

'The reasons children sexually harm others are complicated, varied and not always obvious,' Stop It Now! says.

'Some of them may have been emotionally, sexually or physically abused themselves, while others may have witnessed physical or emotional violence at home.

'Some may have come in contact with sexually explicit movies, video games, or materials that are confusing to them. In some instances, a child or adolescent may act on a passing impulse with no harmful intent, but may still cause harm to themselves or to other children.'

I think back on what Joshua did – or rather, how he did it – and I can't escape the feeling that he knew what he was doing. From the very first time. It wasn't a kind of fumbling around to satisfy a curiosity. It wasn't pushing a button to see what it did, so to speak. He knew that this plus this equals this.

Where did that knowledge come from? And was Joshua himself abused by another kid or an adult …?

It's nearing the end of 2021 and there's a tenuous excitement in the air. After almost two years of strict restrictions on movement, socialising, hospitality, and travel brought on by the coronavirus pandemic, things look to be improving.

Hard borders between the states are opening up. Pubs, restaurants and cafes throw open their doors. Authorities declare an end to the era of rolling lockdowns of cities when there's an outbreak.

I'm preparing for Christmas – my first as a father. Robert and I welcomed our baby in April just gone, in what turned out to be a whirlwind of joy and uncertainty.

She was born via a surrogate in the United States, which meant we had to travel in the midst of a global pandemic when airlines were unreliable, clearing customs was a nightmare, being in a hospital setting was challenging, and getting home again required jumping through many hoops.

We spend three months there in the end, finalising legal requirements, organising citizenship, and coordinating our return to Australia.

It's a pretty wonderful period. Stressful, yes, but also quite special to be in a once-in-a-lifetime bubble, just the three of us.

Suddenly, we're home and the months are disappearing. The cool air is replaced by an oppressive humidity. Beautifully decorated trees go up in shopping centres. Flashing lights are draped on front fences. Mariah Carey's 'All I Want For Christmas is You' is played ad nauseum on the radio.

Given how hard it's been to see loved ones recently, with limits on just about everything, from how far you can move from your house to how many people you can see, and where and when, everyone seems eager to get out and about.

It feels nice. Everyone is enlivened. It's almost like Christmas when you're a kid and time seems to stand still, making that anticipation even more suffocating.

And yet, I catch my mind wandering repeatedly. While I'm giving the baby a bottle in the morning. During meetings at work. While finding more stocking stuffers. As I wrap presents and carefully pile them beneath the tree … I'm thinking about Joshua.

I guess this was inevitable. I've spent a while now reading, exploring, reflecting and talking about what he did to me – what we did – and I've exhausted almost all of the potential avenues for answers and understanding.

There's just one left. Him.

The last I heard from him was seven or eight years back. I was on television, on the news as a kind of expert commentator, when he saw me and looked me up on Facebook. He sent a message saying how proud he was, how well I looked, that kind of thing. I replied without malice or upset.

That was my 'before', when I didn't allow myself to think too much about him or us. Not in a deep way.

I type in his name now in the search bar on Facebook. We're friends. I'm shocked. I spend a fair bit of time there each day, looking at photos, commenting on statuses, pouring through listings in 'buy, swap, sell' pages, catching up on gossip in neighbourhood groups, and uploading photos of the baby. I've never come across anything from him before.

I must've added him as a friend way back when he messaged me, I guess. Maybe he added me? I have no recollection of it.

I'm kind of taken aback. His profile picture shows him behind the wheel of a ute. He wears a dusty red cap and has aviator sunglasses on. I can't get a good sense of what he looks like. I click through his other pictures.

There aren't many. One of him on a small boat with half a dozen other men, smiling while holding a fishing rod. Another of him with his arm around an old, sweet-faced Labrador. As I click through them, I eventually reach one where his face fills the entire frame. If he wasn't smiling and wearing a crisp white polo shirt, it might look like a mug shot. It's taken dead front-on, like a passport photo or a work identification picture.

His hair is still as jet-black as it was when we were kids, but it's thinning now. His hairline has receded a little. His cheeks are puffy and his neck sags. There are fine smile lines around his eyes, which twinkle with happiness like the person behind the camera has made a joke. His lips are thinner than I remember.

But it's Joshua. A wave of memories flood back. We're young again and climbing the gum tree in my backyard, scraping knees and elbows as we slip and trip. There's us tiptoeing through the backdoor of his house late at night during a sleepover to throw pebbles onto the roof of his neighbour's house. We're in his kitchen with a huge mixing bowl, pouring in a coddled concoction of flour, honey, tomato sauce and turmeric, which Joshua insists is the recipe for Gummi Berry Juice, which inevitably I'll be pressured into drinking.

And then we're on his bed, his arm around me, his finger tracing shapes down my back, his face a few centimetres from mine.

I feel myself want to vomit. Bile rushes up from my stomach and burns my oesophagus, building in the back of my throat. I slam shut the lid of my laptop so suddenly that the noise makes my sleeping dog jump.

That will be the end of that, I figure. Maybe I don't need to know whatever he might tell me. But the more I try not to think about him, the longer he occupies my thoughts.

How did he learn to do those things? Surely a child doesn't just come up with it. And the way he did it felt so … deliberate. As though he was repeating the instructions of someone else. So, was he abused? By who?

Did he ever do to anyone else, any other kids, his age or younger, what he did to me? Or was it just some random combination of timing and opportunity that meant it was me?

And what about now? What's Joshua like as a man? Does he have children? Is he married? Is he gay or straight?

There were too many questions to ignore. Too many curiosities to just pretend weren't there. I'd almost certainly go mad if I tried.

Maybe I should jump in the car and go to see him. I could turn up on his doorstep as a surprise, under the guise of catching up after so long, and then pepper him with questions. According to Facebook, he lives in the northern New South

Wales town of Coffs Harbour. I look at my watch. It's just after ten o'clock in the morning. If I throw on a clean shirt, brush my hair and hit the road now, I could be there at about four o'clock.

I play it out in my head. I imagine he lives in a fibro shack near the water, with a neat front yard and a modest sedan parked in the driveway. His furniture would be a mix of stuff inherited from friends and salvaged from kerbside rubbish collections. We'd exchange pleasantries and it would probably be awkward. But then, after a couple of beers on his back deck, we'd get to talking.

What if he had nothing to say? What if he didn't remember it? What if he lied? Or what if he just threw me out of his house and I'd have gone all that way for nothing.

I take the lower stakes, easy way out and message him on Facebook. He's online and replies right away.

He's well, he tells me, explaining that he works in administration at a technical college. Nothing overly exciting, he says, just a bit of management stuff. He doesn't like it too much and has thought about starting his own business, but he's not sure what he'd do.

It's the idea of not working for anyone else, or with anyone else that appeals to him. He likes being on his own, he says.

He asks what I'm up to. He's seen bits and pieces here and there on Facebook, updates on job and life. He's seen the barrage of baby photos. She's very cute, he says.

Joshua isn't married. He doesn't have kids. There's no more

detail about girlfriends or other relationships, about his hopes for starting a family. In all, the conversation is friendly but hard work. He's happy to chat, but it's clear I'll have to do the heavy lifting.

Never gifted at making smooth segues, I ask how much he remembers of what happened when we were kids. I explain that I'm trying to understand more about why I am the way I am, and the things in childhood that shaped the man I've become.

He doesn't recall much, he tells me. Just bits and pieces. 'It was a long time ago,' he writes.

Joshua's replies are so brief that it's impossible to get a sense of tone. I can't tell if he's open to having this conversation or is desperate for it to end.

'I'm just so curious about how it started,' I explain. Surely that kind of thing doesn't come out of nowhere? Did someone show it to him?

'To be honest, I can't remember. I just remember mucking around from time to time. I can't remember specifics.'

I feel a growing sense of dread, like dark storm clouds rolling in. I lose hope that this is going to lead to anything meaningful.

'I've never done anything with anyone else,' Joshua adds.

That strikes me as interesting. I'm surprised that, after dozens and dozens of encounters with me when we were younger, nothing else ever took place with anyone.

I ask if he's straight or gay.

'It's kinda funny you say that,' he begins. 'I always had a soft spot for you. Maybe it was just mutual attraction? If you can have that when you're young?'

It's not really an answer but it feels as close to one as I'm likely to get, so I move on. I ask how he felt about what we did when we were kids, while we were kids. Was there any guilt or shame there? Was there a fear of being caught?

It takes Joshua a long time to answer. I see the little bubble signifying that he's typing pop up, disappear and then pop up again. He's thinking. Perhaps he's struggling with his thoughts.

'That's a tough question,' he eventually replies.

He probably thought about whether it was something we would get in trouble for if anyone found out, he concedes, but he isn't sure he ever thought about it as something that was wrong. He didn't feel any shame – not that he can recall anyway.

I'm not convinced. I distinctly remember how he would get when he was finished with me. He would become cold and distant, as though he was mulling over the severity of what he'd just done. I became so familiar with the emotion of guilt as a result of it. He taught me what it meant. Right now, in this moment, saying that he didn't feel shame then about what we did, Joshua is either lying or fooling himself.

'I guess I knew it was not a kids thing to do and it wouldn't be good if anyone knew,' I tell him.

Joshua asks me if I regret it now. It's not a question I was expecting and I'm kind of floored that he thinks there's a response I could give other than 'yes'.

'I think it was a fairly significant distraction through childhood,' I tell him.

It's the understatement of the year. It haunted me. It still does. It permeated my spirit and infected it with self-doubt, self-loathing, insecurity and embarrassment. How does a kid navigate the world with all that wrapped around their neck? How does an adolescent come to terms with who they are, how that might impact their place in the world, with such a horribly clouded sense of self?

How does an adult have healthy relationships when they don't value themselves at all, when they're just a commodity to be traded for a fleeting self-esteem boost?

'Maybe it was more so for me than you,' I eventually add.

The last time we saw each other, when we were in our early teens, Joshua felt confused after I went home, he tells me.

In spite of everything that had happened, he was under the impression he was a regular, heterosexual young man. And then I burst back into his life briefly, dredging up long buried feelings. He didn't know what to do with them.

'I was like, I like this person, what does that mean for me?' he tells me now. He thought about me afterwards and how the way he thought about me, very differently to how he thought about any other boy, might shape him.

He doesn't say what the outcome was. Has he had a

meaningful relationship with anyone? With women or men? Is he lonely? I get no answers.

But I'm left with the sense that maybe he doesn't have any answers to give. To get to your late thirties and be on your own, with no evidence it was ever any other way, and to be content with that … how does that happen?

Maybe he was more affected by what he did than he knows. In his mind, what happened was not abnormal – it was just kid stuff.

Is he right?

'I guess you have sat in the back of my mind and you pop up every now and again,' he adds. 'I really hope you don't feel any animosity or anything towards me. Because that's not what I want.'

I'm not sure how I feel about him anymore.

I'm speaking to Carol Ronken from Bravehearts when I ask her about a scenario like mine. What if an older boy does something to a younger boy. Is that abuse?

'That's not an easy question to answer,' she says.

'It's complicated. You don't want to isolate a young person and label them as an offender, but at the same time, safety and the protection of the victim as well as other children is really paramount.'

Peer abuse isn't something that's confronted in her space, she tells me. It's an uncomfortable grey area that rightly needs more attention, but which is hard to tackle.

How young is too young to understand that what's being done is wrong? At what age is something no longer an act of childish experimentation? What kind of gap between the perpetrator and the victim, so to speak, is too big or too small?

'There are thirty-eight states in America that have juvenile sex offender registers,' Carol says. 'There is no grey area with young people, even if they're very young. Despite being a criminologist, I don't know how in favour I am of trying children as criminals.

'With the situation in America, some of the people on that sex offender register were eight when an incident occured. They were treated as though they were a culpable adult and branded for life. There are serious consequences with those registers. That stuff terrifies me.'

In fifteen of those thirty-eight states, a juvenile on a sex offender register has their name, home address and photograph published on a website that's freely accessible to the public.

Sure, there are instances when a young person should be dealt with in a particular way. Say, someone in their late teens who has molested a child. And in the other twelve states in America, that's what they do – juveniles convicted in an adult court are added to sex offender registers.

More can and should be done about abuse carried out by

a young person. But Carol isn't sure treating a child like a criminal is helpful in most cases.

'I guess I still have the belief that there's good in everybody, especially children. It might be a blind belief. But we've worked with young people like this to ensure their offending doesn't escalate while they're young, and doesn't continue into adulthood.

'And in fact, research shows that often children and young people "age out" of those sexual behaviours. They are, for the most part, a kind of experimentation, trying to sort out their own identity or understand who they are, or perhaps even a response to trauma, that doesn't last.

'There are some programs out there that work with young people. We have one here at Bravehearts that helps kids aged between twelve and eighteen. In some cases it's gone up to the age of twenty-one, in rare instances to accommodate the developmental age of the person. It's designed to help understand the consequences of what they've done in order to reduce the likelihood they'll continue down that path.'

Wendy O'Brien is a senior lecturer in criminology at Deakin University and followed with interest the Royal Commission's examination of harmful sexual behaviours by children. It's an area that has long been poorly understood.

'During private sessions, the Commission heard that nearly one in six survivors of child sexual abuse had been abused by a person under eighteen,' O'Brien writes in an article for *The Conversation*.

There's a view among many that children with these kinds of behaviours should be viewed in the same light as adults who sexually abuse children. There should be no differentiation, is the misconception, according to the article.

'In many cases, these behaviours in children are a trauma response, a replication of prior abuse, or a reaction to exposure to pornography. The commission reports that children exposed to violence in the home are considerably over-represented in the group of children with harmful sexual behaviours.'

The notion of 'harmful sexual behaviours by children' is in itself problematic, O'Brien notes in her article. The Commission felt the same, expressing some element of discomfort at it being used as a one-size-fits-all descriptor when it could describe a number of incidents.

'At one end of the spectrum, a child's problematic (rather than harmful) behaviour may be outside the developmentally appropriate range, or outside accepted social norms, such as self-stimulation in public. The commission recommends that early and appropriate responses require adults who work with children have knowledge about children's sexual development.

'Where a child's behaviour harms other children, adults, or animals, it is important that the seriousness of the behaviour be acknowledged. Timely reporting and appropriate specialist assessments are also paramount.'

Regardless, the lack of understanding of this grey area – one that's especially taboo and uncomfortable to confront – means that harmful sexual behaviours by children are ignored, brushed under the carpet, or put down to merely being 'child's play'.

'Where adults dismiss or deny harmful incidents, they actively perpetuate the harm for both the child with the behaviours, and children subjected to the behaviours,' O'Brien writes.

In its report, the Commission emphasised the importance of education, to promote prevention and early intervention. But educating children alone, while hugely important, is only part of the solution.

'To address the lack of understanding, the Commission recommends education on preventing harmful sexual behaviours be provided to the broader community,' O'Brien writes. 'This includes parents, carers, and professionals that engage with children.'

In seeking to understand more about the things that happened to me, what Joshua did to me, I searched high and low for research, information, data and specialised support for this kind of behaviour. There was very little around.

O'Brien notes that the Commission's work in this area, helped by the testimony of survivors of harmful sexual behaviours by children, was in many ways pioneering. The report shone a light on something that's been ignored for a long time.

'It is understandable that many people find it confronting to contemplate children engaging in acts that cause such harm. This must now be put aside. It is infinitely more confronting to know that the ignorance or inaction of adults perpetuates harm, and denies children the therapeutic support they need.

'Ensuring that we are educated about developmentally appropriate sexual behaviours is an excellent place to start.'

Chapter Eighteen

I've never told my mum about what happened when I was a kid. I wasn't especially keen to disclose it to anyone for the longest time, and Mum was the absolute last person I wanted to tell.

You need to understand the relationship I have with her. We're more like best friends than mother and son. We always have been. She's this immovable rock in my world that's always stood between me and the harshness of life that I was somewhat more prone to experience due to the challenges I faced at school, and how they shaped who I am and the difficulties I still face.

She's always been my biggest supporter. She's the most excited about anything good that happens to me and is my number one fan. Seriously. Being her Facebook friend must be a nightmare because all she posts, aside from those two-minute Buzzfeed-style videos of cake recipes, is stuff about what I'm up to.

Mum is also fiercely protective. When I was being bullied at school, she would march into the administration building every week or so after I came home with a black eye or bloodied nose, or when I would retreat within myself and close off from the outside world. She demanded action. She hunted down the parents of the worst perpetrators and berated them. She used her influence as a popular hairdresser in our small town to curry favour with whoever she could – a teacher here, the mum of a friendly boy there – to back me up as much as possible.

When I was going to university in Brisbane, during my second year of living out of home, I had this job at a five-star hotel on the outskirts of the city, working in banquets. I was a waiter for events held at the hotel, from business conferences to weddings and birthdays. The head chef was this monster of a man who hated everyone. His way of communicating orders and managing his staff was to bark critiques of poor performance, and his threshold for the acceptable running of the operation was very high.

He hated me. I don't know why. Maybe it was the gay thing? He was this oversized blokey bloke who threw his weight around, literally and metaphorically, and was suspicious of meekness. I was about fifty kilograms of skin, bones and hairspray, and very shy of confrontation, so I tried to shrink into the background whenever I had to be near him.

I think he could smell my fear and discomfort.

He would call out anything he saw as me doing a bad job. He would physically shove me if I was in his way in the kitchen.

He would try to get some of the other chefs, mostly young men who were just as blokey and hardened as him, to join in.

I hated him but I loved the job, and I desperately needed the regular money to get by. One night, after being on the receiving end of his nastiness all night, I called Mum from my car in the staff car park, and broke down.

She was livid. She called my eldest brother, Damien, who was at that stage a policeman in North Queensland. He has also been a fervent lifelong defender of mine, and Mum begged him to do something.

The next evening, he called the hotel, asked to be transferred to the head chef in the kitchen, and had a little chat with him. He outlined how the behaviour was inappropriate, how upset it was making me, and explained that if it continued, he'd jump in his car and drive down to Brisbane to break his spine in half.

The guy never spoke to me, or even really looked at me, ever again.

As the baby of the family – the youngest of four – who always seemed to be in need of a little extra nurturing and care throughout childhood, Mum has always been very present in my life. She doesn't have favourites, of course, but I think she keeps me in a special little compartment in her heart.

For those reasons, I could never tell her what happened. I couldn't have her look at me differently or think about me in a different light. I didn't want her to be ashamed. I didn't want her to ponder the role that five-year-old me played in all of that messiness.

But, as my journey of understanding myself pushed on, there was a need to finally lift the lid on my box of shame and let her have a peek.

Of course, I'm a coward, so I did it via Facebook Messenger. Probably not the best approach, in hindsight.

But that's another thing about my family. We are extremely close. Super tight. My siblings and I getting together is like watching four separate people who are fundamentally very different come together and fit perfectly like puzzle pieces, melding into one. And Mum is the figurehead at the top – the person who sacrificed so much for all of us, including her own happiness. We are indebted to her and carry the weight of that gratitude like some kind of idol.

All of that said, we're fairly insecure about emotions. We feel them, but we don't necessarily share them. For whatever reason, that's just a little too uncomfortable and awkward. I think we're avoiders of conflict – not conflict in the adversarial sense, but in an intimate one – and so the first hint of deepness or raw feelings or, God forbid, tears, and we run.

I went home for Christmas for the first time in two years after Covid and the four siblings were together again at long last. It had been a big and busy year, with lots of ups and plenty of downs, and I was a new father, so I was a touch more emotional than I might have otherwise been.

At the end of the first night, when all of us were drunk, my sister nonchalantly gave me a small box. Inside was a shiny white stone inscribed with a brief quote about the importance of family and the love a sister has for her brother.

I began to weep. Her eyes widened and her shoulders stiffened. She was aghast.

'Jesus Christ, Shannon – it's a fucking rock,' she laughed. 'I got it from the servo. Relax.'

That's how we are as a family. Extremely close, probably willing to take or shoot a bullet for each other, but mentally at arm's length sometimes.

That's why I couldn't bring myself to look my mother in the eye and tell her about Joshua. I couldn't bear hearing her voice down the end of the phone. Hell, the idea of using my own voice to verbalise that chapter of my complicated story made me feel sick to the stomach.

So, I dropped the bomb on Facebook Messenger.

She was livid. Not at me for how I was telling her. Not at what I had done. Not at the three decades of secrecy. She was enraged at Joshua and his actions.

'I will fucking kill him,' she typed at me. 'Where is he? Where does he live?'

What followed was a stream of consciousness full of typos as her furious fingers struggled to keep pace with her racing mind.

She'd always known he was weird, she said. That whole family was weird. The dad was an angry drunk. The mum was airy-fairy and dim-witted. She should never have let me have him as a playmate.

How couldn't she see it, she wondered. Why didn't I say anything at the time?

She demanded to know where he was now. Not literally in a geographic sense, although maybe she was partly serious about tracking him down and killing him. But she needed to know where he was in life. What was he like? Was he still alive? Was he in gaol? In her mind, he – the perpetrator – must've gone on to do equally wrong things. Did he have children of his own? Did he end up gay?

I instantly regretted telling her in the way that I did. It was a horrible thing to drop on a parent from afar. It's the exact same way I told her I was gay when I was fifteen and living in the United States on student exchange – albeit, via the more analogue method known as writing a letter. It was the same thought process, that I couldn't bear to *actually* tell her using my voice. The only way I could tackle something so significant, with such high stakes, that could fundamentally change the nature of our relationship, was with distance. In that case, the distance of the time it took for a letter to be written, addressed, stamped, put in a mailbox, taken across the globe and delivered. But I needed the distance afforded by the absence of direct human connection.

In this case, I needed her to be words inside a blue bubble on a screen, and not my mum, deeply disappointed, wracked by confusion and guilt and anger, in front of me. I couldn't hear her voice. I couldn't hear mine.

I sat with her reaction for a long time. I mulled over how she felt about Joshua – about him being this kind of evil monster in my narrative who'd destroyed my innocence and ruined my childhood.

And after weeks, I realised that I'd come to a different conclusion to her.

I don't think he's the villain in my story. He's another victim. A kid who did something wrong to another kid, for whatever reason. Not a kid who was born evil and maliciously targeted me entirely of his own doing.

His father was an angry drunk. I remember his violent outbursts really clearly. Like the night he went down to the takeaway shop in the centre of town to get pies for dinner, but came back with ones topped with a thick layer of mushy peas. Joshua hated peas. He reminded his dad of this – not even in a bratty or whiny way. But it infuriated his dad, who slapped him across the face so hard that he went flying off the dining room chair and onto the floor with a loud thud.

As Joshua limped towards his bedroom, crying, his dad chased after him, unbuckling his belt and removing it as he did. I sat there frozen and petrified, listening to him beat his son with the belt, again and again, for several minutes.

When he returned and I was still sitting there, he looked at me with a kind of disdain that no adult should feel for a child, and told me to fuck off home.

Maybe that's the kind of trauma that led Joshua down the path that led him to me and that afternoon in his bedroom. Perhaps the deep instability in his home life and his father's violent physical abuse triggered in him a trauma response that I just happened to be in the path of.

Either way, we were young. He was too young to know better.

But if he wasn't the bad guy I can direct all of my rage and blame at, where does that toxic waste of emotions go? Does it just circulate around inside of me until it finds its way to my soul and devours it entirely?

Who can I blame for me being the way I am?

Chapter Nineteen

'I liked therapy,' Will tells me. 'It really helped me come to terms with things and realise that while what happened is obviously not OK, it's OK to feel how I felt in the aftermath. And that how I feel now is OK. And I learnt a lot of coping mechanisms.'

There are times when he still blames himself for what happened to him when he was a boy. There's still a fair amount of shame surging through his body, manipulating the rational side of him and distorting how he sees himself. *How could you let it happen?* it hisses at him.

'But the therapy side of things was turning that on its head,' he tells me. 'It helped me understand the source of this guilt and shame.'

The nightmares will probably never go away. He's come to accept that they're part of who he is and the final big mountain that's just a little too precarious and a touch too tall to conquer.

'My partner gives me a hug and calms me down when I have nightmares. She knows a bit about what happened to me, but we never talk about the specifics. It's the shame aspect.

I don't want her to think of me in these situations, in those horrid positions. I don't want her to know me like that.'

His bouts of blinding anger and the unpredictable outbursts that used to follow are mostly behind him now. It's thanks to therapy, but also the unwavering support of his partner, Trudy.

After he finishes high school, Will is at a crossroads. He's trying to decide whether he heads off to TAFE to study broadcast journalism, or to give this new job he's just landed a go and see where it takes him.

'I'd just started training for this door-to-door sales job flogging second-hand vacuums. I wasn't loving it. I'd been thinking about doing this study in journalism, and so that's ultimately what I did. That's where I met her.

'She's a year and a bit younger than me. She was going through her emo punk phase when we met and I found that very hot.'

Years later, Will was going through a box filled with papers and other odds and ends, doing a bit of a clean-out, when he came across a tattered map. It was torn from a street directory and certain streets were highlighted.

It was from his training for that vacuum sales job. It was where he was going to practise his door-to-door sales techniques the week after he pulled the pin.

'It was my partner's suburb and street – the place she was living at the time,' he recalls. 'If I hadn't decided to go to do this TAFE course instead and met her, chances are I would've knocked on her door and maybe met her that way. I don't really buy into the idea of fate, but it just feels like we were meant to meet each other.'

At the time, he was living in an old nursing home that had been converted into studios and one-bedroom apartments in the western suburbs of Sydney. He was sharing a tiny studio with someone he'd met while trying to find a place to crash. When that guy moved out, Trudy moved in.

'We'd only been going out a few weeks and we were sharing a single bed. It was mad, in hindsight, but it worked out for the best.'

A few months in, the pair travelled to Melbourne to do a study placement for a community radio station. They instantly fell in love with the city, deciding they were 'more Melbourne people than Sydney people'. They returned to Sydney, packed up their stuff, and moved south together.

'We worked in radio for a couple of years at this community station. It was too hard to break into the industry so it eventually faded away.

'I always wanted to be in radio. When I was in high school, I'd come home and listen to this show on Triple M called 'The Shebang' with Marty Sheargold and Fifi Box. I loved it. I listened religiously. I was like, fuck, I want to do this.

'In Melbourne, Trudy and I worked on shows together. We volunteered for a couple of radio shows and then we eventually had our own show about rock music.

'It gained some traction, and we did a lot of interviews for it. It was really cool. We got to meet bands we loved growing up.'

But community radio work doesn't financially support much of a lifestyle. As things got more serious and Will and Trudy started to settle down, they both drifted into more secure work. These days, he works in real estate and she's in insurance.

'We just celebrated twelve years together. We have a son who's two and a bit. Life is really good.'

They each tend to know what the other is thinking. Their connection is strong and intense – just as much as when they first met. Will feels like they share the same brain.

In his darkest times, Trudy has been there by his side. She's his rock, his biggest supporter, and a constant source of encouragement to pick himself up, regroup, and keep going. She's the one who encouraged him to see a therapist for the first time, which started his journey towards healing.

'She's been amazing. She's there for me and she's been a huge support with my challenges. She was the one who gave me the push I needed to address the things that happened to me.'

They live in Victoria with their young son. The couple remains just as in love as they were when they first started dating. A few years ago, they bought a house together and have busily made it into a home.

He has a decent social life. He and his family have big hopes for the future and plenty of shared ambition.

Life now feels a million miles away from the one he knew as a child and adolescent. He's managed, against the odds in many ways, to forge a radically different path to the one he was on.

'Mum lost our family home; I have a lovely family home. I didn't have a stable father figure; I'm a great dad. She couldn't get a good job; I did.'

Jason is a little less advanced in his search for peace, but he also feels a bit more content with where things are currently.

'I don't drink or do anything silly. I have a few friends through work but don't really have much going on out of that, but that's a function of a shitty marriage and partner, and the Covid world situation, as well as how I just am as a person,' he says.

'I feel very lucky. I'm here and alive. I've got my health. I'm relatively content.

'I have a cousin who is two years older than me, who had all the same opportunities that I did. She was abused when she was about five by my uncle. She fried her brain with drugs in her twenties dealing with it.

'My sister-in-law was abused by her grandfather and wasn't believed or supported. She is a functioning alcoholic who thinks about suicide all the time.

'I worked with and had a brief relationship with a woman much older than me who was abused by her father. She had spent years abusing drugs and had been in an abusive marriage. She was on her path to get better but I could see how scarred she was.

'I haven't met or crossed paths with someone who perhaps feels like they are in as good a shape as I am, and that's not a brag or meant to be a suggestion that I'm better or anything, but it's just my observation.

'I wouldn't want to pick silver linings out of it but one thing that maybe I have because of what happened to me is a lot of empathy and time for some people. My expectations and judgement are tempered because you never know where they've been or what they've been through.'

There is a small part of him that worries about how sustainable his current approach is. Will he always feel this way – as though he's able to just push on? Or will there be some point where his resilience is eroded?

Luke isn't entirely sure where his interest in architecture came from but thinks the need for practitioners to be generalists accidentally suits him to a tee.

'Architects have to know a little bit about everything, and I think that's me in a lot of ways. I'm artistically minded but not artistically talented. I can think creatively but I can't paint a pretty picture. I'm interested in science, but I can't solve a complex mathematical formula.

'But I can draw a nice pattern. I can do mathematical art, which is what architecture is really.'

He has a vivid memory of laying on his aunt's lounge room floor when he was a kid, with a piece of paper and some coloured pencils, drawing a floorplan of her house. He was obsessed with trying to figure out how the space worked – how the rooms flowed through to each other, and how the whole place connected.

'I was always building houses out of Lego, or little floorplans out of blocks,' he recalls.

'There was a loft in my dad's office that was lined with bookshelves. I would climb up there and build Lego houses for hours and hours, with dad sitting below me working.'

At high school, when it was time to choose a place to do work experience, his friend's dad lined up a few weeks with the renowned architect Harry Seidler. He was the famed figure's accountant and was able to get Luke in the door.

'I mean, the work experience was not directly with Harry, obviously – he spoke to me probably twice. Once to tell me never to put a kitchen in the corner of a room – galley kitchens only. The second, on my very last day, he gave me some books and said, "Read these and one day you might make something of yourself."

'But it was a pretty amazing experience and I think that kind of decided for me what I was going to do at university.'

On top of liking to draw, he's also fairly structured, organised and disciplined, and those qualities have helped him survive the difficult times he's encountered in life.

And it's those characteristics, coupled with taking on an architecture degree, that probably saved him when things were at their absolute darkest.

'Architecture is one of the hardest degrees you can do. They say it's harder than medicine. It's incredibly intense.

'It's because you do these design tasks that have to impress somebody enough, but to also work functionally – the structure has to stand up – in order to get through to the next year. You redesign and redesign and redesign. You've got to both look ahead and look back, otherwise you'll change something way down the track and then later realise, "Oh no, that's why we made that wall this high."

'In some courses, you can bludge and write an essay the night before it's due and it could be fine. Enough to pass. You can't do that in architecture.

'Then, on top of all of that, is an insane workload. From the second year of uni, most of us were working full-time as well. That's how my university did it – you got credit points for working and had to do certain things. So, I worked thirty hours a week, going to uni seventeen-odd hours a week, then finding time for everything else in between – for life.'

Being that busy and having to be that switched on and doggedly focused meant that he avoided a lot of the vices that might have otherwise been tempting to slip into.

When he hit university, it was a year after he'd told his parents about the abuse he endured as a child. He was still coming to terms with the ramifications of sharing that dark secret, and with the experiences themselves, when he was suddenly thrust into big city life. It was a far cry from the Sutherland Shire.

There's no denying that things were tough. Deciding to go to the police and press charges against his perpetrator opened an entirely new can of worms. So too did dating for the first time and navigating relationships through the lens of his trauma.

But finding a purpose and throwing himself headfirst into the pursuit of it helped to mostly keep his head above water.

These days, he's a gifted architect working for a Sydney firm that does predominantly residential redesigns. In a housing market like this one, it's rare to be able to do a brand-new house totally from scratch, so most of the work consists of renovations or significant rebuilds.

There's something appealing about that, though. To take something that's already there, that has sat in its place for decades and served a good purpose, but that perhaps needs a bit of love and care, and to be able to transform it into something spectacular, is almost transcendant.

He's relatively content. He leads a busy and full life.

A few years ago, Luke found his abuser on Google. He can't remember what inspired his search, if anything specific at all, but he plugged in the guy's name and found him. He dug up a council document for approvals to renovations to his house.

He had his address. His home address. He knew exactly where he was right now.

'I said to my best mate, "I want to go and burn his house down". I wanted to make him pay. I wanted to destroy everything he had, like he did to me. My mate, I think knowing I would never actually do it, he just goes, "OK, let's do it – let's go now and burn it down. I'll drive."

'It was the best thing he could've done. He didn't try to talk me out of it. He called my bluff and was like, yeah, let's go – come on, do it. And I didn't, obviously. And I wouldn't have, obviously.'

But being called on, being forced to think about the extent of his anger and the depths of his hatred and rage, made Luke reassess things. It made him realise that there was a limit to it all, and if there was a limit, it meant that his suffering wasn't absolute. There was room to allow healing.

After his breakdown that night at the bachelor party, Luke went back to therapy in a big way.

That reflection, those conversations with his therapist, presented a fork in the road for Luke. It was an opportunity to change course and try something else for the first time in a long while. He could either keep doing things the way he had since his late teens and hope he could continue merely surviving, or he could give surviving and thriving a go.

'Part of the alternative was feeling like I should speak up about the abuse, about the things that happened to me, and just let it all out in the open. And so that's what I did.'

He's also thrown himself into advocacy and awareness with SAMSN, giving back to the organisation that gave him so much all those years ago when he had little hope and felt desperately alone.

There's so much power in reclaiming his story, he tells me. He's taken ownership of it, and therefore of its ability to dominate his life. To be able to have some agency over himself again gives him a lot of strength.

Chapter Twenty

I decide that it might be time for me to move on from Dr Rolenstein and try something else. Like many big calls, it's one I make fairly spontaneously and handle horribly.

I think I've reached the limit of my eagerness to share. I probably had before I even mentioned Joshua. A few years have passed now, and I feel like I might be running out of things to say. Or rather, things I want to say. Instead, I sometimes find myself wasting time and just making general chit chat to fill the silence.

Talking is good. I've learnt a lot about myself. I understand why I am the way I am so much better. But there's still so much about Joshua and me that doesn't sit right with me. Why did it happen? How did he know what he wanted to do? Why me?

After a while, we reach a point in our sessions where I can't find my way to the answers alone via reflection, like I have been, anymore. And Dr Rolenstein doesn't have any answers.

And so, in early 2019, I break up with Dr Rolenstein via text message. I can't handle the uncomfortable face-to-face conversation. I can't possibly endure his attempts to understand why I want to leave, to change my mind, knowing that he'd be right when he inevitably said that we still had a lot of work to do.

I do what I always do when I feel uneasy about something. I run away and never go back. Just like I did with the group therapy experience – I decide something is over and I smoke-bomb. It's not a very mature thing to do, and I'm aware of it.

Change is easier said than done. I spend a lot of time thinking about all the ways I need to do a better job at living. I need to exercise more. I know it's good for my mental health. I need to eat better. I'm horribly unhealthy and have absolutely no discipline. I need to change my relationship with alcohol. I am rapidly losing my grip on my drinking.

The town I grew up in was small, and so the annual show that came to us was basically the dregs of the bigger regional shows in larger towns. Yeppoon got a few rides, a couple of sideshow alley tents, and half-a-dozen show bag stands. I loved show bags. I still do, come to think of it. There's something exciting about the novelty of getting a little collection of themed items for a flat price.

But with a second-rate show like the one Yeppoon had, pickings were slim to say the least. I remember one year when I was probably six or seven, I took the ten dollars Mum gave me and chose an army show bag. It was shit. There was a plastic cap gun, a camouflage headband and a compass. The compass never worked. The little dial just spun hopelessly around in circles, rendering it totally useless.

That's how I view much of my adult life. I've got the tool that is meant to get me through these challenging times, but it doesn't really work. When I come to a fork in the road – right decision, wrong decision; healthy choice, unhealthy choice – I've got to flip a coin and hope for the best. The device that's meant to guide me is broken.

I start seeing a psychologist who is a little more contemporary in his approach to treatment. He's highly regarded and very friendly, but I don't click with him. I don't really know why. He's so sought-after that he almost never takes on new patients, and he's seeing me as a favour to my husband, so I'm not sure he's totally into the idea of taking me on with all of my bullshit. After four sessions, I pull the pin.

I do a ten-week mindfulness course that I hate at first, then like, and then hate again. I can see the merits of mindfulness. I just don't know how it would help me in my day-to-day life. I give it a good go. I do the homework. I practice. But I just don't like it. There's an exercise where we have to put a sultana in our mouths and then think about how it feels – its texture, surface, roughness, all of that jazz – and I reckon that's the point where I lose interest.

I'm super practical. There's a problem, I find a solution, and then I implement it. The airy-fairy sort of stuff annoys me. I have less and less time to waste as the years roar on by. I probably need someone a bit more hard-nosed to work with.

And so, I'm in between therapists now. The idea of starting all over again with a new one is exhausting. There's so much backstory you've got to fill in, so much context to go with the painting of a pretty messy picture.

'I'm not just fucked up naturally,' I'd want to scream. 'There's more to it!'

But that takes weeks, if not months. I don't know if I'm in a place to commit to that right now. There's a lot of other stuff going on.

For me, I draw so much strength from other people, directly and indirectly.

My husband's pure goodness and kindness makes my heart sing every single day. There's not an ounce of selfishness in his body. He's always patient and extremely empathetic. That lifts me up and cradles me, but it also inspires me to do better and to be better – to be the kind of man and the kind of life partner that deserves those qualities.

I think the loneliness of Covid, with its restrictions, lockdowns and closed borders, has given me a renewed appreciation for the great people in my life. I'm pretty blessed to have a small but wonderful group of friends who I've known through the ups and downs, the good times and bad. Their kindness and compassion is a source of strength for me. It's the fuel that keeps my motor going.

But most of all, more and more, I find myself gravitating towards the kindness in the world. It's still there, even if it doesn't feel like it all of the time – especially lately.

There was a children's television show in the United States called *Mister Rogers' Neighborhood*, which ran from the late '60s until 2001. Hosted by Fred Rogers, it was a beautiful program all about the importance of friendship, community, empathy and kindness.

He was once talking about being a boy and seeing harrowing world events play out on television – wars, famines, natural disasters, man-made horrors – and feeling frightened. He said:

'My mother would say to me, "Look for the helpers. You will always find people who are helping." To this day, especially in times of disaster, I remember my mother's words, and I am always comforted by realising that there are still so many helpers – so many caring people in this world.'

Globally, during the pandemic, when an understandable human response to a highly infectious disease would've been to steer clear of others, it's estimated that rates of volunteerism rose by 25 per cent. In the face of uncertainty and of fear, instead of it being every person for themselves, many of us looked outwards to see how we could help. We became the helpers for others to see, from whom to draw strength and reassurance.

There's a song by Paul Simon called 'I Don't Believe' that I like. It really speaks to my view of the world of late. In one part, he talks about how acts of kindness are like breadcrumbs in the forest that bring light to the darkness and guide us to safety.

Kindness is so powerful. Showing it, benefitting from it, or merely basking in its glorious glow.

My daughter was born in April 2021. It was not the easiest of circumstances. My husband and I began exploring how we might start a family almost four years before Ava arrived. We went down the surrogacy path because it was the quickest and safest option, especially in the United States, where it runs like a well-oiled and legally sound machine.

When we started travelling down the long and winding road, we didn't anticipate the sudden arrival of a global pandemic, which threw quite a spanner in the works. Suddenly, getting out of the country was a much harder prospect. Getting to America when many airlines weren't flying and schedules were changing last-minute was extremely stressful. Jumping through the many legal and immigration hoops after her birth was emotionally taxing and prohibitively expensive. What should've been six weeks on the ground before returning home turned into three months.

But it was all worth it. The week after we brought her home from the hospital to our temporary digs, I was giving her a bottle one afternoon. I sat in an enormous armchair next to a window from which I could see a cloudless, bright blue sky and the tops of trees on the mountain our house was built into. It was quiet and very serene. Just the two of us. She opened her big, steely grey eyes and stared at me intently. Then, with her tiny little hand, she clutched my pinky finger and went back to sleep.

It was a perfect moment. In that instant, my life felt complete. The things I thought I wanted and needed to be happy, to be successful, to be content, melted away. The picture was so much bigger.

I know that's a bit clichéd. I know many who loathe those people who speak of having children like it's some kind of religious experience. The implication is that only those who become parents can live a truly whole life. Of course that's not true. But what she's done by simply existing, by being a part of me, is given me so much more to live for. Not to merely survive for, not to just muddle through for. But to truly live for.

I don't think I would've had that without her.

That said, life hasn't been a blissful nirvana since her birth. There have been some very, very difficult patches. I've felt isolated and lonely. I've been completely overwhelmed. I've doubted myself and my abilities countless times. I've quietly wondered if I'm inevitably going to fuck up her life, either by passing on my eccentricities and personality faults, or by being too much or too little for her.

I remain insecure and anxious. I have bouts of sadness, which oftentimes come from nowhere. I feel angry, usually irrationally so. I am tightly wound.

But there's a new drive to try to fix myself. I feel a little more able to push through the down stretches and the rough days.

Lately, I also care less about being 100 per cent fixed. Perfection is unattainable, regardless of what's happened in the past, and trying to attain it via healing is bound to drive me mad. I'm always going to be a little broken because of my past, but if I can still function, then why shouldn't I be content with that?

The ancient Japanese art of *kintsugi* operates on the principle that few things in life are ever truly broken beyond repair. In a nutshell, the idea is to take broken pottery pieces – dishes, bowls, trinkets and such – and put them back together with gold. It's practical and efficient in that things are recycled and reused as much as possible. But it's also kind of beautiful, in that imperfections are embraced.

Flaws aren't hidden away and repaired in a way that's not noticed. They're shown off. They become an integral part of an even stronger body. The scars become a beautiful and resilient part of the object.

Luke, Will, Jason and Chris have difficult days also. There are rough patches that can crop up quite suddenly. Some are more challenging than others to traverse.

Things are far from perfect. For all the healing, the process is never entirely complete. But what in life is ever really finished? Perhaps part of the human condition is the need to continue growing as people – to find new ways of coping with what confronts us.

These men – myself included, I suppose – were dealt an unfair hand. The game has been much more challenging; the playing field has been overly uneven. But with love and kindness, support and guidance, and a purpose, we've made the most of what we've got.

Hope has also been crucial. The absence of hope allows the monster that is trauma to run wild and out of control within us. Without hope, there is a sense at times that we have no chance of taming that beast and limiting the damage we know it can do.

Shame takes occupancy of us on its own terms. But hope reminds us that we have the capacity to cope with trauma, and so much more, and can shrink that unwieldy shame to a point where we can manage it.

There are many men who don't survive the trauma and the shame. There are a million Joeys out there who, for a variety of reasons, lose the battle.

They can't bring themselves to ask for help and suffer alone. They reach out but there are inadequate supports available to help them. They are disbelieved or shunned or turned away from loved ones. Interventions are left too late. Coping mechanisms are destructive. The trauma is significant. Whatever the cause, those losses are horrendous and devastating and totally avoidable.

Sharing our stories – shining a light on our shame and letting go of our pain – gives hope. So too does taking back the power that was snatched away from us as boys. Deciding to build the future we want, and believing that we deserve it, allows us to write our own story instead of accepting that we're destined to whatever narrative is born from the horrors of our past.

We've healed, to various extents, and continue to heal. We've developed coping strategies. We've emerged from individual wars with battle scars, but with a determination to push on.

Because of what happened. In spite of what happened. And maybe, just a little at least, in stark defiance of it.

Epilogue

Child sexual abuse robs its victims of their innocence and potential. It snatches away their right to the same health and wellbeing outcomes as others, and that's just the beginning.

But in describing it as such, I hope the take-away isn't that survivors are broken beyond repair. I hope the implication of my framing of the seriousness of the trauma that results from abuse isn't that there's no hope for healing.

I hope that my story, but especially the stories of the men I've met through my journey, shows that this isn't the case at all. There is so much capacity for healing and finding some sort of peace.

There remains hurt. Deep scarring never entirely fades from view. Those demons shrink and grow from time to time, but aren't ever completely vanquished from existence.

The men I've met find ways to cope with the ramifications of the horrors they've endured. They heal, with the help of their loved ones and professionals, and develop strategies to carry on – not just keeping their heads above the water enough to keep breathing, but swimming strongly against either calm seas or crashing waves.

That's not to say it's easy. And it's certainly not to say that survivors of child sexual abuse are adequately supported in finding some semblance of peace by authorities, health systems and society more broadly.

Nothing could be further from the truth.

The health system, particularly mental health support services, is horribly broken and shamefully underfunded. We've had multiple royal commissions, at a state and Commonwealth level, in recent years that illustrate just how ill-equipped these systems are to support Australians who find themselves at rock bottom for whatever reasons.

How embarrassing and how deeply offensive that Australia, for all of its wealth and prosperity, is failing millions of people, leaving them to suffer alone with little or no help.

Right now, somewhere in this country, a survivor of child sexual abuse could be mustering every little scrap of courage within themselves to walk into a police station and report what happened to them. But the likelihood of any form of justice following is slim.

Police are the gatekeepers of criminal justice but far too often fail in their responsibilities to take victims seriously, to pursue their complaints, and to bring charges against perpetrators – many of whom could be out free in the community, reoffending and destroying more precious futures.

Those cases that do come before the courts put survivors into horribly adversarial and traumatising environments. Callous judges, indifferent court staff, unpleasant facilities, berating and harassing lawyers, crushing and suffocating environments, little information and zero support. That's what is likely to welcome someone who was sexually abused as a child and has made it to the point of stepping up to ask for justice.

We can do better. We must do better. When an alleged abuser walks into a scenario feeling more confident and at ease than their victim, we should all collectively feel shame and rage and demand more from the legal system.

We should also feel anger and direct it appropriately at those institutions that have overseen the abuse and trauma of countless children, but which still seek to pervert their right to justice in the civil space. For churches, not-for-profit groups and government departments that bear responsibility for the mistreatment of children to obstruct, delay, draw out and re-traumatise survivors, all for the sake of saving a buck, is disgraceful. When this occurs, we should take to the streets and call for blood.

Finally, we as a society can and should do more to end child sexual abuse. And the first big step in doing so is relatively easy to take. All it requires is for us to open our eyes.

It's tempting to look away when things are just too horrific to comprehend. Particularly painful things that no one wants to acknowledge, let alone think about or be haunted by. But the consequence of being able to live oblivious to the suffering of survivors of child sexual abuse – for being spared the horrors they lived through – is that it goes unchallenged.

Pretending it's not there, bar for a few times throughout our lives when we can't ignore it anymore, is deadly.

Child sexual abuse relies on secrecy. The perpetrator needs their victim to stay quiet so the offending can continue. They need the child to remain silent for life to avoid being arrested, charged and gaoled for their unspeakable crimes.

But more than that, the shame that survivors are infected with needs the shadow of secrecy in which to keep feeding on its host and growing ever larger, ever more powerful.

There is death in secrecy. The death of our healthy sense of self and the death of the knowledge of what we deserve in life. Ambition and purpose dies. So too does opportunity. Beneath the crushing weight of shame, we become prisoners inside our own bodies.

We must shine a light on these areas of darkness. We must not look away, even when it's painful.

We need to empower children to feel comfortable in themselves, with their own bodies, and with what's healthy and not, so that they can recognise warning signs and speak up. We must create safe spaces for kids to say anything and everything to trusted adults, so that should something sinister be taking place, they feel like they can and should say something.

We must believe victims when they come forward, at whatever age. We must support survivors who have the courage to step forward, no matter how long after the fact.

We must kill the adversarial element of the legal justice system. We must stop allowing defence lawyers and barristers to scream at survivors and accuse them of being liars, of being tainted or dirty, of seeking a quick buck. We must harness places of respect, consideration and care if we expect anyone to ever embark on the pursuit of criminal justice. We must overhaul the court experience entirely – make them more physically safe spaces, examine every single interaction a survivor has with them, and redesign them to suit.

We must totally rethink and redesign mental health services. Entirely, of course, because the system is completely fucked. Break it down, rebuild it, and plate it in gold. This should especially be the case when it comes to the treatment of trauma. We must adopt holistic, interconnected models of treatment and strive for intervention and prevention.

We must remember that the thousands of cases on Slater and Gordon's books, that Luke and Will and Jason and Chris and Joey and Jack, are not just numbers and names. They're individual people.

Protecting children from sexual abuse is everyone's job. Ensuring offenders are caught, prosecuted and removed from society is everyone's job. Supporting victims to ensure the best possible outcomes for them for the entirety of their lives is everyone's job.

We can start doing our bit right now by pledging to no longer look away.

Additional Resources

If you're a survivor of child sexual abuse and you find yourself troubled by the contents of this book, please reach out to someone to talk to.

In an emergency, dial 000.

Survivors and Mates Support Network
Supporting male survivors of child sexual abuse.
samsn.org.au
1800 472 676

Blue Knot Foundation
An Australian organisation dedicated to empowering recovery from complex trauma.
blueknot.org.au
1300 657 380

Bravehearts
Braveheart is an Australian child protection organisation, dedicated to the prevention and treatment of child sexual abuse.
bravehearts.org.au
1800 272 831

Foundation House
A service dedicated to helping the victims of torture and trauma, predominantly refugees, many of whom have experienced sexual abuse.
foundationhouse.org.au/

Kids Helpline

A confidential 24/7 online and phone counselling service for young people aged 5 to 25.
kidshelpline.com.au
1800 55 1800

MensLine Australia

A national telephone and online support, information and referral service for men with family and relationship concerns, staffed by professional counsellors, experienced in men's issues.
mensline.org.au
1300 78 99 78

No More Silence campaign (Living Well)

A campaign for Aboriginal and Torres Strait Islander men who have survived childhood sexual abuse.
livingwell.org.au

National Sexual Assault, Family & Domestic Violence Counselling Line

For any Australian who has experienced, or is at risk of, family and domestic violence and/or sexual assault. 24 hours, 7 days a week.
1800 737 732

VeryWell Mind

A US-based online resource for up-to-date information on a wide range of mental health topics.
verywellmind.com

Acknowledgements

This book simply wouldn't exist without the immense courage and grace of the men who shared their harrowing stories with me over the span of several months.

Some spoke about their abuse for the very first time to someone who wasn't a therapist or trusted family member. One had never disclosed it to anyone we before spoke. Uttering those words is difficult and painful, whether it's for the first time or the thousandth.

Thank you all so much, for your candour, for your time, for your insights, and for your trust. I'm so very grateful for the faith you placed in me to not just hear your stories, but to retell them here.

A special thanks to Kristy, Joey's partner. I can only imagine how hard it was to let me in and see your broken heart. I was so touched by your intense love and devotion for Joey. Thanks for letting me tell people a little about him.

Thanks to Jarad Grice, who inspired this book. I think you're just wonderful. I'm so thankful for your support and I'm just thrilled that we've become friends.

Thanks to Craig Hughes-Cashmore for telling me your personal story. Your work in establishing the Survivors and Mates Support Network is truly inspiring. Countless men have benefitted from your work and advocacy – me included.

Thanks to Professor Ian Hickie for your extraordinary insights. I'm honoured that you gave up so much of your time to contribute to this book. It would've lacked so much nuance without your voice.

Thank you to Carol Ronken from Bravehearts. You were the first expert I spoke to when I began work on this book. I was so nervous about what I might uncover but your gentle empathy helped put me at ease.

Thanks to Jacqui Eager and Ciara White from Slater and Gordon Lawyers for taking the time to walk me through the extraordinary work you do in helping survivors find some sense of justice. I am in awe of what you do. And thanks to my dear friend Kate van Poelgeest for organising the interview.

I relied heavily on countless pieces of research undertaken by brilliant and brave experts in this field, who've devoted their work to knowing the impacts of child sexual abuse. From local researchers and statisticians to overseas-based clinicians, their work helped to shape not just this book, but my own understanding of my demons.

A special thanks to the supportive literary community that I've been fortunate enough to stumble into. My first book was a pleasant surprise and so I was a little worried I might not entirely belong alongside such brilliant authors, being *just* a journalist. But so many people have welcomed me and offered advice and support during this crazy adventure. Thanks to Caroline Overington, Peter FitzSimons, Brigid Delaney, Trent Dalton, Rick Morton, Christine Jackman, Lech Blaine, Brandon Jack, Ginger Gorman and Frances Whiting, to name but a few. And a huge thanks to Kate Mildenhall, who introduced me to her wonderful agent, which got the ball rolling on this project.

Thank you to Pippa Masson, who's now *my* wonderful agent, for your enthusiasm about this idea and helping me to bring it to life.

Thank you to the incredible Catherine Milne from HarperCollins Australia. It's a true privilege to work with you Thanks for believing in this book. Thanks for believing in me. Thanks also to the broader publishing team – Chris Kunz, Lara Wallace, Kate Butler, Jessica Friedmann and Rebecca Sutherland – for making this all possible.

Thanks to my boss John Healy for being so supportive and accommodating. Thanks for approving so much annual leave!

I'm blessed to have the most incredible friends imaginable. Thanks to Kate Brody, Katherine Feeney, Minnie Cummins, Jen Bini, Kate van Poelgeest, Thea Phillips, Jade Knight, Natalie Patch, and Andrew Churchill, to name just some of them. If I listed them all, that'd be another couple of dozen pages! I am truly so loved and supported. Thank you all.

Thanks to my family for their endless support. My siblings Damien, Trinity and Brett are my favourite people in the whole world – second only to my mother, Donna, of course. Sorry for writing another heavy book, Mum. I'll try to make the next one funny.

Thank you to my second family, the Battisti clan, for your love. I'm especially grateful for the support you showed Robert during the times this book left him as a temporary single dad. Thanks Carlos, Marina, Richie, Matt, Aly, and especially Vicki.

The biggest thanks of all must go to my husband, Robert. You've been so encouraging and understanding, especially during the really challenging parts of this endeavour … which I undertook right after we became parents to lovely little Ava. I know that I've placed a heavy burden on your shoulders. Thanks for giving me the time to get this done. I'll have a break between projects now … maybe.

But in all seriousness, I couldn't have done this without you, my wonderful. Thank you. I love you.

Finally, thanks to you for buying this book. I know it's not an easy read. It's the sort of topic that society understandably shies away from. But the more we confront these horrors and speak about them, the better.

Thanks for not looking away.